Practical Building Law

Construction Technology and Management

A series published in association with the Chartered Institute of Building

The series will, when complete, cover every important aspect of construction. It will be of particular relevance to the needs of students taking the CIOB Member Examinations, Parts 1 and 2, but will also be suitable for degree courses, other professional examinations, and practitioners in building, architecture, surveying and related fields.

Published
Project Evaluation and Development

Other titles in preparation

Building Technology (3 volumes)
The Economics of the Construction Industry
Financial Management in Construction
The Administration of Building Contracts

Practical Building Law

MARGARET WILKIE
WITH A CHAPTER BY RICHARD HOWELLS

MITCHELL · *London*

in association with the Chartered Institute of Building

To DFS in lieu of the PhD conceived on the North Sea,
but washed up on a tide of domesticity

First published 1987

Typeset by Progress Filmsetting Ltd
and printed in Great Britain by
Billings Ltd, Worcester

Published by The Mitchell Publishing Company Limited
4 Fitzhardinge Street, London W1H 0AH
A subsidiary of B. T. Batsford Limited

British Library Cataloguing in Publication Data

Wilkie, Margaret
  Practical building law.—(Construction
  technology and management)
  1. Building laws—Great Britain
  I. Title   II. Howells, Richard
  III. Charterd Institute of Building
  III. Series
  344.103′7869   KD1140

ISBN 0-7134-5042-8 Pbk

Contents

Preface

This book was conceived at the time of drafting the new syllabuses for the Chartered Institute of Building Part I Finals examinations, and is written in part as a textbook for the law syllabus in that examination.

The new syllabus in law, which the author participated in drafting, is intended to have an essentially practical flavour, and careful thought was given to the everyday problems which a practising builder might encounter. The book therefore follows this theme, as its title suggests, and, it is felt, will provide a busy builder with a ready reference on a variety of matters which could arise in the course of his business. In pursuance of a practical approach, a specimen order form for the supply of goods has been included on p. 197. In dealing with such a range of topics, the book cannot be exhaustive in its treatment of any, but it is hoped that on those problems which the book does not answer, it will at least point in the direction of the answer.

I have been selective in my choice of cases and materials, with the construction industry in mind. Although in the first instance for students taking the law examination in Part I of the Chartered Institute of Building examinations, the book will also be of assistance to students taking other professional examinations which often require a general background knowledge of construction-related law. The book deals mainly with those aspects of tort likely to affect the construction industry, and wherever possible, cases involving builders, architects and local authorities have been included. Similarly, the chapters on sale of goods have, where possible, been selective of cases which could affect the construction industry. It is hoped that the chapters on property law and highways will give an outline of useful knowledge in these areas.

The part of the chapter on property law concerned with debt collecting was to have included an outline of bankruptcy procedure, but the Insolvency Act 1985 is currently being introduced and highly relevant detail still remains to be enacted in delegated legislation. There is therefore an appendix on the new bankruptcy law as known at June 1986, but it is necessarily incomplete.

My colleague Dr Richard Howells, who has written a book on The Health and Safety at Work etc. Act 1974 and who has extensive experience in employment law, has kindly contributed the chapter on this topic and I am grateful to him for this.

It will rapidly become apparent to the reader that English law is constantly evolving from the cases before the courts, and since writing the text, there are four cases which the author deems worthy of mention.

Most importantly, perhaps, in *Muirhead* v *Industrial Tank Specialities Ltd* (1985) 3 All.E.R.705, the Court of Appeal has rejected an attempt to apply the principle of liability in negligence for purely economic loss recognised by *Junior Books Ltd* v *Veitchi Co. Ltd* (1982) 3 All.E.R.201 to a situation where a purchaser had his remedy under a contract for the sale of goods. The plaintiff in the case was unsuccessful in his action against the manufacturer of a component for a pump, which was unsuitable for use in England, for purely economic loss not flowing from physical loss, as there was no 'very close proximity' between them. The purchaser had dealt with his immediate supplier and had his remedy against him as a purchaser of goods.

The judgment of the Court of Appeal in *Investors in Industry Commercial Properties Ltd* v *South Bedfordshire District Council and Others* (*The Times*, December 31st 1985) reviews the cases of *Anns* v *Merton Borough Council* (1978) A.C.728 and *Governors of the Peabody Donation Fund* v *Sir Lindsay Parkinson & Co.* (1985) A.C.210. It confirms that the purpose of the Public Health Acts and of Building Regulations made under them is to protect the public against possible dangers to their health and safety and not to give a building owner who fails to comply with them, a right of action for damages against a local authority who negligently pass a defective building. The building owner should rely upon the professional services of his architect or engineer.

In *Gordon and Another* v *Selico Co. Ltd and Another* (*The Times*, February 1986), the court of appeal decided that a vendor who fraudulently concealed a defect in property (in that case, dry rot) could not avoid liability by the application of the doctrine of *caveat emptor*, or a clause in the Law Society's Conditions of Sale imputing to the purchaser full knowledge of the condition of the premises, or by the absence of any warranty as to the state of the premises. Where work has been carried out deliberately and fraudulently to conceal a defect, it is no defence that the purchaser could have discovered the defect for himself by inspection.

In employment law, the Court of Appeal in *Bliss* v *S E Thames R H Authority* (1985) I.R.L.R. 308 (C.A.) refused to follow *Cox* v *Phillips Industries*, holding that, in wrongful dismissals, there can be no damages awarded for frustration, vexation or distress.

Specimen questions from CIOB examination papers are included at the ends of all chapters except the first.

I would like to express my thanks and appreciation to Geoffrey Reeday, who has meticulously and painstakingly read and commented upon the chapters on tort and negotiable instruments, and to Dr Robert Ribiero for similarly reading the chapters on the sale of goods. My husband, a builder, has made relevant comments on the text and has (as every mere woman expects of a man) assisted me in dealing with the vagaries of the word processor, for which I am very grateful.

Table of Cases

Table of Statutes

Abbreviations

The dates and letters following the names of cases in this book are references to the cases in the law reports. The abbreviations for the reports cited are as follows:

A.C.	Court of Appeal
All. E.R.	All England Reports
A.L.T.R.	American Law Times Reports
Build.L.R.	Building Law Reports
Ch. D.	Chancery Division
C.L.R.	Commonwealth Law Reports
C.L.Y.	Current Law Year Book
C.P.	Common Pleas
D.L.R.	Dominion Law Reports
E.G.	Estates' Gazette
Ex.D.	Exchequer Division
I.C.R.	Industrial Cases Reports
I.R.L.R.	Industrial Relations Law Reports
I.T.R.	Industrial Tribunals Reports
K.I.R.	Knights Industrial Reports
K.B.	Kings Bench
LGR	Local Government Reports
Lloyds Rep.	Lloyds Reports
L.T.	Law Times
NELR	New England Law Reports
N.L.J.	New Law Journal
N.S.W.L.R.	New South Wales Law Reports
P.	Probate
Q.B.	Queens Bench
R.L.R.	Rutgers Law Review (American)
R.T.R.	Road Traffic Reports
Sol. Jo.	Solicitors' Journal
T.L.R.	Times Law Reports
W.L.R.	Weekly Law Reports

For the. following older reports, reference is also given to the English Reports (E.R.):

B. & C.	Barnewall & Cresswell's King's Bench Reports. E.R.107–109
B.& S.	Best & Smith's Queens Bench Reports. E.R. 121–122
C.B.	Common Bench. E.R. 135–139
H & C	Hurlstone & Coltman's Reports. E.R. 158–159
H & N	Hurlstone & Norman's Exchequer Reports. E.R. 156–158
M & W	Meeson & Welsby's Exchequer Reports. E.R. 150–153
Ph.	Phillip's Chancery Reports. E.R. 41
Taunt.	Taunton's Common Pleas Reports. E.R. 127–129
W.Bl.	Sir William Blackstone's King's Bench Reports. E.R. 96

Glossary of Latin terms

ex parte – one party only, i.e. a hearing of one party's case only
inter partes – between the parties, i.e. a hearing of both parties' representations
obiter – literally on the journey, by the way, hence an aside
per se – in itself
quia timet – because he is afraid
res ipsa loquitur – the thing speaks for itself
volenti non fit injuria – no wrong is done to a person who is willing

1. Introduction to tort

1. THE NATURE OF TORTIOUS LIABILITY

The law of tort is largely contained in the decisions of judges in cases brought before the courts. For that reason, it is sometimes referred to as a 'common law' subject, being the law as decided by the old common law courts, as distinct from statute law. Many areas of the common law have been codified in statutes however, for example The Occupiers' Liability Act 1957, and sometimes a statute has been passed to reform an area of law, such as the Law Reform (Contributory Negligence) Act 1945.

Several definitions of tort have been made by academic writers, one of the best known being that of Winfield[1]:– 'Tortious liability arises from the breach of a duty primarily fixed by law; this duty is towards persons generally and its breach is redressible by an action for unliquidated damages'. Because each case is decided on its own circumstances, Salmond[2] thought that an overall definition of tort was not possible, and called his book on the subject *The Law of Torts*. Before it is possible to bring an action in tort however, there must be a breach of a duty which the law recognises as redressible, and not all acts or omissions, however culpable, are redressible at law.

The usual remedy for a successful action in tort is unliquidated damages. Unliquidated damages are damages which the court assesses for non-pecuniary injury, such as a broken leg, as distinct from liquidated damages, which are damages claimed by the plaintiff to compensate for a specific loss capable of calculation, such as fares to hospital. A plaintiff may be more concerned to obtain an order for specific performance (that the defendant should do something) or an injunction (that the defendant should refrain from doing something) rather than damages, though, and the court might be prepared to grant an injunction for some torts, for example, in nuisance to abate a noise or remove an obstruction.

The duty imposed upon the defendant in tort is usually determined by that elusive character 'the reasonable man', who has been referred to by Bowen L.J. as 'the man on the Clapham omnibus'[3]. The breach of the duty may be a positive act or a mere omission.

While damage to the plaintiff is essential for a successful claim in most torts, it is not so in some such as trespass and libel, which are actionable '*per se*' (without proof of damage).

The degree of intention may vary from a planned action to total inadvertence. The more intended an act or omission is, however, the easier it will be to attribute the resulting damage to it.

2. THE DISTINCTION BETWEEN TORT AND CONTRACT, QUASI-CONTRACT, CRIME AND BREACH OF TRUST

Winfield's definition states that the duty is owed towards 'persons generally' and this is the main distinction between tortious liability and liability for breach of contract and breach of trust.

Contractual liability derives from the terms of an agreement between the plaintiff and the defendant and is limited by those terms. The damages recoverable for a breach will usually be a liquidated sum, namely, the cost of putting the plaintiff in the position in which he would have been had the defendant carried out his obligations under the agreement. It sometimes happens that the same actions by the defendant will be a breach of contract and a tort giving the plaintiff a right of action in both, although he will not be able to recover damages twice. This would arise for instance where the defendant supplies defective goods to the plaintiff under a contract as a result of which he suffers damage. A person may limit their liability in tort under the terms of a contract[4] but any such limitation is now subject to the Unfair Contract Terms Act 1977.

The plaintiff in an action for a breach of trust will be seeking to recover a sum in compensation for misappropriation of property, and even has rights to 'trace' the property and recover it from someone other than the defendant who misappropriated it. This is a very different action from one for unliquidated damages. The breach of trust by the trustee will be a breach of duty to the beneficiaries under the trust and not to 'persons generally'.

Quasi-contract gives rise to a claim for unjust enrichment, for example, where money is paid by A to B by mistake. B's obligation in these circumstances is to A and not to anyone else and will be for the sum which he has unjustly gained.

Some torts, such as assaults, are also crimes for which the Director of Public Prosecutions or the police, on behalf of the Crown, may bring a prosecution. The object of criminal proceedings is to punish the offender and to deter others from offending, whereas the primary object of an action in tort is to compensate the plaintiff. The fact that the plaintiff, by committing a tort, renders himself liable to an action for damages may of course also deter him, but this is incidental to the main objective of compensation.

3. MOTIVE IN TORT

The defendant's motive, being the reason for his conduct, is generally irrelevant to liability in tort. A good motive will not exonerate the defendant from liability for his tortious act, as in *Kirk* v *Gregory*[5] and a bad motive will not make an act tortious which would not otherwise be so as in *Bradford Corporation* v *Pickles*[6]. However, malice, in the sense of an improper motive, may be a relevant factor in some torts such as malicious prosecution and conspiracy. It may also be relevant in those cases of nuisance involving interference with comfort and amenity, where it will operate to negative the reasonableness of the interference with the plaintiff's rights. It will destroy two defences in defamation, namely, qualified privilege and fair comment.

4. FAULT

Although culpability underlies every action in tort, it is not an essential ingredient. The object of the action is to redress an injury and not to punish the defendant. Nevertheless value judgments of the defendant's, or the plaintiff's, conduct may be relevant in determining the amount of damages awarded or the extent of the duty owed. A plaintiff who contributes to an accident by his own negligence may have his damages against the defendant for negligence reduced proportionately[7] and a defendant's duty under the Occupiers' Liability Acts for dangerous premises is less onerous if the plaintiff is a trespasser than if he is an invitee.[8]

5. THE INSURANCE BACKGROUND TO TORT CLAIMS

Many torts where accidental damage is caused are covered by insurance policies. There are two kinds of accidents arising from torts for which it is compulsory by law to insure. These are injuries to third parties in motor accidents, and injuries at work[9]. Although the defendant is sued in his own name, in the event of liability, damages will be paid by the insurance company. If a person is absent from work as a result of an accident, he can claim sickness benefit and is only required to refund half of this for the first five years if he recovers the loss of wages in a subsequent action in tort. An action in tort costs more and takes longer[10] than a claim for social security benefits, however, and there is always an element of risk in a court case. To what extent then should the law of tort be replaced by insurance and State benefit schemes? The Pearson Commission, which was appointed in 1973 following the thalidomide cases, spent five years hearing evidence and deliberating on this and reported in 1978[11]. They decided that the only area where social security benefits should be available, apart from industrial injuries where they already are, is road accidents. They justified this on four grounds:

(i)   the large number of road accidents;
(ii)   that road accidents are not confined to any particular group of persons but affect the population generally;
(iii)   road accidents are likely to be serious;
(iv)   road traffic is an essential part of modern living.

There were two further recommendations of the Commission's which, if implemented, would be likely to diminish the role of tort:

(i)   that no damages should be awarded for pain and suffering for the first three months following an accident and
(ii)   the whole of any social security payments received should be offset against any damages recovered in tort.

Both of these recommendations would discourage many smaller claims in tort.

The Commission considered the systems operating in other countries, including New Zealand, where personal injuries resulting from any accident are compensated from a state fund regardless of fault[12]. This would greatly reduce the significance of the law of tort. The Commission was not prepared to recommend any such far-reaching changes however and compromised by recommending an extension of the present state benefits for industrial injuries[13] to cover also motor accidents.

There are two state-administered schemes for compensation for personal injuries only, where any action in tort is likely to be unrewarding. The Motor Insurers' Bureau pays compensation to anyone injured by an uninsured driver and the Criminal Injuries Compensation Board pays compensation to the victims of crime.

CONCLUSION

As with any branch of law, tort is constantly adapting in order to deal with the changing social conditions of modern living. Negligence will often be the cause of an accident, for most damage is caused by inadvertence rather than intention, but in recent years the courts have developed the tort of negligence itself to the point where it has encroached upon other torts considerably.[14]. There have been increased trends towards state or other compulsory insurance systems, which must, to some extent, replace the law of tort.

NOTES TO CHAPTER 1

1. *Winfield & Jolowicz on Tort*, 12th Ed.

2. Salmond, *The Law of Torts*, 2nd Ed.

3. Citing Greer L.J. in *Hall* v *Brooklands Auto Racing Club* (1933) 1 K.B.22

4. For example, Section 2(1) of the Occupiers' Liability Act 1957 provides for exclusion of the occupier's duty under the act 'by agreement or otherwise'.

5. *Kirk* v *Gregory* (1876) 1 Ex.D.55
Someone who moved some jewellery which she believed to be at risk to a place she thought safe was liable for trespass to it when it was stolen as she failed to show that it was necessary to move it.

6. *Bradford Corporation* v *Pickles* (1895) A.C.587
Mr Pickles resented the fact that Bradford Corporation would not purchase his land for a water supply scheme. Water percolated from his land to that of the corporation's on a lower level. He therefore drilled a shaft on his land which diminished the water percolating through to the Corporation's land. As he had not committed any tort, however, his malicious motive was irrelevant.

7. Law Reform (Contributory Negligence) Act 1945.

8. This was the position under the common law and now has statutory embodiment in the Occupiers' Liability Act 1984.

9. Road Traffic Act 1972; Employers' Liability (Compulsory Insurance) Act 1969 and Employers' Liability (Defective Equipment) Act 1969.

10. The Pearson Commission estimated that costs of an action in tort amounted to 85% of the compensation paid, but the cost of recovering social security benefits was only 11% of the amount recovered. Where damages of over £5,000 were recovered in tort actions, over 50% of the cases took over two years to realise payment compared with an average period of nine and a half months to recover social security benefits.

11. *Report of the Royal Commission on Civil Liability and Compensation for Personal Injury*, Cmnd. 7054, 1978.

12. Accident Compensation Act 1972 and Accident Compensation Amendment Act (No.2) 1973.

13. National Insurance (Industrial Injuries) Act 1946.

14. For example, it is doubtful since the case of *Letang* v *Cooper* (1964) 2 All.E.R. 929 whether it is possible for the tort of trespass to be negligent, and an action for negligent trespass should be brought in negligence itself.

2. Vicarious Liability

1. INTRODUCTION

Vicarious liability arises when A is liable for damages to C for the tort of B. B will also remain liable, so that A and B are jointly liable and A may be able to recover the whole or part of the damages paid by him from B under the Civil Liability (Contribution) Act 1978.

Vicarious liability derives from the relationship between A and B and has been recognised to exist between principals and agents and partners. The most common situation which gives rise to vicarious liability however is employment, where the employer (A) is liable for damage caused by the tort of his employee (B) in the course of his employment to a third party who is injured (C).

For A to be liable, it is necessary to establish two things:

(a) that B is an employee of A's under a contract of service and not an independent contractor, and

(b) that tort was committed by B in the course of his employment.

In both these requirements, the courts have leaned heavily in favour of finding a vicarious liability as the employer will be covered by insurance and able to meet the claim for damages, whereas the employee will not. The cases therefore often reflect a very artificial application of the criteria.

(a) Is a person employed as an employee (or 'servant') or as an independent contractor?

It is often difficult to distinguish a contract of service from a contract for services undertaken by an independent contractor. At one time, great emphasis was placed on what is known as the 'control' test, that is, that in a 'master–servant' relationship (to use the terminology of the old cases which are often still applicable) the master can tell the servant not only what to do, but also how to do it. Although this test is still accepted as important today, it is not conclusive, and is often not suitable for modern employment situations where employees are highly skilled. The contract must be looked at as a whole and all other factors affecting the employment must be considered. Professor Street has said that in order to decide whether there is sufficient control to make the contract one of employment, it is necessary to have regard to seven factors:

   (i)   the extent to which the employer can control the details
of the work;
  (ii)   whether the method of payment is on a time or job basis;
 (iii)   whose tools, equipment and premises are to be used;
  (iv)   the skill called for in the work;
   (v)   the intention of the parties;
  (vi)   the freedom of selection of labour by the employer;
 (vii)   the power to dismiss.

It should be particularly noticed that although a specific provision in the contract between the parties as to the nature of the contract is one factor to be taken into account, it is not conclusive. (*Ferguson* v *John Dawson & Partners (Contractors) Ltd*[1]).

   By contrast, an independent contractor is a person employed to do only a specific task, whose employment will cease on its completion. The tasks may vary enormously and may be the very kind of work for which a servant is emloyed under other circumstances. This is neatly illustrated by the judgment of Denning L.J. in *Stevenson, Jordan & Harrison Ltd* v *Macdonald* (1952) where he said:

It is often easy to recognise a contract of service when you see it, but difficult to say wherein the distinction lies. A ship's master, a chauffeur and a reporter on the staff of a newspaper are all employed under a contract of service; but a ship's pilot, a taxi-man and a newspaper contributor are employed under a contract for services. One feature which seems to run through the instances is that, under a contract of service, a man is employed as part of a business, and his work is done as an integral part of the business; whereas under a contract for services, his work, although done for the business, is not integrated into it but is only accessory to it.

The test of whether the work is an 'integral part of the business' would seem to be as good a way as any of identifying a contract of service.

   Further complications may arise when a servant is hired (often together with machinery which he is operating) to another employer. Does he remain the employee of the original employer, or does he become the employee of the hiring employer?

   The burden of proof to show that he has become the employee

of the hiring employer is on the original employer, and the more skilled the employee is, the more difficult it will be to discharge it. (*Mersey Docks & Harbour Board* v *Coggins & Griffith (Liverpool) Ltd*)[2]. Again, a clause in the contract of hire stipulating that the employee is to become the servant of the hirer is not conclusive, although it may enable the original employer to claim a contribution or indemnity (*Spalding* v *Tarmac Civil Engineering Ltd*[3]).

The concept of a master–servant relationship has been extended artificially to cover a driver of a vehicle who is driving at the owner's request for a purpose in some way of interest to the owner (*Ormrod* v *Crosville Motor Services Ltd*[4]). Salmond says that a person may be a servant for a single transaction only and even though his service is gratuitous. An employer will not be liable, however, for the use of his car by an employee for purposes other than his business, even though he pays a mileage allowance (*Nottingham* v *Aldridge*[5]).

(b) Was the tort committed by the servant in the course of his employment?

The underlying policy of finding the master, who is insured, liable wherever possible for the torts of his servant is most evident in the liberal interpretation by the courts of what acts are within the course of employment, and many of the cases in this respect are very artificial. Finnimore J. said in *Staton* v *National Coal Board* (1957) 'there is no one test which is exhaustive by which this particular problem can be solved'.

It may be said however that a servant will be acting in the course of his employment in the following circumstances:

(a) If his act is expressly or impliedly authorised by the master

Clearly acts expressly authorised by the master will be within the course of employment and the onus is on the master to ensure that there is a safe system of work. Acts by a servant not expressly authorised may also be within the course of his employment, however, if they are in furtherance of the master's interests, for example, to protect his property (*Poland* v *Parr*[6]) or to keep order on his premises (*Petterson* v *Royal Oak Hotel*[7]).

(b) If it is an unauthorised way of doing an authorised act

Examples of this are the over-zealous railway porter in *Bayley* v *Manchester, Sheffield & Lincs. Railway*[8], and the driver of the fork lift truck who moved a lorry blocking access to his warehouse in *Kay* v *I.T.W. Ltd.*[9]

More controversially, acts expressly forbidden by the employer are also included if they are in the course of furthering the employer's business. See *Rose* v *Plenty*[10], *L.C.C.* v *Cattermoles*[11] and *Ilkiw* v *Samuels & Others*[12].

An act will not be in the course of employment however if the servant is 'on a frolic of his own' (per Parke B. in *Joel* v *Morison* (1834)). For example, a servant giving a lift to a passenger when expressly forbidden to do so was held to be acting outside the scope of his employment as it was in no way in the interests of the master (*Twine* v *Beans Express* 1946).

If the driver of a vehicle makes a diversion from his authorised route, will this amount to a 'frolic of his own' or not? In each case, it depends upon the extent of the diversion and the purpose of it, and the cases of *Harvey* v *R.G. O'Dell*[13] and *Hilton* v *Thomas Burton (Rhodes) Ltd*[14] may be contrasted.

(c) An act which is incidental to the servant's employment

This may include not only acts which are impliedly authorised, as in *Kay* v *I.T.W. Ltd*[19] but also acts which, although not part of the employment, are incidental to it (see *Staton* v *National Coal Board*[15]). The most remarkable case of an incidental act held to be in the course of employment is that of *Century Insurance Co. Ltd* v *Northern Ireland Road Transport Board*[16].

In the case of *Harrison* v *Michelin Tyre Co. Ltd*[17] Comyn J. had to consider whether a practical joke by an employee which resulted in injury to a fellow-employee was in the course of his employment or whether it was (quite literally) a frolic of his own. On the facts of the case, he decided that it was 'part and parcel' of his employment, distinguishing the case from other practical joke cases held to be outside the scope of the employment. In one, the plaintiff had failed to establish a failure in supervision by the employers[18]. In a case where the employers were aware of the mischievous nature of the practical joker however, they were held liable[19].

(d) Can deliberate criminal acts be within the course of employment?

The cases of *Petterson* v *Royal Oak Hotel*[7] and *Lloyd* v *Grace, Smith & Co.*[20] indicate that even criminal acts may be within the course of employment, and in the latter case it was made clear that this is so notwithstanding that they are entirely for the benefit of the servant and in no way for the benefit of the master. The rationale for this is the ostensible authority which the employer has bestowed upon the servant. Even this ostensible authority will not extend however to 'moonlighting' by the servant (*Kooragang Investments Property Ltd* v *Richardson & Wrench Ltd*[21]) or to an act which constitutes an offence whith it is not within the servant's ostensible authority to perform.

2. AN EMPLOYER'S LIABILITY FOR THE TORTS OF HIS INDEPENDENT CONTRACTOR

At the beginning of this chapter, in considering who is an employee, a distinction was made between an employee and an independent contractor, who is employed to carry out a particular task only and is not 'integral' to the employer's work. As Denning L.J.'s judgment makes clear (see above, p. 34), it is not the nature of the work itself but the relationship between the parties which determines whether a person is employed as a servant or an independent contractor. It is crucial to an employer's liability however to determine in which capacity a person is employed, as generally an employer will not be liable for the torts of his independent contractor.

To this general rule, there are a number of qualifications.

The first obligation on a person who employs an independent contractor is to take reasonable care to ensure that the contractor is competent for the work which he is employed to do. If the work is skilled, then he cannot be responsible for overseeing it (*Haseldine* v *Daw & Sons Ltd*[22]) but he will be responsible for unskilled work such as cleaning (*Woodward* v *Mayor of Hastings*[23]).

Secondly, a person cannot escape liability for 'extra-hazardous' activities by employing an independent contractor and the duty in such undertakings is to see that care is taken (*Honeywell & Stein Ltd* v *Larkin*[24]).

Thirdly, there are certain circumstances where the law imposes a strict (or absolute) liability on someone which he cannot avoid by delegating work to another person. Work on a highway comes within this category (*Gray* v *Pullen*[25], *Tarry* v *Ashton*[26]). However, where an apparently competent independent contractor was employed to remove a tree in a garden, which fell on to telephone wires causing them to fall on to the highway, there was no liability because the work was not on the highway but near the highway (*Salsbury* v *Woodland*[27]). Also within this category is any work which causes subsidence to neighbouring land. A right of support to land is a natural right of a landowner and a neighbour's duty in relation to this is absolute. This was recognised in the early cases of *Dalton* v *Angus*[28] and *Bower* v *Peate*[29]. In the Australian case of *Stoneham* v *Lyons & Others*[30] however, the employer was not liable where builders who had been expressly told not to excavate without the architect's instructions to do so nevertheless did so, causing damage to a garage on adjoining land.

The Rule in *Rylands* v *Fletcher* (see Chapter 6) and damage from fire are further instances where strict liability is imposed on a person for the acts of an independent contractor employed by him (*Balfour* v *Barty-King*[31]). There is certainly strict liability for some acts in nuisance, as shown by the case of *Mantania* v *National Provincial Bank*[32] and possibly also for acts not inherently dangerous but involving negligence by the contractor (*Spicer* v *Smee*[33]).

Finally, an employer may be liable for the negligence of an independent contractor employed by him provided that the negligence is in the performance of the work and not incidental to it (*Reedie* v *L. & N.W. Ry*[34]). Of that case Chapman wrote:

I am not liable if my contractor in making a bridge happens to drop a brick . . . but I am liable if he makes a bridge which will not open . . . The liability of the employer depends on the existence of a duty . . . it only extends to the limit of that duty. I owe a duty with regard to the structure of the bridge; I owe a duty to see that my bridge will open; but I owe no duty with regard to the disposition of bricks and hammers in the course of construction.

Although there may be sound reasons for the liabilities imposed on an employer for the torts of his independent contractor in negligence and extra-hazardous undertakings, as Glanville Williams has pointed out, the result may be unfair both morally and socially. From the moral point of view, liability should go with culpability, and socially, it may result in severe hardship to a person who employs an independent contractor who will often be a private individual and uninsured for any damage resulting, whereas the contractor himself may well be insured.

QUESTIONS

1. Officebuild plc entered into a contract with Cranehire plc for the hire of a crane. The contract provided that Cranehire plc would provide a competent operator whose wages would be paid by them. Owing to the negligence of the operator, an accident occurred on the site as a result of which one of the employees of Officebuild plc was seriously injured.
   (a) Consider the liability of:
      (i) Officebuild plc
      (ii) Cranehire plc
   (b) Would the answer differ if the contract had provided that the wages of the operator were to be paid by Officebuild plc? (Specimen paper)

2. Discuss the liability of an employer for wrongful acts committed by his employees, and by those who are not his employees but are doing work for him. (1985 paper)

3. Cranehire plc entered into a contract with Goodbuild plc to hire a crane with a competent driver. This contract stated that the crane driver's wages were to be paid by Cranehire. The crane driver, in negligently operating the crane, trapped and injured one of Goodbuild's employees. Brown, another employee of Goodbuild plc, injured his back in helping to free his trapped workmate.
   Consider:
   (a) the liability of Cranehire plc
   (b) the liability of Goodbuild plc
   (c) the position if the hire contract had stated that the crane driver's wages were to be paid by Goodbuild plc.
   (*Note*: This question also raises the issue of *volenti non fit injuria* and rescue cases, discussed under Defences to Tort in Chapter 3).

NOTES TO CHAPTER 2

1. *Ferguson* v *John Dawson & Partners (Contractors) Ltd* (1976) 1 WLR 1213
A building worker expressly stipulated orally that he was a 'self-employed labour only sub-contractor'. The Court held that there was nevertheless a master-servant relationship and that he was an employee. Having regard to the remainder of the contract (such factors as the site agent being able to tell him what work to do, to move him from one site to another, to dismiss him, the tools were provided by the employers and the hourly

payment was in reality a 'wage') the relationship was typically one of master and servant and he was a party to a contract of service.

2. *Mersey Docks and Harbour Board* v *Coggins & Griffith (Liverpool) Ltd* (1947) AC 1

The Harbour Board hired out a crane, together with the crane driver, to some stevedores for unloading a ship. The contract of hire provided that the crane driver was to be the servant of the stevedores, but the Harbour Board paid him and could dismiss him. Owing to the negligence of the crane driver, someone was injured. It was held by the House of Lords that the Harbour Board were solely liable. Although the stevedores could tell the crane driver what to do, they could not tell him how to do it, and therefore did not have the required degree of control over his work to make him their employee.

3. *Spalding* v *Tarmac Civil Engineering Ltd* (1966) 1 WLR 156

The 1st defendants were employed by a local authority to carry out construction work at an airfield. They hired an excavator and operator from the 2nd defendants. The plaintiff was an engineer employed by the local authority who was injured by the excavator. Culpability for this was apportioned as to 60% the negligence of the operator and 40% defective brakes on the excavator due to lack of maintenance. The contract of hire made the operator the servant of the 2nd defendants and stated that they were liable for all claims. Held – they were liable for 60% of the claim but the 1st defendants were liable for 40% as the responsibility for maintenance remained with them and was not removed by the contract of hire.

4. *Ormrod* v *Crosville Motor Services Ltd* (1953) 1 WLR 409

The owner of a car asked his friend to drive it from Birkenhead to Monte Carlo where they were to start a holiday together. Held – owner was vicariously liable for his friend's negligent driving as he had an interest in the journey he was making. It was irrelevant that the friend was also acting in his own interests.

5. *Nottingham* v *Aldridge* (1972) 2 All ER 717

The plaintiff and the defendant were required by their employers to attend a course at a residential training centre. The defendant borrowed his father's van in order to drive himself and the plaintiff there on Sunday evening. The plaintiff was injured due to his negligent driving. Held – even though the defendant could claim a mileage allowance for himself and the plaintiff, not within the course of his employment. No duty to drive himself and the plaintiff there and not delegated by his employers to do so.

6. *Poland* v *Parr* (1927) 1 KB 236

A carter assaulted a boy whom he suspected of stealing sugar from his master's cart – held that this was in the course of his employment and the master was liable as he was acting to protect his master's property.

7. *Petterson* v *Royal Oak Hotel* (1948) N.E.L.R. 136

A customer in a public house threw a glass at the barman after being refused a drink. The barman threw a piece of the glass at the customer as he was leaving and injured him. Held – this was in the course of his employment as it was a way, although a wrong way, of keeping order.

8. *Bayley* v *Manchester, Sheffield & Lincolnshire Railway* (1873) L.R.8 C.P.148
The defendant's porter, mistakenly believing a passenger to be on the wrong train, pulled him off the train forcibly. Held – he was acting in the course of his employment.

9. *Kay* v *I.T.W. Ltd* (1967) 3 WLR 695
A storekeeper employed by the defendants wanted to move a fork lift truck which he was driving back to the warehouse. He found the entrance blocked by a lorry belonging to a customer, and so moved the lorry. In doing so, he injured the plaintiff, another employee of the defendant's. Held – this was in the course of his employment as it was to enable him to carry out his work.

10. *Rose* v *Plenty* (1976) 1 All.E.R. 97
A milkman employed by the defendants allowed a boy aged 13 to assist him with his round, contrary to an express prohibition from his employers. The boy was injured by the negligent driving of the milk float. Held – this was nevertheless in the course of the milkman's employment, as the prohibition extended only to the way in which the work was done and did not limit the scope of the work itself, and the employers were liable.

11. *London County Council* v *Cattermoles (Garages) Ltd* (1953) 1 WLR 997
It was part of the work of a garage hand employed by the defendants to move cars by hand, but he was expressly forbidden to drive them. He injured the plaintiff while driving a car to move it. Held – this was in the course of his employment and his employers were liable.

12. *Ilkiw* v *Samuels & Others* (1963) 2 All. E.R. 879
W, a lorry driver employed by the defendants, allowed a workman (not employed by the defendants) who had been helping with loading it to move the lorry without enquiring as to his driving ability. The workman, who was not used to driving a heavily loaded lorry, injured the plaintiff when the lorry ran into a conveyor belt upon which the plaintiff was standing. Held – this was in the course of the lorry driver's employment, even though he had strict instructions not to allow anyone else to drive the lorry, as the lorry was under his control and he had been negligent in allowing someone inexperienced to drive it.

13. *Harvey* v *R.G. O'Dell* (1958) 2 QB 78
An employee of the defendant's drove himself and another employee into a town five miles away to buy some tools and to have a mid-day meal. Due to his negligent driving, there was an accident on the way back in which he was killed and his passenger was injured. Held – this was in the course of his employment, and would have been so had the journey been made solely for the purpose of having a meal.

14. *Hilton* v *Thomas Burton (Rhodes) Ltd* (1961) 1 WLR 705

A van owned by their employers was used to transport a gang of workmen to a demolition site some 30 miles away, and was driven by one of the workmen, an employee. The workmen went for lunch at a public house and then returned to the site. Three of them decided to go for tea at a cafe 7 to 8 miles away, but before they reached the cafe, decided that they were too late and turned back. There was an accident on the way back owing to the employee's negligent driving and the plaintiff was injured. Held – this was not in the course of their employment. They were 'on a frolic of their own'.

15. *Staton* v *National Coal Board* (1957) 1 WLR 893

T, an employee of the defendants, had finished work and was cycling to the wages office to pick up his wages. There was an accident as a result of his negligence in which the plaintiff's husband, another employee of the defendants, was killed. Held – T was acting in the course of his employment as it was part of an employer's duty to pay wages, and wages were only paid at the wages office, to which T therefore had to go.

16. *Century Insurance Co. Ltd* v *Northern Ireland Road Transport Board* (1942) AC 509

The driver of a petrol tanker employed by the defendants lit a cigarette and threw away the match while unloading petrol from the tanker into an underground tank. There was an explosion and fire which damaged the plaintiff's garage. Held – although the act was done for his own benefit, it was nevertheless still in the course of his employment, and was a negligent and unauthorised way of doing what he was employed to do. Comyn J. in *Harrison* v *Michelin Tyre Co. Ltd* has said of this case '. . . the word "frolic" is an understatement: I would have thought a madness of his own'.

17. *Harrison* v *Michelin Tyre Co. Ltd* (1985) 1 All. E.R. 918

The defendant was pushing a truck along a passageway indicated by a chalk line. He diverged two inches to push it under the duckboard of a machine on which the plaintiff was standing so that the plaintiff fell off and was injured. Held – in the course of his work and his employers were liable.

18. *Coddington* v *International Harvester Company of GB* (1969) 6 K.I.R. 146

The plaintiff lit a tin of paint thinners which he and another employee X sat near for warmth. A third employee M who was passing kicked the tin nearer to X who was scorched and in jumping kicked the tin over and the plaintiff was badly burned. Held – employers not liable, since although M known as a practical joker, they had no reason to believe he was a danger in the foundry. The plaintiff had failed to establish that M's act was in the course of his employment.

19. *Hudson* v *Ridge Manufacturing Company Ltd* (1957) 2 All. E.R. 229

Employee had been persistently troublesome to fellow-employees for four years by tripping them up, and had been reprimanded by his foreman for this. Tripped up the plaintiff, a cripple, injuring him. Held – employers liable since knew of his mischievous nature.

20. *Lloyd* v *Grace, Smith & Co.* (1912) AC 716
A managing clerk employed by the defendants, a firm of solicitors, obtained money from a client by fraudulently inducing her to sign documents transferring property to him, with which he then absconded. Held – the defendants were liable and the act was in the course of his employment although entirely for his own benefit.

The clerk was carrying out the sort of work which he was employed to do and the employers had held him out to be responsible and trustworthy for the work.

21. *Kooragan Investments Pty Ltd* v *Richardson & Wrench Ltd* (1982) AC 462
An employee of the defendants, a firm of valuers, carried out valuations for a group of companies whom the defendants had instructed him to do no more work for, although they had previously done work for them. The valuations were on the defendants' headed notepaper, although the defendants did not know and did not benefit from the work in any way. The plaintiffs, who invested on the strength of the valuations, lost money. Held – the defendants were not liable. Their employee was 'moonlighting' and was not acting in the course of his employment. Authority could not be inferred from the fact that the work was of the type which he was employed to do.

22. *Haseldine* v *Daw & Sons Ltd* (1941)
A firm of contractors who specialised in the maintenance of lifts were employed by the defendant to repair a lift. Due to their negligence, the lift broke down very shortly after they had attended to it, injuring the plaintiff. Held – the employer was not liable as he could not be expected to realise that the lift had been negligently repaired.

23. *Woodward* v *Mayor of Hastings & Anor* (1945) KB 174
A charwoman working at a school failed to clear away loose snow from a step, as a result of which the plaintiff slipped and was injured. Held – the employers were liable as they were able to oversee her work. (Du Parcq L.J. said 'The craft of a charwoman may have its mysteries, but there is no esoteric quality in the nature of the work which the cleaning of a snow-covered step demands'.)

24. *Honeywill & Stein Ltd* v *Larkin Bros Ltd* (1934) 1 KB 191
A photographer who was employed to take photographs in a cinema used a flashlight, which caused a fire and damaged the cinema. Held – the employers were liable for the damage to the cinema as the use of a flashlight there was potentially hazardous.

25. *Gray* v *Pullen*(1864) 5 B. & S.970
The defendant employed an independent contractor to put a drain under the road to connect his own drain with the main sewer. The contractor filled in the trench which he had dug badly as a result of which the plaintiff, a road user, was injured. Held – the defendant was liable, even though not negligent himself.

26. *Tarry* v *Ashton* (1876) 1 QBD 314

A heavy lamp projecting from the defendants' property over the highway was repaired negligently by an independent contractor employed by them. The lamp subsequently fell and injured a passer-by. Held – the defendants were liable. The highway, for which there was strict liability, extended to the soil beneath the highway and the airspace over it. Also, there was a continuing liability for the structure after the contractors had finished the repair.

27. *Salsbury* v *Woodland* (1970) 1 QB 324

The defendant employed an apparently competent independent contractor to remove a tree in his garden which adjoined the highway. The tree fell on to some telephone wires, causing them to fall into the road, as a result of which the plaintiff, a road user, was injured. Held – the defendant was not liable. The removal of the tree was not an extra-hazardous act, and although near the highway, the work was not on the highway.

28. *Dalton* v *Angus* (1881) 6 App C 740

Over 20 years previously, a house had been converted into a factory and girders inserted into the brickwork stacks, the effect of which was to increase the pressure on the soil of the adjoining land. The house on the adjoining land was demolished by an independent contractor employed by the owner, which caused damage to the factory. Held – the owners were liable even though the contractor had been instructed to shore up and support the factory. A right of support to the factory had been acquired as an easement since it had been enjoyed for over twenty years.

29. *Bower* v *Peate* (1876) 1 QBD 321

The defendant employed an independent contractor to demolish his house and rebuild it, the contractor undertaking to do all that was necessary to support the plaintiff's adjoining house. Held – defendant was liable for damage caused by subsidence to adjoining house.

30. *Stoneman* v *Lyons & Others* (1975) 50 ALTR 370

The appellants employed the builders to erect a supermarket and the builders were instructed not to excavate without the architect's instructions to do so. They did so and the respondent's garage, on the boundary of his adjoining land, was damaged as a result. Held – the builders had been negligent in doing something which they were forbidden to do and the appellants were not liable.

31. *Balfour* v *Barty-King* (1957) 1 QB 496

Plumbers employed by the defendant to thaw frozen pipes used a blow lamp on pipes which were lagged causing a fire. Held – the employer was liable for the fire.

32. *Mantania* v *National Provincial Bank* (1936) 155 LT 74

The tenants of the second floor of a building employed independent contractors to carry out alterations. The dust and noise made by them stopped the plaintiff, who was a tenant on the first floor of the building, from giving piano lessons for three months. Held – the defendants were liable in nuisance to the plaintiff.

33. *Spicer* v *Smee* (1946) 1 All. E.R. 489

A fire caused by the negligent re-wiring of a bungalow by an independent contractor destroyed an adjoining bungalow. Held – employer liable.

34. *Reedie* v *L.&N.W.Ry* (1849) 4 Ex.244

Contractors employed by a railway company to build a bridge negligently allowed a stone to fall on to a passer-by below. Held – railway company not liable as this was an act of collateral negligence.

3. General Defences and Remedies

There are certain defences and remedies which apply specifically to particular torts. For instance, statutory authority may be a defence to an action in nuisance, and abatement of the nuisance is a possible remedy, whilst entry onto another's land to abate a nuisance may itself be a defence to an action for trespass. There are some defences and remedies which apply generally to all or most torts however, and these can be looked at separately.

1. GENERAL DEFENCES

(a) *Volenti non fit injuria*

This is a Latin phrase used to express the maxim that a person who willingly accepts a risk cannot complain of an injury, which is in itself a tort, arising from it[1].

The majority of cases where it has been successfully pleaded as a defence are actions arising out of sporting activities where either a spectator or a participant has been injured. In *Hall* v *Brookland Auto-Racing Club*[2] for example, a spectator who was injured when a racing car crashed through some iron railings failed in his action in tort as motor racing is recognised as a dangerous sport and a person who goes to watch it voluntarily accepts the possible risks involved. In *Simms* v *Leigh Rugby Football Club*[3] it was held that a rugby player accepts the risk of sustaining a broken leg in a rugby tackle and this amounts to a defence in an action for the injury.

For the defence to apply, the consent must be to the particular activity which causes the injury, so that where the injury is caused by some extraneous act, the plaintiff will not be deemed to have consented to that. Thus in a Canadian case, *Payne & Payne* v *Maple Leaf Gardens*[4] a spectator who was injured by an ice hockey stick in the course of a fracas between two of the players was still able to sue successfully, as although he had consented to the risks inherent in the game, he had not consented to risks arising from a fight between the players. In *Gillmore* v *L.C.C.*[5] a member of a physical training class who was injured by falling on a slippery floor was held not to have consented to the extra risk caused by the slippery floor.

The strict application of the principle has led to difficulties where the cause of action is negligence, and some writers[6] have expressed the view that the defence has no application in an action for negligence as a plaintiff can never be said to have consented to the defendant's negligence. In *Slater* v *Clay Cross Co. Ltd*[7] the plaintiff was found to have consented to the normal risks of walking along a private railway line through a tunnel, but not to the negligence of the train driver, who failed to slow down and whistle on entering the tunnel, whose train then struck her. A more questionable decision is *Dann* v *Hamilton*[8] where a person who accepted a lift with a drunken driver was held not to be '*volens*' to his negligent driving. In *Owens* v *Brimmell*[9] however, a passenger's knowledge of a driver's drunkenness was treated as contributory negligence and 20 per cent damages deducted.

The acceptance of the risk may be express, as for instance where a notice makes it clear that a person accepts no responsibility for injury arising from a particular activity[10] or where there is a contract which exempts the defendant from liability for injury. The freedom to include such exemption clauses in a contract is now severely restricted by the Unfair Contract Terms Act 1977 which relates to business activities or premises. This allows only a reasonable exemption for damage to property caused by negligence, and no exemption at all for death or personal injury caused by negligence. Moreover, the Act specifically provides that knowledge of a contract exemption of this sort does not indicate acceptance of the risk[11]. More frequently, however, consent is implied from the plaintiff's participation in the activity. This is particularly apparent in the case of *Murray* v *Harringay Arena*[12] where a six year old boy, who was a spectator at an ice hockey match, was struck in the eye by the puck, but the owners of the rink were held not to be liable to ensure a spectator's safety from obviously foreseeable risks arising from the game, although it is unlikely that a six year old had a full appreciation of the risks involved.

The consent must be freely given, and consent given under fraud or duress, or any element of compulsion, will not be sufficient. Thus in *Smith* v *Baker*[13], a workman who was working in a cutting over which heavy stones were being moved by a crane was held not to have voluntarily accepted the risk because he was under an obligation to carry out his employer's orders. This case is also authority for mere knowledge of a risk not amounting to consent to it. The workman knew that the crane was operating overhead, but that in itself did not make him '*volens*' to the risk. Lord Herschell said in this case:

> . . . does the mere continuance in service, with knowledge of the risk, preclude the employed, if he suffers from [the employer's] negligence, from recovering in respect of his employer's breach of duty? I cannot assent to the proposition that the maxim '*volenti non fit injuria*' applies to such a case, and that the employer can invoke its aid to protect him from liability for his wrong.

In some cases, there may be an overlap between the defence of '*volens*' and contributory negligence, but the two were nicely distinguished in *I.C.I. Ltd* v *Shatwell*[14]. Two brothers, who were working in a quarry, deliberately ignored their employers' regulations, made in accordance with a statutory order, as to testing detonators and there was an explosion which injured both of them. The House of Lords held that their deliberate act, which they knew to be in breach of the regulations and to involve a certain risk, allowed their employers to plead successfully the defence of *volens*, which meant that the employers were not liable at all for the breach of the statutory requirements. Had their conduct been merely negligent, the defence of contributory negligence might have applied to reduce their damages, although it should be noted that it is open to the court to find a defendant 100 per cent contributorily negligent, thus effectively cancelling out the defendant's liability.

The defence of '*volens*' is usually pleaded in cases of personal injury and the similar defence of 'leave and licence' may be available in torts against property.

(b) Necessity

It is a defence to an action in tort arising out of an injury to another person or his property that the act which caused the injury was done to protect the person or property of the defendant or someone else.

The defence is strikingly illustrated by the South African case of *Grayvenstein* v *Hattingh*[15] where the defendants were held to be justified in entering the land of a third person and scaring a plague of locusts coming towards their land back on to the land of the plaintiff, where they devoured the plaintiff's crops. In this country, preventive measures against flooding, which result in the inadvertant flooding of a neighbour's land, are within the scope of the defence provided that all reasonable care is taken[16]. In *Dewey* v *White*[17] a house adjoining a highway became dangerous after a fire, and in demolishing it, damage was caused to an adjoining house. This was held to be covered by the defence of necessity. In *Burmah Oil Co. Ltd* v *Lord Advocate*[18], however, Lord Upjohn expressed doubts as to the extent to which the defence can apply nowadays, and pointed out that it must be obsolete in many situations where it would have applied in earlier times. For example, a person whose house was threatened by fire spreading from his neighbour's house could send for the fire brigade, and the availability of such a service might not justify him in entering on to his neighbour's land to demolish his neighbour's house.

The defence is more likely to succeed if the act causing injury is to protect persons rather than property. In *Southport Corporation* v *Esso PetroleumLtd*[19], where a cargo of oil which was jettisoned to save the ship polluted the beach, Devlin, J. said 'The safety of human lives belongs to a different scale of values from the safety of property. The two are beyond comparison and the necessity for saving life has at all times been considered a proper ground for inflicting such damage as may be necessary upon another's property'. The action must be judged as reasonable or not in the circumstances prevailing at the time and not with the value of hindsight, so that in the case of *Cope* v *Sharpe*[20], where the defendant's gamekeeper set fire to a strip of heather on the plaintiff's land to prevent a fire from spreading to the defendant's land where there were nesting pheasants, and the fire was later brought under control and extinguished, the defence of necessity was held to apply nevertheless to an action by the plaintiff for trespass as the gamekeeper's act had been reasonable at the time.

The defence will only apply if there is some measure of emergency. It was therefore held inapplicable as a defence to trespass against squatters who occupied an empty building[21] and against defendants who trespassed on to neighbouring land to carry out repairs to their property, even though there was no other means of doing so[22].

It is possible that a quasi-contractual claim for compensation, as distinct from a claim for damages in tort, may lie for damage resulting from an act of necessity. In *Southport Corporation* v *Esso Petroleum Ltd*[19] Devlin J. said:

I am not prepared to hold without further consideration that a man is entitled to damage the property of another without compensating him merely because the infliction of such damage is necessary to save his own property. . . . For example, whether it is permissible to do £5,000 worth of damage to a third party in order to save property worth £10,000.

(c) Statutory authority

An act which is a tort may be the inevitable result of carrying out work under the authority of a statute, and this will be a defence. The statute may impose a duty to carry out the work or be merely permissive in authorising it.

The most common application of this defence is in actions for nuisance[23]. Whether the statute authorises the tortious act or not depends upon the actual wording of the statute, and the presumption is that Parliament did not intend to encroach upon the rights of private individuals. Thus if the tort committed is due to the work authorised by the statute being carried out badly or carelessly, and no tort would have been committed if the work had been carried out properly, then the statutory authority will not be a defence. In *Manchester Corporation* v *Farnworth*[24] the plaintiff's crops were destroyed by fumes from an electricity generating station erected under statutory authority. The plaintiff obtained damages, and Viscount Sumner said that the defendants 'have failed to show that they have used all reasonable diligence and taken all reasonable steps and precautions to prevent their operations from being a nuisance to their neighbours'.

(d) Limitation of actions

The law provides for a limitation period, after which a plaintiff is barred from bringing an action for a tort committed against him. This is to avoid unfairness to the defendant, who may be prejudiced by a plaintiff's delay if he is unable to trace witnesses and obtain evidence as to events which happened some years ago.

The Limitation Act 1980 provides that an action arising out of 'negligence, nuisance or breach of duty'[25] will be barred six years from the date when the cause of action accrued, or three years from the date of accrual if the claim is for personal injuries. Breach of duty includes an action for breach of contract and the Section has been held to include actions for personal injuries arising from other torts such as trespass[26].

The date when the action accrues

The action accrues and time begins to run from the date when the plaintiff could succeed in an action against the defendant. In torts which are actionable *per se* (without proof of damage) such as trespass, this will be the date of the tort, but where damage is an essential element of the tort, such as in negligence, it will be the date on which the damage is suffered. As regards personal injuries however, the period may be extended to three years after the plaintiff knows that he has a cause of action, and knowledge is statutorily defined by Section 14 of the Limitation Act as when the plaintiff is aware:

  (i)   that the injury is significant;
  (ii) that it was attributable wholly or in part to the alleged tort[27];
  (iii) of the identity of the defendant[28]; or
  (iv) if it is alleged that the act or omission was that of a person other than the defendant, the identity of that person and the additional facts supporting the bringing of an action against the defendant. (This could arise in the case of an employer's vicarious liability for a tortious injury by his employee).

Section 14(3) provides that a person is deemed to have knowledge which he might be expected to have from facts observable or ascertainable by him, or facts which would have been ascertainable by him with the assistance of expert advice which it would have been reasonable for him to obtain.

Section 33(1) gives the court a general discretion to extend the limitation period, having regard to any hardship to the plaintiff or prejudice to the defendant, and the court is directed to consider six factors:

  (i)   the length of, and reasons for, the plaintiff's delay[29];
  (ii) the effect of the delay on evidence in the case;
  (iii) the defendant's conduct after the cause of action arose, including his response to the plaintiff's request for information;
  (iv) the duration of any disability of the plaintiff after the cause of action accrued;
  (v)   whether the plaintiff acted promptly and reasonably once he knew he might have a claim;
  (vi) any steps taken by the plaintiff to obtain medical, legal or other expert advice and what the advice was.

These factors are not exhaustive, however, and the court may consider other matters[30].

Disability or fraud

Where the plaintiff is under a disability, such as infancy or unsound mind, the limitation period runs from when the disability ceases.

Section 32(1) provides that where the plaintiff's action is based on fraud, or his cause of action has been deliberately concealed, then time does not begin to run until the plaintiff discovers, or could have discovered with reasonable diligence, the fraud or concealment[31].

Latent damage

A matter of great importance to the construction industry is the date at which time begins to run in respect of a tort which causes a latent defect in a building, which may not become known to a plaintiff until some years later.

Where there is any deliberate concealment or 'conscious wrongdoing' time will clearly not run until discovery of the damage, so the problem will arise almost exclusively in connection with claims in negligence. The Court of Appeal has held however that proceeding with a job does not amount to deliberate concealment[32].

In *Pirelli General Cable Works Ltd* v *Oscar Faber & Partners Ltd*[33], the House of Lords reversed an earlier Court of Appeal decision and decided that time runs under the Limitation Act from the date the damage occurs, and not from the date on which it was first discovered. The case concerned an unsuitable chimney, negligently designed by the defendants, in which cracks must have occurred in 1970 shortly after it was built. The plaintiffs did not discover, and could not have discovered the cracks, until 1977. It was nevertheless held that their action in 1978 was barred as time ran from 1970 when the cracks occurred. Moreover, time does not start to run again for the purchaser of a defective building, so that his action may be barred before he even acquires it. Lord Fraser explained in the Pirelli case that 'No owner in the chain can have a better claim than his predecessor in title'.

The problem of balancing fairness to a plaintiff and the heavy burden imposed on professional people in the construction industry by a claim many years later was the subject of a Law Reform Committee's Report[34]. The Committee agreed with the decision in Pirelli that time should run from the date of damage but recommended an extension of three years from the date of discovery. They recommended a 'cut-off' point fifteen years after the commission of the tort however, which should not be extendable at the court's discretion.

An action for personal injuries caused by a latent defect in a building would not be barred as time would not run until the plaintiff had knowlege of his claim, as defined by Section 14.

Under the Defective Premises Act 1972, a cause of action runs from the time when the building was completed.

2. JUDICIAL REMEDIES

(a) Damages

By far the most frequent and important remedy which a court can award is damages, and there are very few cases where damages are not claimed, even though some other remedy may be claimed in addition. Damages are essentially monetary compensation for the injury which the plaintiff has suffered. As regards material losses actually incurred, such as claims for damaged clothing or travelling expenses to hospital, it will be a comparatively simple arithmetical exercise to arrive at a figure to compensate the plaintiff, but damages for future financial loss and pain and suffering will be more speculative and will require the court to make its own assessment of what amounts to reasonable compensation in each case.

The most difficult assessments of damages arise in actions involving personal injuries, and it is therefore convenient to consider these cases separately from claims for damage to property.

Damages in actions for personal injuries

The law distinguishes between general damages, such as damages for pain and suffering, which will be presumed, and special damages, being damages peculiar to the plaintiff's case which must therefore be specifically set out in his statement of claim. Special damages will be all those expenses which the plaintiff has incurred up to the date of the hearing, and will therefore be calculable, whereas general damages will mostly not be readily calculable and will be assessed by the court. It is incumbent upon the plaintiff to take any reasonable steps to mitigate his loss in respect of both types of damages.

In an action for personal injuries, general damages will be awarded to cover future estimated financial loss and also non-pecuniary loss.

(i) Future financial loss
Loss of earnings up to the date of the trial will be recoverable as special damages, but loss of prospective earnings until the anticipated date of recovery, or until death or retirement, are general damages for assessment by the court. At present, such damages can only be awarded as a lump sum, although Section 6 of the Administration of Justice Act 1982 (not yet in force) provides for an interim payment and postponement of a final award in cases

where the plaintiff's condition is likely to deteriorate. Deductions are made from the sum awarded for income tax and national insurance contributions which the plaintiff would have had to pay[35] and for any benefits which he receives as a result of the accident, such as a disability pension or redundancy payment if he is made redundant as at result of the accident[36]. Under the Law Reform (Personal Injuries) Act 1948, one half of sickness benefit, industrial injuries benefit and industrial disablement benefit payable during the first five years from the date when the action accrued are deductible. Pensions, National Health Service benefits and insurance moneys payable on a private insurance policy are not deductible, however, but wages or sick pay which an employer is contractually bound to pay are, although *ex gratia* payments made by an employer are probably not[37].

Where the plaintiff's expectation of life is reduced by the injury, he may recover for loss of earnings which he might have been expected to make based on his life expectancy before the accident[38], although a claim in general damages for loss of life expectancy has now been abolished by section 1(1)(b) of the Administration of Justice Act 1982.

Although loss of future earnings is likely to constitute the main claim for general pecuniary damages, there may be other claims peculiar to the plaintiff's case, such as special equipment or services required by the plaintiff due to his disability, or the loss of a car provided by his employer for his personal use[39]. In *Donnelly v Joyce*[40] it was held that the wages of a mother who gave up work to nurse her son were recoverable by the plaintiff and the fact that he was under no obligation to pay for her services was irrelevant as far as the defendant was concerned.

The court should disregard inflation when making an assessment of future pecuniary loss, as this will be to some extent set off against interest earned on a lump sum payment[41] and is in any event highly speculative[42].

(ii) Non-pecuniary loss

The plaintiff is entitled to damages for pain and suffering, including nervous shock, as a result of his injury. The assessment is subjective, so that a plaintiff who never recovers consciousness cannot claim damages under this head. Although damages are not now recoverable for loss of expectation of life, they are recoverable for a persons's suffering in realisation of this (Section 1(1)(a) of the Administration of Justice Act 1982).

Injuries causing some measure of permanent disablement, such as loss of an eye or a limb, will obviously affect considerably a plaintiff's enjoyment of life. The courts have adopted a 'tariff' system for the injury itself, so that unless the plaintiff's circumstances are in some way exceptional, he may expect to receive a substantially similar payment to any other plaintiff suffering a similar loss, and in order to maintain some uniformity, awards are published monthly in *Current Law*. Loss of amenity and quality of life will vary with the particular plaintiff however, and could include for instance inability to pursue a particular sport or hobby. Unlike damages for pain and suffering, damages for loss of amenity are still recoverable by a plaintiff who is unconscious and therefore unaware of his loss[43]. It has been said that the Court of Appeal should not lightly interfere with damages awarded by a court under this head as the assessment is not susceptible of a precise calculation[38].

Because interest is payable at different rates on special damages and on general non-pecuniary damages, but not payable at all on future pecuniary damages, the court should apportion damages between pecuniary and non-pecuniary loss[44].

By Section 1(1) of the Law Reform (Miscellaneous Provisions) Act 1934, all causes of action (other than for defamation) vested in a person on his death survive for the benefit of his estate. But Section 1(2)(a) of the Administration of Justice Act 1982 provides that damages for loss of expected income after death are not recoverable by his estate as such damages are now recoverable by the 'dependants' of a deceased victim under the Fatal Accidents' Act 1976, and this could give rise to a duplicity of claims. They are recoverable by a deceased victim, however, for the period after the injury but before death, along with damages for pain and suffering and loss of amenity. No deductions or accretions to the estate by reason of death are to be made, except that funeral expenses may be claimed. The Law Reform (Contributory Negligence) Act 1945 applies to a claim by the victim's estate as it would to a claim by the plaintiff himself.

Section 1(1) also provides that causes of action 'subsisting' against a defendant at the time of his death shall survive against his estate, and by Section 1(4) an action is deemed to subsist against him at his death even though damage is not suffered, and the tort (if damage is an essential ingredient, as in negligence) is not complete, until after his death.

Claims by dependants of a deceased victim

By Section 1(1) of the Fatal Accidents Act 1976, where death is caused by 'any wrongful act, neglect or default' which would have given rise to an action in tort by the victim had he survived, then the dependants of the victim may claim damages against the defendant.

'Dependants' are widely defined in Section 1(3) of the Act to include, among others, a spouse or common law spouse of two years' cohabitation, parents, children (including step children or adopted children), brothers, sisters, uncles or aunts and their issue.

Although the right of action by the dependants is an entirely new one and in most cases the limitation period runs from the date of death, there is no action at all unless the deceased victim himself would have had one. As Lord Dunedin said[45] 'one must consider the hypothetical ability of the deceased to sue as at the moment of his death, with the idea fictionally that death has not taken place'. It follows therefore that if the deceased himself was barred from bringing an action because he had accepted a settlement of his claim, or if there was a defence, such as *volenti non fit injuria*, against him, then any such defence will apply to a claim by the dependants. The Law Reform (Contributory Negligence) Act 1945 also applies to any claim brought by the dependants in the same way in which it would have applied to a claim brought by the deceased victim himself.

Since 1982, a spouse or parents of an unmarried minor may bring an action for damages for bereavement, and these damages are fixed at £3,500[46].

A much more substantial action however is the action which the dependants may bring for loss of support. The Act itself gives no guidance as to how such damages should be assessed other than that they are to be 'proportioned to the injury resulting from the death to the dependants respectively'[47] but Pollock C.B. said that damages should be assessed 'in reference to a reasonable expectation of pecuniary benefit as of right, or otherwise, from the continuance of the life'[48]. Although 'pecuniary benefit' has been widely defined to include the advantages of a mother's upbringing[49] and voluntary financial assistance[50], there must be some financial loss, so that where a father paid his son a full wage for his work with him, there was no claim[51].

An assessment of the loss to the dependants necessarily involves the court in having regard to the circumstances of the dependants, and obviously the loss of a father to a young child is more than the loss of a husband to an elderly or infirm wife whose expectation of life is limited. In a case where the deceased victim's wife died before judgment, damages were limited to the period for which she survived him[52]. A widow's remarriage prospects are not now to be taken into account when assessing her damages[53], but they may be when damages for the children of the deceased are being assessed[54].

The process of assessment is similar to that for assessment of expectation of future earnings and will be scaled down by various factors such as the victim's life expectancy and regularity of employment. No deductions are made except for the victim's anticipated living expenses, and no account is taken of possible inflation in wages.

Damages for injury to chattels

Where the injury results in the loss or destruction of the chattel, damages will be the market value, and therefore the cost of replacement, at the date of the loss. The plaintiff may also recover consequential damages for loss of use, including loss of profits which use of the chattel would have earned him. To some extent, the usefulness of a chattel may be reflected in its market price, so that the courts may be cautious in awarding general non-specific damages for loss of use, although specific damages attributable to loss of use will be recoverable. Thus in *Liesbosch Dredger* v *S.S. Edison*[55] the plaintiff's dredger was sunk as a result of the defendant's negligence. The plaintiffs were able to recover the cost of a new dredger and for loss of profit on their dredging contract up to the time when they could have been expected to replace the dredger. The plaintiffs were unable to afford to replace the dredger however and had to hire another dredger in order to fulfil their contract. The additional cost of hiring was held not to be recoverable as it was due to the plaintiffs' impecuniosity. With economic loss more readily recognised as recoverable by the courts nowadays, it is possible that such a loss might be recoverable in a future case and Donaldson L.J. has expressed the opinion that a plaintiff's lack of financial means would merely be one element of foreseeability to be taken into account in assessing damages[56].

Where the injury results in damage to the chattel, the plaintiff is entitled to recover the cost of repairs, provided that this does not exceed its replacement value, and compensation for loss of its use while undergoing repairs.

Damage to land and buildings

A plaintiff may recover the cost of reinstatement of a building which is destroyed, even though this may be more than the diminution in its value, provided that it is not excessively more. He may recover the cost of repairs to a building which is damaged, and the cost is assessed at the date when he could first be reasonably expected to carry out the repairs, taking into account his financial circumstances[56].

Contemptuous and nominal damages

These damages are an exception to the general rule that damages are awarded to compensate the plaintiff.

Contemptuous damages may be awarded where the plaintiff proves his case but the court considers his conduct unworthy and the defendant's conduct possibly justified.

Nominal damages are awarded where the plaintiff proves his case but does not suffer any real damage, as for example in a case of trespass where the trespasser does not cause any damage to the property.

Exemplary damages

Exemplary damages are damages in excess of compensation and are therefore punitive in nature. This confuses the functions of the criminal process and the civil law, and in *Rookes* v *Barnard*[57] Lord Devlin said that exemplary damages should only be awarded in cases of oppressive or unconstitutional action by government employees, or where the defendant's tort was the result of a deliberate calculation that his gain would exceed the risk of the plaintiff obtaining damages against him. In the latter class of cases, exemplary damages are justifiable as a deterrent.

The costs of a case are in the court's discretion, and where only contemptuous or nominal damages are awarded the court may decline to award costs to the plaintiff, and may even make an order for costs against him, so that he would have to pay not only his own but also the defendant's costs.

(b) Injunctions

An injunction is an order of the court restraining someone from doing something. It is an equitable remedy, and is therefore granted at the court's discretion, and the court will be unlikely to exercise its discretion to grant an injunction if damages are a sufficient remedy, or if the damage suffered by the plaintiff is trivial or temporary.

Although an injunction is a remedy generally available in tort, it will usually be sought to prevent or stop a nuisance or a trespass or an infringement of copyright. The fact that the action which amounts to a tort against the plaintiff is for the public good will not be a ground for refusing an injunction, although the injunction may be restricted in such cases to excessive interference with the plaintiff's rights[58].

In cases of urgency and extreme damage, an interlocutory injunction may be granted *ex parte*. This enables a plaintiff to obtain an immediate injunction which will preserve his present position until the merits of his case can be heard. Before making an interlocutory injunction, the court will usually require an undertaking from the plaintiff to indemnify the defendant against any loss he suffers should the injunction be found to be unjustified when the action is tried on its merits, and the court should consider whether this will adequately safeguard the defendant's interests.

Although injunctions are usually prohibitory in nature, the court may grant a mandatory injunction requiring a defendant to take positive steps to ameliorate damage. The principles upon which the court should grant such an injunction were laid down in the case of *Redland Bricks Ltd* v *Morris*[59] and are that damages will not be an adequate remedy to the plaintiff, that the cost of remedying the damage is not excessive to the defendant, and that the action to be taken by the defendant is made clear to him.

A *'quia timet'* injunction may be granted to prevent an anticipated imminent wrong.

Damages may be granted in lieu of an injunction where the hardship of an injunction to the defendant is extreme and the injury to the plaintiff is not significant[60].

3. SELF-HELP REMEDIES

The law permits a person to take reasonable measures himself to remedy a wrong done to him. These measures are as follows:

(a) Defence of persons and property

A person may use reasonable force to protect himself and his family from harm, although the force used should be proportionate to the harm threatened. This probably extends to the protection of other persons against the use of force which constitutes a crime as there is a general right to take reasonable steps to prevent the commission of a crime.

A trespasser can be expelled from one's land with such reasonable force as is necessary. A wall or house which a trespasser has erected may be demolished[61]. The liability of a landowner to a trespasser for dangerous premises is now governed by the Occupiers' Liability Act 1984 (see Chapter 5), but he must not use dangerous traps in order to protect his premises.

A person may take reasonable steps to protect his property and the property of others, and if this results in injury to a third person, the original wrongdoer will be liable as there will not be any interruption in the chain of causation[62].

The essential element in all these forms of private defence is reasonableness in the circumstances, and no doubt the law would tolerate harsher measures for protection against bodily injury than it would for protection of property.

(b) Re-entry on to land

A person may recover possession of land against a trespasser by re-entry using no more force than is necessary (see Chapter 6(1)).

(c) Recaption of chattels

A person may recover his goods from a person who wrongfully takes them, and from a third person provided that he has not acquired a good title to them, for example by buying them in the open market. He may enter the land of the wrongdoer to recover them, although it is dubious whether he may enter the land of another in order to abate a third person and he may not do so if the third person himself has not committed any tort[63].

In all cases he should, again, use no more force than is reasonable in the circumstances.

(d) Abatement of nuisance

A person may enter on to the land of another in order to abate a nuisance but should, if at all possible, give notice of his intention to do so. The only circumstances where entry without notice might be justifiable would be a degree of urgency where lives or property are at risk.

Notice need not be given however if it is possible to abate the nuisance without entering on to the land of another, such as by cutting off the branches of an overhanging tree[64], although the branches are the property of the owner of the tree and should be returned to him. The position with regard to intruding tree roots is less certain[65], and notice should probably be given to the owner.

Even where notice need not be given, it may be wiser to do so, as the law does not look kindly on self-help in the abatement of a nuisance, and the abatement may destroy any action which the plaintiff may have for damages.

If there is more than one way of abating a nuisance, the least mischievous must be followed[66].

(e) Distress damage feasant

A landowner may withold a trespassing chattel until he has been compensated for any damage caused by it. The defence used to apply to trespassing cattle, but has now been replaced as far as cattle are concerned by the statutory provisions of the Animals Act 1971.

QUESTIONS

See question 3, Chapter 2, above as to *volenti non fit injuria*.
1. (½ question only)
   In 1970 a contractor built a house for a private client. In1975 cracks appeared in the chimneystack. In 1980 the houseowner sold the house to a new purchaser. The chimney recently had to be demolished as it was unsafe.
   Advise the contractor as to his liability to:
   (i) the original purchaser
   (ii) the new purchaser
   (Specimen paper)
   (*NOTE* This question also relates to Chapter 5(i) – liability for dangerous premises and Chapter 4 – negligence.)

NOTES TO CHAPTER 3

1. Not all risks which a person takes involve a tortious act. For example, painting a ceiling from a ladder or climbing a tree to pick apples do not involve risks arising from a tort.

2. (1933) 1 K.B. 205

3. (1969) 2 Al.E.R. 923
Section 2(5) of the Occupiers' Liability Act 1975 is a statutory embodiment of the defence ('The common duty of care does not impose on an occupier any obligation to a visitor in respect of risks willingly accepted as his by the visitor . . .'). In this case, there was some evidence that the plaintiff's injury might have been caused by his being thrown against a wall round a rugby pitch, but it was held that the plaintiff had willingly accepted the risk of playing on a field which complied with bylaws.

4. (1949) Dominion Law Reports 369

5. (1938) 4 All.E.R.331

6. Sir Frederick Pollock. This opinion was also expressed by Diplock L.J. in *Wooldridge* v *Sumner* (1963) 2 Q.B.43.

7. (1956) 2 Q.B.264

8. (1939) 1 K.B.509
Note that this case was not followed in a later Australian case.

9. (1976) 3 All.E.R.765

10. There have been cases where a notice in a car warning anyone who accepted a lift from the driver that they did so at their own risk was effective to render them '*volens*', although this would not be so since the Road Traffic Act 1972, S.148(3) became law.

11. Section 2.

12. (1951) 2 K.B.529

13. (1891) A.C.325

14. (1965) A.C.656

15. (1911) A.C.355

16. *Nield* v *L.&N.W. Railway* (1874) L.R.10 Ex.4
The defendants owned a canal and erected planks to divert threatened flooding from a river, with the result that the plaintiff's nearby land was flooded. Held – they were not liable.

17. (1827) M & M 56

18. (1965) A.C.164

19. (1956) A.C.218

20. (1912) K.B.496

21. *Southwark London Borough* v *Williams* (1971) 1 Ch. 734

22. *John Trenberth Ltd* v *National Westminster Bank* (1979) 123 Sol.Jo.388
The plaintiffs refused to give permission for the defendants or their contractors to enter upon their land to carry out repairs to the defendants' property, although the repairs could not be carried out without entry. The defendants erected scaffolding, part of which was on the plaintiff's land. The plaintiffs obtained an injunction against them for trespass, and the court refused to suspend this as in *Woollerton & Wilson Ltd* v *Richard Costain Ltd* (see 'Trespass', in Chapter 5), and doubted whether this case was correct, trespass being a tort which is actionable without proof of damage.

23. See Chapter 6 (2)

24. (1930) A.C.171

25. Section 11, Limitation Act 1980

26. *Letang* v *Cooper* (1965) 1 Q.B.232

27. *Pickles* v *National Coal Board* (1968) 2 All.E.R.598
A miner developed silicosis six years after he had left mining. He applied

to his union for advice as to whether he had a cause of action and this took a further year. Held – his action was not barred as he did not know until he received advice from the union's head office that he had a cause of action.

28. *Simpson* v *Norwest Holst Southern Ltd* (1980) 2 All.E.R. 471
A worker on a building site suffered an injury due to his employers' negligence and breach of statutory duty. His contract of employment was with 'Norwest Holst Group', which included four companies. His pay slips were from 'Norwest Holst'. He instructed solicitors to act for him and they obtained a legal aid certificate to sue 'Norwest Holst Construction Co. Ltd'. The Solicitors were unable to obtain the name of the employers from the insurance company and were finally informed that they were 'Norwest Holst Southern Ltd' in time to issue a writ just outside the three years' limitation period. Held – the action was not barred as the plaintiff did not know the defendant's identity within three years.

29. *Thompson* v *Brown Construction (Ebbw Vale) Ltd* (1981) 2 All.E.R.296
The plaintiff was injured when some scaffolding collapsed due to negligence. His solicitors delayed issuing a writ until after the three years' limitation period. Held – court would exercise its discretion to grant leave to issue a writ outside the limitation period. The fact that the plaintiff had a good action in negligence against his solicitors was one factor to be considered in exercising this discretion, but not a reason for refusing leave, as the plaintiff would still have had to start a new action.

30. *Firman* v *Ellis* (1978) 2 All.E.R.851

31. *Beaman* v *A.R.T.S.* (1949) 1 All.E.R.465
In 1935 the defendant company undertook to store four packages for the plaintiff who went abroad. Owing to the war, the plaintiff was unable to return, and the company, which was Italian, closed down. The packages were given to the Salvation Army. In 1946 the plaintiff returned and demanded the packages. Held – the company's conversion of the packages had been concealed from the plaintiff. The limitation period was therefore postponed and she had a right of action.

32. *William Hill Organisation* v *Bernard Sunley & Sons* (1983) 22 Build.L.R. 1
Contractors were employed to put stone cladding on to a building and this was defective. The contract for the work was in 1960 and the final certificate was issued in 1963. Cracks first appeared in the cladding in 1971 and there was movement in 1974. It was then found that defective fixings had been used. The plaintiff's employers claimed that their action for negligence was not statute-barred as there had been 'fraudulent conceal-ment' but did not call any evidence to support this and had had their own supervisor on the site. Held by Court of Appeal – the defendants' getting on with the work did not amount to fraudulent concealment.
NOTE. The Law Reform Committee's *Report on Latent Damage* (HMSO Cmnd. Paper 9390) suggests that the words 'deliberate concealment' in Section 32 of the Limitation Act would cover simply getting on with the job as in this case.

33. (1983) All.E.R.65

34. Law Reform Committee, *24th Report (Latent damage)*, HMSO Cmnd. 9390.

35. *British Transport Commission* v *Gourley* (1956) A.C. 185

36. *Wilson* v *National Coal Board* (1981) S.L.T.67.
This will not apply however if he is made redundant independently of the accident.

37. *Parry* v *Cleaver* (1970) A.C.1.

38. *Pickett* v *British Rail Engineering Ltd* (1980) A.C.136

39. *Clay* v *Pooler* (1982) 3 All.E.R.570

40. (1974) Q.B.454
No doubt a claim for wages would have to be limited to a reasonable one and a claim for loss of very high wages would not be justifiable.

41. Per Lord Diplock in *Mallet* v *McMonagle* (1976) A.C.166

42. Per Lord Scarman in *Lim* v *Camden Health Authority* (1980) A.C.174

43. *West* v *Shephard* (1964) A.C.326
A woman who was paralysed and only partially conscious was able to recover damages for loss of amenity.

44. *Cookson* v *Knowles* (1979) A.C.556 where guidelines for apportioning damages were laid down by the House of Lords.

45. In *British Columbia Electric Railway* v *Gentile* (1914) A.C.1034

46. Section 1(A) of the Fatal Accidents Act 1976, inserted by section 3 of the Administration of Justice Act 1982.

47. Section 3(1) of the Fatal Accidents Act.

48. In *Franklin* v *S.E. Railway* (1858) 3 H & N 211

49. *Hay* v *Hughes* (1975) Q.B.790

50. *Sykes* v *N.E. Railway* (1875) 44 L.J.C.P.191

51. *Williamson* v *John I. Thornycroft Ltd* (1940) 2 K.B.658

52. This only applies to a 'widow' and not to a common law spouse, or to the mother of a child dependant of a victim.

53. Fatal Accidents Act 1976, Section 3(3)

54. *Thompson* v *Price* (1973) 2 All.E.R.846

55. (1933) A.C.449

56. In *Dodd Properties Ltd* v *Canterbury City Council* (1980) 1 W.L.R.433

57. (1964) A.C.1129

58. *Kennaway* v *Thompson* (1981) Q.B.88, where only excessive noise from the defendant's water sports was restricted.

59. (1970) A.C.652

60. Lord Cairns's act 1858, now Section 50 of the Supreme Court Act 1981.

61. *Perry* v *Fitzhowe* (1846) 8 Q.B.757

62. *Scott* v *Shepherd* (1773) 2 W.Bl.892
A threw a lighted squib which landed on the gingerbread stall of B. A person nearby threw the squib and it landed on C's stall. C threw the squib again and it hit D, exploding in his face and blinding him in one eye. Held – A was liable for D's injury and not the other persons who had thrown it to protect property.

63. *British Economical Lamp Co. Ltd* v *Empire Mile End Ltd* (1913) 29 T.L.R.386.
The defendant terminated the lease of a cinema, and some detachable lamps which the tenant had hired from the plaintiff were still on the premises. Held – the defendant could refuse permission to the plaintiff to enter onto the premises to remove the lamps as he himself had not committed any tort with regard to the lamps.

64. *Lemmon* v *Webb* (1895) A.C.1.

65. *Butler* v *Standard Telephone & Cables Ltd* (1940) 1 K.B.399.
A row of houses had been damaged by the roots of poplar trees which had grown under the foundations and extracted water from the clay soil during a dry period, causing subsidence and damage to the houses. Lewis J. approved an Irish decision which drew no distinction between overhanging branches and roots, and held that the roots could be cut and damages recovered.

66. *Lagan Navigation Co.* v *Lambeg Bleaching, Dyeing & Finishing Co. Ltd* (1927) A.C.226.

4. Negligence

Negligence as a mental factor may be present in other torts, but the tort of negligence itself is conduct arising from mental inadvertence. It has been defined by Winfield as 'the breach of a legal duty to take care which results in damage, undesired by the defendant, to the plaintiff'[1].

It will be seen that there are three ingredients in the definition which the plaintiff must prove in order to succeed:
1. the existence of a legal duty of care;
2. breach of that duty by the defendant;
3. resulting damage to the plaintiff.

1. THE EXISTENCE OF A LEGAL DUTY OF CARE

The first attempt to lay down a general rule as to when a duty of care exists was made in a famous speech by Lord Atkin in the case of *Donoghue* v *Stevenson* in 1932[2]. Few students have difficulty in remembering the facts of the case, which was an action by the plaintiff for damages for injury suffered from drinking ginger beer from an opaque bottle found to be contaminated with a decomposed snail. The plaintiff was unable to sue the manufacturers in contract as the ginger beer had been bought for her by a friend, so that she was not a party to the contract of purchase. Her only remedy therefore lay in tort, and she brought an action in negligence. The House of Lords decided that the manufacturer owed her a legal duty to ensure that the ginger beer was not contaminated, and, in considering when a legal duty of care is owed to someone, Lord Atkin said:

The rule that you are to love your neighbour becomes, in law, you must not injure your neighbour; and the lawyer's question 'Who is my neighbour?' receives a restricted reply. You must take reasonable care to avoid acts or omissions which you can reasonably foresee would be likely to injure your neighbour. Who, then, in law is my neighbour? The answer seems to be – persons who are so closely and directly affected by my act that I ought reasonably to have them in contemplation as being so affected when I am directing my mind to the acts or omissions which are called in question.

The definition by Lord Atkin is based on foreseeability, but this alone has not proved adequate to define the limits of a legal duty of care. Situations may arise where the test of foreseeability will clearly impose liability, but liability is for some reason undesirable or unwarranted. In these situations, the courts have to decide, as a matter of policy, whether the plaintiff has an interest which should be protected by law or not. As MacDonald J said in a Canadian case[3],

When upon analysis of the circumstances and application of the appropriate formula, a court holds that the defendant was under a duty of care, the court is stating as a conclusion of law what is really a conclusion of policy as to responsibility for conduct involving unreasonable risk. It is saying that such circumstances presented an appreciable risk of harm to others as to entitle them to protection against unreasonable conduct by the actor.

In that case, it was held that pilots were under no duty of care to avoid the plaintiff's mink farm, although planes on the flight route disturbed the 'noise conscious mink'. Harm to the mink from the noise of the planes was foreseeable, but the court decided that the plaintiff's interest was not one which should be protected, bearing in mind the public utility of the airline's operations.

Another case where the court declined to find a duty of care on the ground of public policy is that of *Rondel* v *Worsley*[4], in which it was held by the House of Lords that a barrister cannot be sued by his client for negligence in the conduct of advocacy in court proceedings. The House of Lords took the view that to decide otherwise would raise the spectre of endless litigation which would, in effect, be a re-trial of the case in which negligence was alleged. This immunity extends to pre-trial matters closely linked with the conduct of the case in court but the majority of the Lords in *Rondel* v *Worsley* felt that the immunity should not apply further than the demands of public policy required, and that a barrister should be liable for negligence in 'paper-work' in chambers, such as drafting a document or giving an opinion[5]. In *Ross* v *Caunters*[6] a solicitor was held liable in negligence for failing to warn the spouse of a beneficiary named in the will that his attestation of the will would invalidate the gift.

A further factor which the courts have been mindful of in defining the extent of a duty of care is that known as the 'floodgates' argument. Given a situation where the defendant's negligent conduct could cause injury or damage to a large number of people, would damages be recoverable by all of them? In *Weller & Co. Ltd* v *The Foot and Mouth Disease Research Institute*[7] it was assumed that the foot and mouth virus had escaped from premises where the defendants were carrying out research on it. An order was made stopping all cattle markets in the area, and the plaintiffs, cattle auctioneers, sued for loss. The court held that the defendants owed no duty of care to the plaintiffs. The ability to foresee one's actions resulting in an indirect or economic loss to someone does not automatically impose a duty of care to avoid that loss. To do so would give rise to endless possible actions for damage caused by the spread of the disease. In *Electrochrome Ltd* v *Welsh Plastics Ltd*[8] the plaintiffs, who had lost a day's work in their factory because their water supply was cut off due to the defendant's lorry driver negligently damaging a hydrant, were unable to recover damages for this. Lane J. said in this case

. . . it may seem inequitable that a person who has undoubtedly suffered loss in this manner should have no right of action against the person who started off the train of events but . . . in the case of water being cut off in this manner one can imagine a whole series, maybe hundreds, of actions being brought against the defendants on this type of negligence and . . . the complexity of society would mean that there might be no end to the concatenation of resulting damage.

Nevertheless, the general trend has been for the limitations imposed on the duty of care for reasons of public policy to be whittled away. The courts have been more and more prepared to compensate for foreseeable injury to the plaintiff caused by the defendant's negligence, and there are previous immunities which the courts will not now uphold, and other immunities where considerable qualifications have been established. The position is probably now as stated by Lord Wilberforce in *Anns* v *London Borough of Merton*[9] that

. . . the question has to be approached in two stages. First one has to ask whether, as between the alleged wrongdoer and the person who has suffered damage there is a sufficient relationship of proximity or neighbourhood such that, in the reasonable contemplation of the former, carelessness on his part may be likely to cause damage to the latter, in which case a *prima facie* duty of care arises. Secondly, if the first question is answered affirmatively, it is necessary to consider whether there are any considerations which ought to negative or reduce or limit the scope of that duty or the class of person to whom it is owed or the damage to which a breach of it may give rise.

The extensions of the duty of care and consequent diminishing qualifications to it can be conveniently considered under various heads, although some cases where the courts have refused to find a duty of care may reflect more than one principle for failing to do so.

(a) Dangerous property

At common law, the vendor or landlord of property was not liable to a purchaser or lessee for defects making it dangerous, such transactions falling within the well-known maxim of *'caveat emptor'* (buyer beware). The Defective Premises Act 1972, which came into effect on the 1st January 1974, modifies this immunity as regards all building work carried out after that date. Section 1 imposes a statutory duty to ensure that 'construction, repair, maintenance or demolition or any other work' to a dwellinghouse is carried out in a workmanlike or proper manner, with proper materials. The duty is owed to all persons 'likely to be affected', and continues notwithstanding the subsequent disposal of the house. It applies to owner-builders as well as to builders carrying out work in the course of a business, and by section 6, the duty cannot be restricted or excluded unless the house is the subject of an agreement under a scheme approved by the secretary of State (the most common one being the N.H.B.C. scheme). By Section 3 of the Act, the *'caveat emptor'* rule is abolished, and Section 4 imposes obligations as to the condition of property he is letting as a landlord.

In the case of *Dutton v Bognor Regis UDC* in 1972[10], before the Act came into force, the Court of Appeal had already found a local authority vicariously liable for the negligence of its building inspector in approving the foundations of a house – as he was required to do under the building byelaws[11] – which were built inadequately on a rubbish tip liable to subsidence. This decision was applied by the House of Lords in *Anns v London Borough of Merton*[9] where it was said that a local authority owes a duty to owners and occupiers of property to apply its byelaws without negligence. The duty is still owed to an owner who employs a builder, provided that the owner's loss is not caused by his own negligence[12]. A builder who does not comply with the byelaws will also be liable to the owner, but the local authority will not be liable to the builder for failing to ensure that he does comply with them, as there is generally no liability in tort for an omission to act[13].

It was at one time believed that liability in negligence for defective buildings covered only physical damage. The courts have been increasingly prepared to compensate a plaintiff for purely financial loss, however, and damages in *Dutton v Bognor Regis UDC* were for cracks in the wall making the house potentially unsafe. In a more recent case[14] damages were recovered for a threatened structural failure, and in *Junior Books Ltd* v *Veitchi Co. Ltd*[15] purely economic loss resulting from bad workmanship was recoverable.

(b) Trespassers

Trespassers, to whom at one time no duty of care was owed, are now owed a limited duty of care under certain circumstances under the Occupiers' Liability Act 1984 (see Chapter 5).

(c) Omissions

As already noted in the case of *Peabody Donation Fund* v *Sir Lindsay Parkinson & Co. Ltd*,[13] the law does not generally impose an obligation upon a person to act so as to avoid harm to another. It has been well established for some time however that a person who feels compelled by a moral obligation to go to the rescue of a person placed in jeopardy by the defendant's tortious act will not be barred from recovering damages for any injuries he sustains by the general defence of '*volenti non fit injuria*' (see Chapter 3). Those in charge of children are under an obligation to prevent harm befalling them and the 'careful parent' standard of care applies to education authorities and to schools[16]. Street has said that liability for an omission would arise in circumstances where the defendant's conduct has misled the plaintiff into a false sense of security[17].

(d) Statutory authorisation

Acts, not negligent in themselves, authorised by a purely permissive or enabling statute, will not result in liability for damage ensuing[18] However, in *Anns* v *London Borough of Merton*, it was pointed out that a local authority is under an obligation to consider whether it should make byelaws, and that a decision not to do so might be negligent if it failed to consider adequately the interests of persons likely to be affected by them, or *ultra vires*, that is, outside their powers. As has been seen in that case, there is liability for negligence in the performance of duties under an enabling statute, for as Lord Salmon said 'the exercise of power without responsibility is not encouraged by the law'. This followed the case of *Home Office* v *Dorset Yacht Co.*

Ltd[19] where the Home Office, in carrying out their statutory obligations to maintain a borstal institution, were held liable for damage done by escapees to yachts in the vicinity.

(e) Economic loss

The courts have been reluctant for a long time to recognise a duty of care as regards purely financial loss.

Such loss may result from physical damage, or be pure economic loss independent of any physical damage, and the courts have in the past been more ready to find a duty of care with regard to the former than the latter.

Thus in *Spartan Steel Alloys Ltd* v *Martin & Co. (Contractors) Ltd*[20], the defendants negligently damaged an electric cable supplying the plaintiffs' factory, causing the power to be cut off. The plaintiffs claimed for (i) loss of profit on the melt in the furnace when the electricity supply was cut off (damaged by pouring liquid oxygen on to it to avoid it solidifying and damaging the furnace) and (ii) loss of profit on four further melts which they would have poured that day. The Court of Appeal held that the first head of damage was recoverable, as the economic loss was the direct consequence of physical damage to the melt, but the second head of damage, being purely economic, was not. The more recent case of *Junior Books Ltd* v *Veitchi Co. Ltd*[15] casts doubt upon the decision as regards the second head of loss. It must be emphasised however that in *Junior Books* the court found a very close degree of proximity between the plaintiffs and the defendants 'falling only just short of a direct contractual relationship'[23] and it is possible that a future case may be distinguished if such a close proximity does not exist. As Lord Fraser said:

It would surely be wrong to exclude from probation a claim which is so strongly based, merely because of anxiety about the possible effect of the decision on other cases where the proximity may be less strong. If and when such other cases arise they will have to be decided by applying sound principles to their particular facts.

As regards liability for negligent mis-statements, again the courts have been more sympathetic to claims for physical damage resulting than to claims for economic loss independent of physical damage. Thus in *Clay* v *Crump*[21] an architect was held liable for a negligent assurance as to the safety of a wall which subsequently collapsed. In *Hedley, Byrne & Co. Ltd* v *Heller & Partners Ltd*[22] however, the House of Lords changed the previous law as regards economic loss resulting from a negligent mis-statement by indicating that such a claim would lie where there was a special relationship between the parties. Lord Devlin referred to this as a relationship equivalent to contract. Subsequent cases have found such relationships to exist between a barrister and client in work outside court[5], in work done by solicitors affecting adversely persons other than their clients[6], in accounts prepared by accountants who knew that they would be seen by prospective bidders in a take-over[23] and in a certificate given by an architect as to work done under a building contract[24].

In *Argy Trading Co. Ltd* v *Lapid Developments Ltd*[25], though, it was held that there is no obligation to correct earlier statements which have since become incorrect, and there will not be liability for statements made casually, for example on a social occasion.

(f) Nervous shock

There has always been liability for nervous shock resulting from an intentional act[26], but liability for nervous shock caused by negligence is another area where the judges have found it difficult to draw a line. Nobody would suggest, for instance, that a person who is nervously affected after seeing an alarming film should be able to sue for damages for it. On the other hand, someone suffering shock after being involved in a car accident in which their husband was injured would clearly be a person within the scope of foreseeability of injury to whom a duty is owed[27]. Between these two extremes, the courts have been presented with some difficult cases, as a result of which a formula was established whereby a victim of nervous shock could only recover damages if he was himself near to the accident. Although originally the person involved in the accident had to be a close relative, this was extended to strangers in *Chadwick* v *British Railways Board*[28].

In *McLoughlin* v *O'Brian*[29] however, the House of Lords held that a mother, who was two miles away from an accident in which her husband and two children were injured and another child was killed, and who suffered nervous shock when she was told about it by a neighbour and went to the hospital, could recover damages. Lord Wilberforce expressed the opinion that a plaintiff suffering from nervous shock has a sufficient degree of proximity to be within the duty of care owed by the defendant if he is close to an accident in which close relatives of his are involved; if he himself has a proximity to the accident in time or space; or if he is very soon afterwards at the aftermath of the accident, as in the case of a parent or spouse who is likely to go there as soon as possible.

It should be noted that the 'egg-shell skull' rule which applies generally to damages in tort, applies to nervous shock cases, so that in *Malcolm* v *Broadhurst*[27] a wife whose nervous condition was exaggerated by her own involvement in the accident was able to recover damages for this.

2. BREACH OF DUTY OF CARE

Assuming that the plaintiff in an action for negligence is able to show that he was owed a duty of care by the defendant, he must also show that the defendant's behaviour amounted to a breach of that duty.

This element of the tort requires consideration of the defendant's behaviour, which is to be assessed according to the standards of that mythical creature, 'the reasonable man'. As Alderson B. said[30], 'Negligence is the omission to do something which a reasonable man, guided upon those considerations which ordinarily regulate the conduct of human affairs, would do, or doing something which a prudent and reasonable man would not do'.

The standard is objective in that it does not take account of the individual idiosyncracies of the defendant, but subjective in so far as it does have regard to the circumstances of the defendant and the situation in which he finds himself. The standard of care is a matter of law, but it is a question of fact in each case as to whether the defendant falls short of it. It is only in exceptional cases nowadays that cases of negligence are tried before a jury, and usually the judge will therefore determine both the facts and the law, but if the case is heard before a jury, then it is for the jury to decide the issues of fact.

Circumstances relating to the defendant which the court will take account of in determining the standard of care applicable to his conduct are:

(i) Any particular skill which the defendant professes to have

A skilled person is expected to show average competence for a person of his training and experience. Thus the actions of a doctor, carpenter or builder are judged according to the hypothetical standards of doctors, carpenters and builders of averagely competent ability. A householder may reasonably be expected to carry out minor repairs in his home without achieving the standard of a professional carpenter, provided the work is averagely competent[31].

If the defendant does not hold himself out as having any particular skill, then he will not be expected to show any[32], although a learner driver has been required to show the standard of care of an average driver[33].

(ii) Knowledge of the defendant

The conduct of the defendant must be judged according to the knowledge which he had at the time. This is illustrated by the case of *Roe* v *Minister of Health*[34] where the plaintiff was paralysed when he was given a spinal anaesthetic for a minor operation. It was subsequently found that the glass ampoule containing the anaesthetic, which had been stored in phenol solution, had an invisible crack through which the phenol penetrated. This possibility was not known to the medical profession at the time, however, and the hospital authority were held not to be liable. Thus, hindsight is not negligence.

Factors relating to the accident which the court may take into account in deciding whether the defendant is in breach of a duty of care are:

(i) The magnitude of the risk of injury and the practicability of precautions against it

If the risk of damage or injury is slight, it may not be reasonable to expect the defendant to take expensive precautions against it. Thus in *Bolton* v *Stone*[35] a cricket club was not liable to a woman injured by a cricket ball hit out of the ground into the road where she was standing, as evidence was given that balls had only been hit into the road about six times in twenty-eight years and a very high fence would have had to have been erected to stop the ball.

In *Latimer* v *A.E.C.*[36] a slippery factory floor caused by flooding did not justify closure of the factory, which would have been necessary to clean the floor.

(ii) The seriousness of any injury resulting

Factors making the consequences of a breach of duty more serious are relevant. Thus an employer's duty of care to a one-eyed welder to ensure that he wore goggles was higher than had the man been normally sighted, as injury to his remaining eye had more serious consequences[37].

(iii) Purpose of the defendant's conduct

There are some risks inherent in modern living, such as traffic and trains travelling at a reasonable speed. Small risk to achieve a worthwhile end may be justifiable, and the two must be balanced. In *Watt* v *Hertfordshire County Council*[38] a fireman was injured by a jack in a lorry in which he was travelling shifting on to him when going on an urgent call to a trapped woman critically injured. It was pointed out by Denning L.J. however that the slight risk of the jack shifting would not have been justified had the purpose of the journey been merely to save property at risk.

(iv) The circumstances of the plaintiff

Account must be taken of the fact that certain persons will be more vulnerable. Children and elderly persons may not exercise the same degree of care for their own safety as others and the standard of care towards them is therefore higher. In *Haley* v *London Electricity Board*[39] the defendants were liable to a blind man who fell into an excavation in the pavement, although a sighted person would not have done so. Conversely, a trained person may be expected to be aware of possible dangers attendant on his job[40].

(v) Conformity with approved practice

If the defendant can show that his conduct conformed with generally approved practice, or an established system of working, this will usually be sufficient to discharge the duty of care and to rebut any allegation of negligence against him. This will still apply if there are conflicting views on what is a proper practice[41]. It will not apply however if the system itself can be shown to be negligent[42].

Conversely again, if there is an approved practice which the defendant fails to comply with, this will be *prima facie* evidence of negligence.

The burden of proof

The plaintiff must establish, on a balance of probabilities, that the defendant was in breach of the duty of care. Therefore, if the circumstances of an accident are completely unknown, the plaintiff may not be able to do this[43].

The burden of proof rests on the plaintiff to prove his case, but there are two circumstances where negligence will be assumed in his favour and the burden of proof is then shifted to the defendant to show that he was not negligent. These are:

(i) Where the defendant has been convicted of a criminal offence with regard to his conduct

The Civil Evidence Act 1968 allows evidence of the conviction to be given in a civil action, and the defendant must then show that he has not been negligent. The most usual example of this is where the defendant is convicted of a driving offence and the conviction is used in a subsequent civil action for damages.

(ii) Where the doctrine of 'res ipsa loquitur'[44] applies

The doctrine applies to relieve the plaintiff of the burden of proving negligence 'where the thing (causing the accident) is shown to be under the management of the defendant or his servants, and the accident is such as in the ordinary course of things does not happen if those who have the management use proper care'[45]. The doctrine has been applied to bags of sugar which fell from a warehouse on to a customs officer below[45] and to a barrel falling which fell on to a passer-by in a street below[46].

For the doctrine to apply, the following requirements must be satisfied:

1. The thing in question must be in the sole control of the defendant.

Thus the doctrine applied to the door of a metropolitan train which opened shortly after the train had left Great Portland Street station[47], but not to the door of an express train seven miles after its last stop[48] for as Goddard L.J. said 'It is impossible to say that the doors of an express corridor train travelling from Edinburgh to London are continuously under the sole control of the railway company'.

2. The accident is one which 'in the ordinary course of things does not happen'.

This is illustrated by the two cases above as bags of sugar and barrels do not usually fall from warehouses without negligence on someone's part.

3. There is no evidence as to how the accident happened.

If there is evidence, then the inference in favour of the plaintiff does not apply and the court must decide, on a balance of probabilities, whether the defendant was negligent or not[49].

Where the doctrine applies, there is a presumption of negligence, but it is still open to the defendant to prove that he was not negligent. If he cannot show how the accident happened, he may do this by showing that he took all due care and precautions[50]. Alternatively, he may show how the accident happened and that it was not due to any negligence on his part. It is not sufficient, however, to adduce in evidence a number of possible explanations for the accident, only one of which excludes negligence on his part[51].

3. REMOTENESS OF DAMAGE

The third requirement for a plaintiff to prove in order to sue successfully for negligence is damage resulting from the defendant's breach of duty.

Theoretically, all events are causally linked and the most unlikely results may sometimes ensue from the defendant's tort. The courts have to decide, as a matter of law, what ensuing damage is sufficiently linked to the defendant's negligence to be recoverable, and what is too remote. Somewhere along the chain of causation, there will be a 'cut-off' point where, for reasons of policy, fairness or common sense the defendant's liability will end. The very nature of the exercise requires that each case has to be treated individually, and it is only possible to draw certain broad principles from the decisions. Even then, there are cases which, because of their own particular circumstances, do not fit neatly into the principles.

Remoteness of damage is dealt with in relation to the tort of negligence because damage is an essential ingredient of the tort, and in negligence it is usually impossible to attribute to the defendant that degree of intention necessary to make a clear causal connection between the tort and the resulting damage. Nevertheless, the same rules are now generally applicable in all torts, except perhaps torts of strict liability, where limitation of damage recoverable is not easy to reconcile with an absolute liability.

Tests for remoteness

In the case of *Re Polemis*[52], stevedores who were unloading the ship *Polemis* dropped a plank. Because of petrol vapour in the hold of the ship, a spark from the plank caused a fire which destroyed the ship. The Court of Appeal held the charterers who employed the stevedores vicariously liable for the loss of the ship.

This was a direct consequence of their negligent act, however unforeseeable.

In the *Wagon Mound*[53], a case heard by the Judicial Committee of the Privy Council on appeal from the Supreme Court of New South Wales, *Re Polemis* was not followed and different principles of liability, based on foreseeability, were established. In that case, the defendants' employees on board the ship the *Wagon Mound*, were refuelling at a wharf in Sydney harbour, and because of the negligent way in which this was done, fuel oil was spilt on to the water. The oil was carried across the water to the plaintiff's wharf, where welding operations were in progress. The manager stopped the operations to enquire whether it was safe to continue, and as, in the light of scientific knowledge at that time, it was believed that fuel oil on water would not ignite, he was assured that it was safe. In the event, a piece of cotton waste floating on the water was ignited by the welding operations, this ignited the fuel oil, and the wharf and the ship on which work was being carried out were damaged. The Privy Council decided that the damage to the wharf was not recoverable as not being foreseeable.

The decision of the Judicial Committee of the Privy Council is not binding on English courts, but as the appellate court of the House of Lords is constituted from the same law lords as the Judicial Committee, it is of strong persuasive value, and the *Wagon Mound* has generally been taken to represent the law as to remoteness. It received approval from the House of Lords in *Hughes* v *Lord Advocate*[54]. In fact however the two tests are not as inconsistent as they might at first appear, because in most cases direct consequences will be foreseeable, and it is only in exceptional circumstances that they are not[55].

Although there are a number of fine distinctions in the decisions as to what damage is recoverable, it is possible to extract some well-established principles from them. These are as follows:

(i) The damage must be attributable to the defendant's tort

If the damage is not due to the defendant's tort, he will not be liable for it. Thus in *Barnett* v *Chelsea & Kensington Hospital Management Committee*[56], three night watchmen attended hospital complaining of vomiting and the doctor sent them home without examining them. Later that day one of them died, death being caused by arsenic poisoning. The evidence suggested strongly that he would have died in any event, however, so that his death was not attributable to the doctor's negligence in failing to examine him and the Hospital Committee were not liable.

Moreover, there must be clear evidence that the harm suffered was due to the defendant's negligence, and in the absence of such evidence, the claim will fail[57].

Problems sometimes arise where the plaintiff's injury is caused partly by the defendant's tort and partly by other factors. There are two conflicting cases here which it is difficult to distinguish on any very sound ground. In *Baker* v *Willoughby*[58], the defendant was liable for an injury to the plaintiff's leg. The plaintiff was subsequently attacked by robbers as a result of which his leg had to be amputated. The defendant was nevertheless held to be still liable for the plaintiff's deprivation due to his negligence. In *Jobling* v *Associated Diaries Ltd*[59], however, a plaintiff who suffered a back injury, for which the defendant was liable, subsequently developed a disease which made him unfit to work. The defendant was held not liable in damages for loss of earnings which would have been recoverable for the back injury, and Lord Bridge said 'To hold the tortfeasor, in this situation, liable to pay damages for a notional continuing loss of earnings attributable to the tortious injury, is to put the plaintiff in a better position than he would be in if he had never suffered the tortious injury'. Attempts to distinguish the two cases by describing the plaintiff's disease in Jobling as one of the 'vicissitudes of life' (per Lord Russell) whereas the contributory cause in Willoughby was another tort, are not convincing, and it must therefore be a matter of conjecture as to which way future cases will be decided.

(ii) The damage suffered must be of a type likely to result from the defendant's tort

It is important here to distinguish between the kind of damage suffered by the plaintiff and the extent of the damage. Provided the nature of the damage is such that it was likely to result from the defendant's tort, it does not matter that it was considerably more than likely in extent. This is illustrated by the House of Lords case of *Hughes* v *Lord Advocate*[54] where a boy aged eight was extensively burned by a paraffin lamp exploding. The lamps had been left unattended outside a canvas shelter over an excavation, and the boy and his friend were playing with them when one fell into the hole, causing an explosion, which caused the boy also to fall into the hole. The defendants were held liable for his extensive injuries because it was foreseeable that young children might play with lamps left unattended and suffer burns as a result. The fact that the burns were severe because the lamp fell into the excavation and exploded only affected the extent of the injury and not the nature.

Conversely, in *Tremain* v *Pike*[60], where a farmhand contracted a rare disease (Weil's disease) from rats on the defendant's farm, this was held to be unforeseeable in nature. Although rat bites or food contamination would have been foreseeable as a result of the defendant's negligence in failing to control the rat infestation on the farm, a rare disease contracted by contact with rats' urine was not.

(iii) Intended consequences will never be too remote

If the defendant commits a tortious act which is likely to cause injury, then he will be liable for any injury resulting, notwithstanding that the injury is more than the defendant intended. In *Scott* v *Shepherd*[61] the defendant threw a lighted squib at a fair. It landed on a stall, the owner threw it off, another person threw the squib again, and it exploded blinding the plaintiff in one eye. The defendant was held liable.

(iv) The 'egg-shell skull' rule

As already mentioned, provided the damage suffered by the plaintiff is the type of damage which might be expected to result from the defendant's tort, the defendant is still liable even though it is more excessive than might have been expected. What is the position if the damage is more extreme because of some pre-existing physical or mental weakness of the plaintiff?

The rule (known as the 'egg-shell skull' rule) is that a tortfeasor must take his victim as he finds him. In *Robinson* v *Post Office*[62], the plaintiff, an employee of the Post Office, slipped on an oily rung on a ladder and was given an anti-tetanus injection as part of his treatment at hospital. He proved to be allergic to this and developed encephalitis as a result. The Post Office were held liable. In *Malcolm* v *Broadhurst*[63] the plaintiff was able to recover damages for nervous illness exacerbated by a pre-existing nervous condition at the time of the accident.

(v) Resulting economic loss

It follows from the egg-shell skull rule that damages for loss of earnings will be more if the plaintiff is a surgeon than if he is a male nurse. As far as damages for financial loss are concerned however, the courts have limited these to direct consequential loss, so that increased loss due to the plaintiff's own peculiar circumstances will not be recoverable. Thus in *Malcolm* v *Broadhurst*[63], although the wife was able to recover loss of earnings from her full-time job, she was unable to recover for loss of earnings as a part-time secretary for her husband as this was due to her own special domestic circumstances. In *Liesbosch Dredger* v *S.S. Edison*[64], a dredger was sunk due to the negligence of the crew of the *Edison*, a ship owned by the defendants. The plaintiff dredger company was carrying out a contract for which a guarantee as to time of completion had been given and there were penalties for exceeding the specified time. Because they could not afford to buy another dredger, they were obliged to hire one in order to carry out the contract. The hire charge was held not to be recoverable as it was an additional expense due entirely to the plaintiff's impecuniosity, and was extrinsic to the defendant's tort.

(vi) 'Novus actus interveniens' *(a new act intervening)*

Where an extraneous act occurs which breaks the chain of causation, this will terminate the defendant's liability. For example, in *Lamb* v *Camden London Borough*[65] the plaintiff's house was damaged due to the defendant's nuisance and left unoccupied. Squatters moved in and caused further damage. The defendants were held not liable for the squatters' damage as it was not a necessary result of their nuisance.

The '*novus actus interveniens*' may be an act of nature[66], an act of a third party, as in *Lamb* v *Camden London Borough*[65], or an act of the plaintiff himself. If the act of the plaintiff or a third party is reasonable and predictable under the circumstances however, it will not constitute a '*novus actus*'. The case of *Scott* v *Shepherd*[61] (see above, p. 80) illustrates this, the plaintiff's loss being attributable to the original tort of the defendant as it was not unreasonable that a lighted squib should be thrown on in the heat of the moment. This is particularly relevant to the 'rescue' cases, where an element of moral compulsion and emergency may make an act reasonable which would not otherwise be, so that it is still within the chain of causation for which the defendant is liable[67]. If the further injury or damage is entirely as a result of the predicament in which the plaintiff finds himself due to the defendant's tort, it will not amount to a '*novus actus*' and the defendant will still be liable[68].

Contributory negligence

It is possible that, although the accident is caused primarily by the defendant's negligence, the plaintiff's own negligence may also have contributed to it. In these circumstances, the damages recoverable by the plaintiff will be reduced according to the percentage of blame for the accident which the court attaches to the plaintiff. The Law Reform (Contributory Negligence) Act 1945 gives the court a very wide discretion to reduce the plaintiff's damages 'to such an extent as the court thinks fit having regard to the claimant's share in the responsibility for the damage' (Section 1(1)). The court may decide that the plaintiff is entirely to blame, notwithstanding the defendant's tort, so that the plaintiff's damages are extinguished[69].

In the case of contributory negligence, it does not matter that the injury sustained by the plaintiff is different in nature to the injury which he was risking[70].

There are certain classes of plaintiffs, however, where the courts will be more reluctant to find contributory negligence. These are people who are less able to care for themselves, such as children[71] or elderly or disabled people. Equally, in a case where a workman of known low intelligence failed to comply with instructions, the court refused to find contributory negligence, finding instead that this was relevant to the standard of the duty of care owed to him by his employers[72].

QUESTIONS

1. See Question 1 under Chapter 3.
2. Jones commissioned Smith, an architect, to design and supervise the building of a house on land he owned. Builders Ltd contracted to build the house. During the construction work Middletowns Council's building control officer made the usual inspections under the Building Regulations.

    Five years after completion Jones noticed cracks in an exterior wall of the house. Investigation revealed that the foundation to the wall was inadequate and not to the standard of the building regulations. Expensive repairs are now necessary. Consider the common law liability of all concerned in the matter.

    (1985 paper)

    (*NOTE* This question is also relevant to Chapter 5(i))
3. Conversions plc contracted with Smith to convert a farm building he owned into a house. Smith lived in the house for two years and then sold it to Jones. Three years later Jones discovered that some of the work done by Conversions plc was defective and that expensive repairs were necessary.

    (a) Consider the liability of Smith to Jones.

    (b) Consider the common law liability of Conversions plc to Jones.

(c) Consider the liability under the Defective Premises act 1972 of Conversions plc to Jones.

(1986 paper)

(*NOTE* This question is also relevant to Chapter 5(i))

NOTES TO CHAPTER 4

1. *Winfield & Jolowicz on Tort*, 12th Ed. 69.

2. (1932) A.C.562

3. (1951) 2 DLR 241

4. (1967) 3 All.E.R.993

5. *Saif Ali* v *Sydney Mitchell & Co.* (1978) 3 All.E.R.1033
A barrister failed to advise amendment of writ in claim for damages arising out of a car accident. House of Lords held he was liable in negligence as professional immunity only extended to pre-trial matters intimately connected with the conduct of the case in court.

6. (1980) Ch.297

7. (1965) 3 All.E.R.560

8. (1968) 2 All.E.R.205

9. (1977) 2 All.E.R.492

10. (1972) 1 Q.B.373

11. These are now replaced by Building Regulations under the Public Health Act 1961.

12. *Acrecrest Ltd* v *W.S. Hattrell & Partners & Another* (1983) 1 All.E.R.17
A land development company employed architects and building contractors to build a block of flats. The foundations were dug to a depth of 3'. The building inspector said that the foundations should be dug to 5' where there were tree roots, but that 3'6" to 4' would be sufficient elsewhere. The building suffered from subsidence and cracks. The architects admitted that the foundations should have been dug to 5', and joined the local authority as third party in an action for negligence. Held – the local authority owed a duty of care to the owners provided their own negligence was not the cause of their loss. In relying upon their architects and the local authority's building inspector, the owners had not been so negligent as to cause their own loss, and the fact that the owners had employed architects and builders did not take them outside the scope of the local authority's duty of care. Both the building inspector and the architects had been negligent, and damages were apportioned 25% against the local authority and 75% against the architects.

13. *Peabody Fund* v *Sir Lindsay Parkinson & Co. Ltd* (1983) 3 W.L.R.754
The local authority approved plans for a development of 245 houses with a drainage system with flexible pipes. The artchitects subsequently substituted rigid pipes for the flexible ones and the developers agreed to this. The drainage system failed to pass on testing and had to be reconstructed, causing three years' delay. Held local authority not liable. They had discharged their duty to see that an adequate drainage system was installed by requiring plans to be deposited. They owed no further duty of care to stop the developers from acting unlawfully by not complying with the building regulations.

14. *Batty* v *Metropolitan Realisations Ltd* (1978) A.C.728
Builders erected houses on a steep slope without having the land surveyed and the subsoil tested. Three years after the plaintiff had bought one of the houses, there was a landslide on nearby land and within ten years the house's foundations would slip. Held – the house was 'doomed' and the plaintiff could recover damages for its diminution in value.

15. (1982) 3 All.E.R.201
Nominated sub-contractors were employed by builders to lay a floor in a factory. The floor was defective and had to be replaced; the plaintiffs (the owners who had employed the builders and the architects who had nominated the sub-contractors) sued the sub-contractors for the cost of replacement and for loss of profit from having to close the factory while the work was carried out. The House of Lords held that such loss was recoverable, that the sub-contractors, called in for their specialist knowledge in flooring, owed a duty of care to the owner, and that the loss resulting from closing the factory was entirely foreseeable.

16. *Beaumont* v *Surrey County Council* (1968) 112 S.J.704

17. *Street on Torts*, 7th Ed. 100

18. *East Suffolk Catchment Board* v *Kent* (1941) A.C.74
The Catchment Board exercised a purely permissive and enabling statutory power to repair a sea wall, in such a way that the plaintiff's farm was flooded for a longer period than it would have been had they repaired the wall in a different way. Held – not liable. Only duty was not to add to the damage that would have been caused if they had done nothing.

19. (1970) A.C.1004.

20. (1972) 3 All.E.R.557

21. (1963) 3 All.E.R.687

22. (1964) A.C.465
Bankers gave a reference for clients on the strength of which advertising agents placed copy and suffered a loss of about £17,000. House of Lords indicated that the bankers would have been liable if the reference had not expressly disclaimed liability and that liability would arise where there is a special relationship such that the person making the negligent misstatement knows that his skill and judgment is being relied upon.

23. *Jeb Fasteners Ltd* v *Marks, Bloom & Co.* (1983) 1 All.E.R.583

24. *Sutcliffe* v *Thackrah* (1974) 1 All.E.R.859
An architect certifying the value of work done was held to be exercising his professional skill and judgment and was therefore liable for negligence. The immunity which he would have had while acting as arbitrator under the contract on grounds of public policy did not extend to this situation.

25. (1977) 1 W.L.R.444

26. *Wilkinson* v *Downton* (1897) 2 Q.B.57
As a practical joke, the defendant told the plaintiff that her husband had broken both his legs in an accident. Held – she could recover damages for the nervous shock she suffered as a result.

27. *Malcolm* v *Broadhurst* (1970) 3 All.E.R.508

28. *Chadwick* v *British Transport Commission* (1967) 1 W.L.R.912

29. (1982) 2 All.E.R.298

30. *Blyth* v *Birmingham Water Works* (1856) 11 Ex.784

31. *Wells* v *Cooper* (1958) 2 Q.B.265
A householder repaired a handle on his back door. A fishmonger, delivering fish, pulled the door shut behind him and fell from some steps up to the door when the handle came away. The handle had been operative for about five months. Held – no evidence of incompetence and not liable.

32. *Phillips* v *William Whiteley Ltd* (1938) All.E.R.566
A jeweller pierced ears for a customer. Held – he could not be expected to take the medical precautions which a doctor would take and was not liable for injury.

33. *Nettleship* v *Weston* (1971) 2 Q.B.691
The plaintiff was injured in an accident caused by the negligence of the learner driver he was escorting. The Court of Appeal held by a majority that she was liable for failing to show care. This case appears to be out of line with the general rule, and the decision was probably influenced by the insurance situation.

34. (1954) 2 Q.B.66

35. (1951) A.C.850

36. (1953) A.C.643

37. *Paris* v *Stepney Borough Council* (1951) 1 W.L.R.117

38. (1954) 1 W.L.R.835

39. (1965) A.C.778

40. *Roles* v *Nathan* (1963) 1 W.L.R.117
Chimney sweeps called out to clean the flue of a coke-burning boiler were

warned to seal off the sweep-hole and the inspection chamber before the boiler was lit. They did not and died from poisonous fumes. Held – defendant (owner of the premises) was not liable.

41. *Bolam* v *Friern Hospital Management Committee* (1957) 2 All.E.R.118
The plaintiff sustained a broken pelvis in the course of receiving E.C.T. Medical opinion differed as to whether a patient should be physically restrained during such treatment or given relaxant drugs. In directing the jury, McNair J. said '. . . a man is not negligent if he is acting in accordance with a practice merely because there is a body of opinion who would take a contrary view'.

42. *Lloyds Bank* v *Savory* (1933) A.C.201
A bank's practices were held to be negligent and they were therefore held liable for collecting for employees' cheques which they had stolen from their employer.

43. *Wakelin* v *L.S.W. Railway Company* (1886) 12 App.Cas.42
The plaintiff's husband was found dead on the railway line, but there was no evidence as to how the accident had happened. Held – no evidence which established negligence by the railway company.

44. Literally translated from the Latin, this means 'the thing speaks for itself'.

45. Per Erle C.J. in *Scott* v *London & St Katherine's Docks Co* (1865) 3 H & C 722

46. *Byrne* v *Boadle* (1863) 2 H & C 722

47. *Gee* v *Metropolitan Railway Company* (1873) L.R. 8 Q.B.161

48. *Easson* v *L.N.E.R.* (1944) 2 K.B.421

49. *Barkway* v *South Wales Transport Co. Ltd* (1950) 94 S.J.95
A motor coach ran off the road due to a defective tyre. Held – *res ipsa loquitur* did not apply as the cause of the accident was known, but on the facts there was evidence of negligence on the part of the defendants.

50. *Swan* v *Salisbury Construction Co. Ltd* (1966) 1 W.L.R.204
The plaintiff was injured when a crane his employers were using collapsed. It collapsed because the ground under one of the four wheels holding the chassis on which the crane was mounted subsided. Held by the Privy Council on appeal from Bermuda – as the trial judge had found, as a finding of fact, that as the defendant employers had used all due care in positioning the crane, they had discharged the burden of proving that they had not been negligent.

51. *Moore* v *R. Fox & Sons* (1956) 1 Q.B.596
A workman was killed by an explosion of gas accumulated under a de-rusting tank. Held – *res ipsa loquitur* applied and the employers had failed to discharge the burden of proof that they had not been negligent. It was not sufficient to show several hypothetical causes of the accident

inconsistent with negligence on their part. They had either to give an explanation of the accident showing they were not negligent, or to show that they had taken all due precautions.

52. *Re Polemis & Furness, Withy & Co. Ltd* (1921) 3 K.B.560.

53. *Overseas Tankship (UK) Ltd* v *Morts Dock & Engineering Co Ltd* (1961) A.C.388.

54. (1963) A.C.837, per Lord Reid.

55. In the second action arising out of the circumstances of *The Wagon Mound* and brought by the owners of the ship being repaired, the court accepted evidence that the damage was foreseeable. As Winfield points out, the court were wrong to hear expert evidence to the effect that fuel oil on water would not ignite, as the relevant factor as to a breach of duty of care was the belief of the defendants. It has also been pointed out that the petrol vapour in the hold of the *Polemis* made it highly inflammable, and it was therefore foreseeable that any minor incident could cause a serious fire.

56. (1969) 1 Q.B.428.

57. See *Wakelin* v *London & South Western Railway*, Note 43 above.

58. (1970) A.C.467

59. (1982) A.C.794

60. (1969) 1 W.L.R.1556

61. (1773) 1 W.B1.892

62. (1974) 1 W.L.R.1176

63. (1970) 3 All.E.R.508
A husband and wife were involved in a car accident caused by the defendant's negligence. The wife claimed damages for (i) nervous illness, exacerbated by a nervous condition from which she was suffering at the time of the accident and by the strain of coping with her husband's changed personality after the accident and (ii) loss of earnings from her full-time job and from her previous part-time job as her husband's secretary, he being unable to work. Held – the defendant was liable for increased damages due to the aggravated nervous condition and for loss of earnings from her full-time job, but not from her part-time job as this was because of her own particular domestic arrangements.

64. (1933) A.C.448

65. (1981) Q.B.625

66. As in *Carslogie Steamship Co. Ltd* v *Royal Norwegian Government* (1952) A.C.292, where a ship, delayed from sailing by repairs after a collision with the defendant's ship due to the defendant's negligence, was subsequently damaged by being in heavy weather in the Atlantic when she did sail. The heavy weather was held to be a new factor, extraneous to the

defendant's negligence, and the defendant was not liable for the damage caused by it.

67. *Haynes* v *Harwood* (1935) 1 K.B.146

The plaintiff was injured while trying to stop two bolting horses left unattended in a street. Held – plaintiff's action was foreseeable and not a *novus actus interveniens*.

68. *Wieland* v *Cyril Lord Carpets Ltd* (1969) 3 All.E.R.162

The plaintiff suffered a neck injury due to the defendant's negligence and had to wear a collar. She was further injured when she fell downstairs, as she was unable to use her bifocal glasses to see properly because of the collar. Held – defendants were liable for her further injuries.

69. *Jayes* v *I.M.I. (Kynoch) Ltd* (1984) 81 L.S. Gaz. 3180

The plaintiff, an experienced man employed as a production supervisor, injured his finger when he used a rag to wipe oil from the belt of a moving machine. The guards had been removed by fitters called in to deal with a lubrication problem. The defendant's employers were liable for a breach of statutory duty as to fencing the machine, but the plaintiff was held to be 100 per cent contributorily negligent and received no damages for his injury.

70. *Jones* v *Livox Quarries Ltd* (1952) 2 Q.B.608

The plaintiff, riding on the towbar of a taxcavator, was injured when a vehicle drove into the back of it. Held – his damages should be reduced for contributory negligence. Although the obvious danger he risked was being thrown off, he had made himself more vulnerable in the accident which in fact happened.

71. *Yachuk* v *Oliver Blais & Co. Ltd* (1940) A.C.386

A shopkeeper who sold gasoline to a nine year old boy was held to be liable in negligence when the boy burned himself with it, but the boy was not contributorily negligent as he could not have appreciated the inflammable quality of it.

72. *Baxter* v *Woolcombers* (1963) 107 Sol.Jo.553.

5. Liability for dangerous premises and structures

1. OCCUPIER'S LIABILITY

The law as regards an occupier's liability for dangerous premises was radically changed by the Occupiers' Liability Act 1957. Before then, the extent of the duty of care owed to a visitor depended upon the status of the visitor, that is, whether his entry on to the premises was as an invitee, licensee or trespasser, or under the terms of a contract. The basic change made by the 1957 Act was to establish a common duty of care owed to all lawful visitors. The terms of a contract will still govern entry under that contract, although, as we shall see, the occupier is restricted in some ways as to the terms he is able to impose, and the Occupiers' Liability Act 1984 now determines an occupier's liability towards a trespasser.

(a) Liability of occupier to lawful visitors

(i) Who is an occupier

A person is an occupier if he has control over the premises, or over activities in progress on the premises. An owner with legal title to the property will be an occupier if he himself is resident there. There may be two or more joint occupiers of premises however, so that an owner may also be an occupier jointly with his servants who are resident and conducting operations there[1]. Because the Act covers not only the dangerous state of the premises but also premises which are dangerous due to 'things done or omitted to be done on them', dual occupation will often arise where one person is resident and another person is carrying out work there, such as a building contractor[2].

(iii) Who is a lawful visitor?

A lawful visitor to whom a duty of care is owed under the Act is anyone with express or implied permission to enter on to the premises, or anyone who enters under a right conferred by law, such as a meter reader or an inspector carrying out duties under the Building or Health and Safety at Work Regulations. It includes the former categories of invitees and licensees, but clearly does not include a trespasser, defined by Lord Dunedin[3] as 'one who goes on the land without invitation of any sort and whose presence is either unknown to the proprietor, or if known, is practically objected to'. A licence will not be implied from repeated trespasses.

A lawful visitor may become a trespasser if he remains on the premises when his permission to do so has been withdrawn, although he should probably be given a reasonable time to leave and to remove his property. He will also become a trespasser if he exceeds the terms of his invitation. As Scrutton L.J. said[4] 'When you invite a person into your house to use the staircase you do not invite him to slide down the banisters'.

The categories of express or implied invitees and trespassers are not clear-cut, however, and leave a residual indeterminate class of visitors who are uninvited but whose entry is not unlawful or unjustifiable. Examples of such visitors would be canvassers or persons delivering leaflets, or competitive observers. Such persons are probably within the scope of the 1957 Act unless a notice prohibiting them makes them trespassers, such as a notice 'No hawkers or circulars'. Persons exercising private rights of way or public rights of access would be non-visitors, however, and outside the scope of the Act.[5]

(iii) The scope of the Act

The Act applies not only to buildings but to a 'fixed or moveable structure', such as a tunnel or machine in it[6], a grandstand, electricity pylons, ships, trains, cars and aeroplanes.

It applies to 'things done or omitted to be done' on the premises, which clearly covers repairs or a want of repair. It is debateable whether it also covers activities in progress on the premises, but in any event a visitor would have an action in negligence against a person carrying out an activity without due care[7] and in such cases there may be an apportionment of liability between the occupier and the person responsible for a negligent activity[8].

The Act applies to damage to property as well as injury to persons, including damage to property of persons who are not visitors[9]. Where there is a contract of bailment however, such as where goods are deposited in a warehouse, then the terms of the contract will determine liability and not the Act, which only replaces the previous common law cases. There is no liability either for goods stolen by a third person[10].

(iv) The duty of care under the Act

Section 2(2) provides that an occupier has a 'duty to take such care as in all the circumstances of the case is reasonable to see that the visitor will be reasonably safe in using the premises for the purposes for which he is invited or permitted to be there'. In determining what is reasonable, regard may be had to the care which a skilled tradesman may be expected to show with regard to the dangers of his trade – Section 2(3) (b)[11] – and to the fact that children may be expected to be less aware of dangers than adults – section 2(3) (a)[18]. Contributory negligence by a visitor may reduce the damages recoverable[12] by him or voluntary acceptance of a known risk may operate as a defence[13].

If the occupier is aware that visitors enter his premises at night, then adequate lighting should be provided[1]. A warning by an occupier to a visitor – for example, 'mind your head' – does not in itself absolve the occupier from liability, unless in all the circumstances it was enough to enable the visitor to be reasonably safe (Section 2(4) (a)).

If the danger arises from 'faulty execution of any work of construction, maintenance or repair by an independent contractor employed by the occupier', then the occupier will not be liable if he was acting reasonably in entrusting the work to an independent contractor, and took reasonable steps to satisfy himself that the contractor was competent and the work was properly done (Section 2(4) (b)). If the work is of a specialised and complex nature, the occupier's only duty will probably be to make adequate enquiries to ensure that he has engaged a competent contractor[14], but if the work is unskilled, then he may be expected to oversee it and will still be liable if it has not been carried out properly[15]. If the occupier carries out repairs himself, then provided they are the everyday running repairs which an occupier might be expected to do himself and they are done with reasonable competence, he will not be liable[16].

Section 2(1) provides that the occupier may 'in so far as he is free to and does, extend, restrict, modify or exclude his duty to any visitor or visitors by agreement or otherwise'. The words 'or otherwise' would clearly include a notice such as 'visitors enter at their own risk' or 'no liability accepted for any injury howsoever arising'.

Where the premises are business premises, however, the Unfair Contract Terms Act 1977 provides that an occupier cannot restrict or exclude his liability for death or personal injury resulting from negligence, by contract or notice. The effect of this is to reverse the decision in *Ashdown* v *Samuel Williams & Sons*[17] where a notice was held to exempt the occupier from liability for injury from shunting trucks, and presumably a notice under Section 2(1) would only be effective since 1977 as regards private property. The 1977 Act does provide however that a notice or contract which 'satisfies the requirement of reasonableness' may exclude liability in negligence for loss or damage to property.

(b) Liability of occupier to entrants other than lawful visitors

This is now governed by the Occupiers' Liability Act 1984 which came into force in May of that year.

It has already been pointed out that, in addition to trespassers, there are certain other 'non-visitors', such as persons using a right of way or a public access overland, and these people are included in the 1984 Act as well as trespassers.

Like the 1957 Act, it covers injuries arising from the state of the premises or from 'things done or omitted to be done' on them, but it does not apply to loss of or damage to property. The occupier is the same as for the purposes of the 1957 Act, and under Section 1(3) of the Act he will only be liable for the duty imposed by the Act to a non-visitor if three conditions are fulfilled:

   (i)   he is aware, or has reasonable grounds to believe, that the danger exists, and
   (ii)   he knows, or has reasonable grounds to believe, that the non-visitor is in the vicinity, or may come into the vicinity, of the danger, and
   (iii) it is reasonable, under all the circumstances, that he should offer some protection against the risk.

Under (ii) above, it seems probable that many of the old cases on what amounts to an 'allurement' enticing children on to the land, so that the occupier is aware that their presence is likely, will still apply[18].

If these three requirements are satisfied, then an occupier's duty to a non-visitor is to take such steps 'as are reasonable in all the circumstances' to give warning of the danger or discourage persons from taking the risk. The reasonable steps which he is required to take will vary according to who the non-visitor is, so that for instance a notice might not be sufficient to warn young children or blind persons, whereas it would be to warn a burglar.

In *Phipps* v *Rochester Corporation*[19] it was held that a very young child aged five, who was injured when he fell into a trench on a building site while accompanied by his sister aged seven, could have been expected to be under parental supervision, and the defendants were not liable. This decision could presumably still be relied upon as regards very young child trespassers.

2. LIABILITY OF A NON-OCCUPIER FOR DANGEROUS PREMISES

A person other than the occupier for the purposes of The Occupiers Liability Act may be liable for injury or damage arising from defective premises. Building contractors may be liable for negligence, as in *A.C. Billings & Sons Ltd* v *Riden*[20], where contractors working on the front of a house made access to it unsafe and a visitor was injured. In *Dutton* v *Bognor Regis UDC*[21] a local authority were held liable for the negligence of their building inspector in passing defective foundations; and in *Anns* v *Merton Borough Council*[22] for failing to carry out their statutory duty of inspection properly. The Defective Premises Act 1972, which came into effect on the 1st January 1974, now imposes a statutory liability for injury or damage arising from defective premises independently of occupation.

Liability of a contractor

In addition to liability in negligence as mentioned above, Section 1(1) of the Defective Premises Act provides that

A person taking on work for or in connection with the provision of a dwelling (whether the dwelling is provided by the erection or by the conversion or enlargement of a building) owes a duty to see that the work which he takes on is done in a workmanlike or, as the case may be, professional manner, with proper materials and so that as regards that work the dwelling will be fit for habitation when complete.

The section applies only to dwellings which are not within the N.H.B.C. Scheme however (an 'approved scheme' under Section 2 of the Act), and as most new houses are within the scheme, the section is probably most relevant to conversions. The duty applies to architects and surveyors involved in the construction as well as builders, but a person who carries out work properly according to instructions is not liable[23], so that a contractor or subcontractor carrying out work according to specifications may not be liable.

The limitation period of six years after which an action for damage is barred runs not from the time when the damage occurs[24] but from the completion of the dwelling, although the period of three years' limitation on a claim for personal injuries still runs from the date of the injury.

Section 3 of the Act provides that a claim survives notwithstanding subsequent disposal of the premises, so that a vendor or a lessor who has carried out repairs himself may remain liable as well as a builder or other professional person.

It may be more attractive financially for an aggrieved owner with defective premises to sue the local authority for failing to carry out their obligations properly under the Building Regulations, as in *Anns* v *Merton Borough Council*. Frequently, the builder and the local authority will be joined in the same action, and in *Worlock* v *S.A.W.S.*[25], where both the builder and the local authority were sued, the Court of Appeal held that the builder's negligence was the primary cause of the defects in the plaintiff's bungalow, and apportioned damages 75% against the builder and 25% against the local authority, this being a usual apportionment nowadays in such cases.

Liability of a landlord

In addition to a landlord's possible liability under Sections 1 and 3, Section 4 of the Act provides that where he is under an obligation to repair premises which he has let, he is liable to take reasonable care to see that persons 'who might reasonably be expected to be affected by defects in the state of the premises' are reasonably safe from personal injury or damage to property caused by a defect due to his failure to repair. The duty is owed not only to the tenant and his family, but to anyone who might reasonably be expected to be on the premises, or a passer-by.

The obligation to repair may arise from an express covenant to repair contained in the lease, or from the obligations implied by statute[26] or by case law[27]. The landlord will not be liable, however, unless he knows, or should have known, of the want of repair, so that in *O'Brien* v *Robinson*[28], where neither the landlord nor the tenant knew of a latent defect which caused the ceiling to collapse, the House of Lords held that the landlord was not liable.

QUESTIONS

1. *Nuisance.* A contractor is to start work shortly on demolishing and rebuilding a shop front. It will be necessary to leave building skips in the road.
    Advise the firm:
    (a) as to what applications it should make, and to whom, in order to do so, and as to its criminal liability if it should fail to do so.
    (b) as to its civil liability in tort if the skips obstruct the pavement and also the entrance to the adjacent shop.
    (Specimen paper)
    (*NOTE* This question is also relevant to the chapter on Highways.)
2. *Trespass and Nuisance.* Highbuild plc has contracted to build an office block on a restricted site. During the course of the work, the crane on the site swings over the adjoining building of Alpha plc. Building materials for the project have also been deposited on adjacent land belonging to Beta plc without permission.
    Consider the legal position of all concerned and the remedies available to a court to deal with any claim by Alpha plc and Beta plc.
    (1986 paper).
    (*NOTE* Also relevant to remedies in Chapter 3).
3. *Strict liability, Rylands* v *Fletcher, Fire.* (½ question). Describe the liability of occupier for spread of fire from his premises.
    (Specimen paper).
4. Brown engaged Wellbuild Limited to extend his house. The excavation for the extension was in water-logged ground so continual pumping was required. One night whilst Wellbuild's workers were off the site a coupling on the pump became disconnected, with the result that the garden of Green's house next door was flooded, destroying a special collection of rock plants. When the building work was completed, one of Wellbuild's workers set fire to some rubbish. Sparks from the fire ignited a local farmer's field of corn.
    Consider the legal position.
    (1985 paper).
    (*NOTE* Also slightly relevant to Nuisance under this chapter).

NOTES TO CHAPTER 5

1. *Wheat* v *Lacon & Co. Ltd* (1966) A.C.552
The defendant brewers, owners of a public house, allowed their licensee's wife to take in paying guests. A guest fell while going down, at night, unlit stairs, on which the handrail finished three steps from the bottom. Held – the brewers had joint occupation with the licensee. However, as there was no evidence as to why the guest had fallen, and the brewers could not possibly have known that the light bulb was broken, they were not liable.

2. *A.M.F. International Ltd* v *Magnet Bowling Ltd* (1968) 1 W.L.R.1028
Magnet employed building contractors under the R.I.B.A. form of contract to construct a building to be used as a bowling alley. The bowling alley was to be installed by A.M.F. when they were notified by Magnet that the building was ready. Magnet duly notified A.M.F. who installed bowling equipment. The building was not completed, however, and because of this was flooded in a heavy rainfall, which damaged the bowling equipment. Held – (i) Magnet, who were occupiers under the Occupiers' Liability Act, had not checked that the work had been properly done by their contractors and were therefore liable; (ii) liability under Section 3(1)(b) of the Act for damage to property did not limit the damages to the actual property damaged, but the normal rules as to remoteness of damage applied, and liability extended to consequent financial loss; (iii) the building contractors were also occupiers for the purpose of the Act and liable; and (iv) although Magnet could not claim an indemnity against the building contractors for their own negligence under the Act, they could under the R.I.B.A. contract.

Even if the building contractor is not deemed to be an 'occupier' within the Act, he may be liable in negligence: see *A.C. Billings & Sons Ltd* v *Rider* (1957) 3 All.E.R.1, where the House of Lords held the appellant contractors liable because they were in breach of the ordinary duty to take reasonable care that all persons who might be expected to visit the premises where they were working should not be exposed to danger by this work.

3. In *Addie* v *Dumbreck* (1929) A.C.358.

4. In *The Calgarth* (1926) P.93

5. A private right of way is exercised 'as of right', this being one of the essential requirements for its acquisition by prescription. Thus in *Holden* v *White* (1982) 2 W.L.R.1030, a milkman who tripped over a defective manhole cover while delivering milk along an access which was a private right of way was unable to recover damages for his injury, as it was held that the owner of the land over which the right of way went was under no duty to maintain it.

6. *Bunker* v *Brand (Charles) & Son Ltd* (1969) 2 Q.B.480
A machine was hired to the defendants for use in constructing a tunnel in building the Victoria Line. The plaintiff, an employee of the engineering firm cutting the tunnel, was injured by the machine. Held – the defendants were occupiers of the machine, and of that part of the tunnel

in which the machine was, for the purposes of the Occupier's Liability act. The plaintiff's knowledge of the danger did not absolve them from the common duty of care under the Act.

7. A case before the Act on this is *Slade* v *Battersea & Putney Group Hospital Management Committee* (1955) 1 All.E.R.429, where a visitor who slipped while the floor was being polished was able to recover damages.

8. *Fisher* v *C.H.T. Ltd* (No.2) (1966) 2 Q.B.475
The first defendants ran a club, which included a restaurant which was run by the second defendants. They employed the third defendants, who were plasterers, to re-plaster a ceiling, and one of the third defendants' employees was injured by touching a live wire on the ceiling. Held – both the first and second defendants were occupiers under the Occupiers' Liability Act, but under the Factories Act the person conducting operations was also deemed to be an occupier, so that the third defendants were also liable. Per Denning L.J., as between the first and third defendants, the third defendants were more liable. Liability was apportioned between all three defendants.

9. Section 1(3)(b) of the Act. The example of damage to a non-visitor which would fall within the Act given in *A.M.F. International Ltd* v *Magnet Bowling* (Note 2 above) is a tile falling from the roof of a house and damaging a car parked outside the property.

10. This was the position before the Act, and in *Tinsley* v *Dudley* (1951) 2 K.B.18, a publican was not liable for the theft of a motor cycle from the yard of his public house.

11. *Roles* v *Nathan* (1963) 1 W.L.R.1117
The plaintiffs were two chimney sweeps who were warned about the danger of fumes from a defective coke-burning boiler if it was lit. Held – the owner was not liable for their deaths.

12. *Sole* v *W.J. Hallt Ltd* (1973) Q.B.574
Builders who were building houses employed plasterers. The plaintiff, a plasterer, was injured when he stepped back into a stair well. No guard rails or boards had been provided. Held – the common duty of care under the Occupiers' Liability Act required that boards should have been provided, but the plaintiff had also been negligent, and his damages were reduced by one third.

13. Section 2(5) of the Act provides that an occupier has no obligation 'in respect of risks willingly accepted' by a visitor and specifically applies the common law cases on '*volenti*' in deciding whether the risk was so accepted.

14. *Haseldine* v *C.A. Daw & Son Ltd* (1941) 2 K.B.343
The landlords of a block of flats had a service contract with engineers for the maintenance of a lift. The lift was defective as it was not put back correctly after greasing, and a person using it was injured. Held – the landlords, who had employed competent engineers to maintain the lift, were not liable, although the engineers were.

See also *A.M.F. International Ltd* v *Magnet Bowling* (Note 2 above) for a case where the occupier's obligation to oversee the work done by his independent contractor was not discharged properly.

15. *Woodward* v *Mayor of Hastings* (1945) K.B.174 where there was liability for the work of a charwoman who failed to clear snow from an icy step properly.

16. *Wells* v *Cooper* (1958) 2 Q.B.265
A householder who repaired the handle of a door with reasonable competence was not liable when it came away injuring a visitor some months later.

17. (1957) 1 Q.b.409

18. *Southern Portland Cement* v *Cooper* (1974) A.C.623, a Privy Council case on appeal from Australia.
The appellants dumped sand in the course of quarrying, creating a sandhill from which an electric cable could easily be reached. They told children from the nearby town that the quarry was out of bounds to them. Held – they were liable to a child injured playing on the sandhill, even though he was a trespasser, since they had created the danger, and knew that the sandhill was an allurement to children and that children played there.

19. (1955) 1 Q.B.450

20. (1958) A.C.240

21. (1972) 1 All.E.R.462

22. (1977) 2 All.E.R.492

23. Section 1(2) and (3).

24. See Chapter 3(1)

25. (1982) 265 E.G.774

26. Under the Housing Act 1961 Sections 32 and 33, a covenant is implied, in leases not exceeding seven years, that the landlord will maintain the structure and installations for water, gas, electricity and sanitation. The Housing Act 1957 requires a landlord to keep a house let at a very low rent (not exceeding £80 per annum in London and £52 elsewhere) fit for habitation, provided that this can be done at reasonable cost (*Buswell* v *Goodwin* (1971) 1 All.E.R.418)

27. In *Smith* v *Marrable* (1843) 11 M & W 5, it was established that there is an implied obligation that furnished premises are fit for habitation at the commencement of the tenancy.
In *Liverpool City Council* v *Irwin* (1977) A.C.239, a landlord was held liable to take reasonable care to maintain the common parts of a building leased.

28. (1973) 1 All.E.R.583

6. Other Torts relevant to the Construction Industry

1. TRESPASS TO LAND

Trespass to land has been defined by Winfield[1] as an 'unjustifiable interference with the possession of land'. It differs from nuisance in that it is a direct interference, usually involving a physical incursion, and it was said in *Entick* v *Carrington*[2] that 'every invasion of property, however minute, is a trespass'.

Mistake is no defence to trespass to land and negligent trespass would still presumably be a trespass, although as regards negligent trespass to the person, the court has indicated that an action should be brought in negligence rather than trespass[3]. Trespass to land, like other forms of trespass, is actionable *per se* (without proof of damage), however, whereas negligence is not, so that it is conceivable that an action for negligent trespass might succeed where an action for negligence might fail.

Trespass to land may take any one of the following forms:

(i) Wrongful entry on to the land

This is the most commonly recognised form of trespass and the type of trespass referred to in the notices 'Trespassers will be prosecuted'. The notice is in fact inaccurate. Prosecution is for a criminal offence and the tort of trespass is a civil wrong for which an action for damages or an injunction lies.

Because the definition of land includes the airspace above and the subsoil below, an action for trespass lies for interference with these. Unlawful tunnelling below the surface would be a trespass and in the case of *Cox* v *Glue*[4] damages were awarded for trespass to the subsoil by digging holes in the land to erect poles and a booth. In *Kelsen* v *Imperial Tobacco Co*[5] a signboard projecting only eight inches over the plaintiff's land was nevertheless held to be a trespass, and in *Woollerton & Wilson Ltd v Richard Costain Ltd*[6] a crane swinging over the plaintiff's land was a trespass. Concessions are made to aircraft flying over the land at a reasonable height, however, under the Civil Aviation Act 1982, and a consequential, indirect intrusion, which is not the result of a positive act by the defendant, will not be a trespass, although it may well be a nuisance. For example, the branches or roots of a tree which have grown over or under the plaintiff's land will be a nuisance which the plaintiff may abate, subject to minimal damage being caused and notice to the defendant in some cases.

An entry on to land in the exercise of a right, which is abused by misuse, will also constitute a trespass. An example of this type of trespass is the use of a highway for purposes other than access[7].

(ii) Trespass by remaining on the land

An entry under licence will become a trespass when the licence is withdrawn and the licensee has been given a reasonable time to leave by an appropriate route. A visitor to a house on lawful business will have an implied licence unless a notice expressly prohibiting callers negatives it and makes him a trespasser.

Where a person, who is lawfully on land for a purpose, abuses his authority by a positive act of misfeasance, such as stealing, as opposed to a mere act of nonfeasance[8], his entry becomes a trespass which relates back to the moment he enterd on to the land. This principle is known as trespass '*ab initio*'.

(iii) Trespass by placing things on the land

A trespass is committed if objects are placed on the land of another, even though there is no physical entry on to the land. Examples of this type of trespass are throwing stones onto the land, or depositing rubbish or a ladder against a wall[9]. There is no right to enter another's land without permission to carry out repairs to adjoining land[10] unless the owner has acquired the right to do so as an easement[11]. It is generally conceded that the law as to entry on to adjoining land for the purposes of carrying out repairs is unsatisfactory and the problem is the subject of a Law Commission's Working Paper[12].

Continuing trespass

The tort of trespass is committed for so long as the unlawful entry continues and the plaintiff may bring subsequent actions. This is ilustrated by the case of *Holmes* v *Wilson*[13] where buttresses were built on the plaintiff's land to support a road. The plaintiff recovered damages but the defendants did not remove the buttresses, and the plaintiff was able to bring a further action for damages.

A continuing trespass must not be confused however with continuing damage from a trespass which has ceased. As Salmond points out[14],

cases of continuing trespass must be distinguished from cases of the continuing consequences of trespass which is over and done with. If I trespass on another's land, and make an excavation there without leaving any rubbish on the land, the trespass ceases as soon as I leave the land, and does not continue until I have filled the excavation up again. Consequently, only one action will lie, and in it full damages are recoverable for both the past and the future.

Defences to Trespass

(i) Licence

A licence is permission to enter on to the land. It is usually given for a purpose, and if the purpose is exceeded or abused, the entry will be in excess of the licence and become a trespass.

(ii) Legal authority to enter

Entry by a bailiff under a warrant, or by a police officer exercising a power of search, is not trespass. A private citizen also has limited rights of entry to prevent a serious crime.

(iii) Inadequate title of the plaintiff

Since trespass protects possession of land, a person who is not in immediate possession, such as a landlord, cannot bring an action for trespass[15]. If the defendant has occupied land adversely to the owner for twelve years, then the owner's right to recover possession will be extinguished under the Limitation Act 1980. The occupation must be adverse however, and occupation which is not inconsistent with the owner's ultimate intentions as to user of the land will not be adverse[16].

Remedies for Trespass

(i) Re-entry on to the land

Subject to the protection given to tenants under the Rent Acts whereby it is unlawful to re-enter without a court order, the plaintiff is entitled to repossess his land, although in doing so he must not use more force than necessary[17].

(ii) Legal action for possession (formerly ejectment)

As the law protects possession, a person dispossessed may recover the land from his dispossessor, even though his own title is merely possessory and not legally authenticated. His right to do so, as in the case of the true owner, is extinguished after twelve years' adverse possession. The adverse possession may be by successive 'squatters', whose total 'squats' add up to twelve years.

(iii) Damages

The plaintiff is entitled to compensation in the form of damages for any injury done to his property. As previously mentioned, trespass is actionable *per se*, but the plaintiff is only likely to recover substantial damages in practice if an injury has been done.

If the plaintiff has been dispossessed, his damages are known as mesne profits, which are normally assessed as the letting value of the property. Mesne profits are usually claimed in an action for recovery of possession.

(iv) Injunction

The plaintiff is entitled to a court order restraining the defendant from trespassing. This will be particularly relevant in cases of continuing trespass. An injunction is a discretionary remedy however, and will not usually be awarded by the court unless for some reason damages are inadequate, or have been refused[18].

2. NUISANCE

The nature of nuisance

It is necessary to distinguish between private nuisance, a tort involving interference with the proprietary rights of an individual, and public nuisance, which is not basically a tort at all.

The forms of nuisance are similar in that they both affect the environment in some way, but there the similarity ends. Both are nowadays controlled and superseded to some extent by statutes passed for the protection of the environment, such as the Control of Pollution Act 1974 (Part II of which replaces the Noise Abatement Act 1960), the Clean Air Acts and the Public Health Act 1936. These statutes are enforceable by public bodies, usually local authorities, although occasionally they may provide for an individual to make a complaint for enforcement – for example, under Section 59 of the Control of Pollution Act 1974 an occupier can bring summary proceedings for premises affected by noise.

Public nuisance

A public nuisance is principally a criminal act for which a prosecution can be brought in the magistrates' courts. In more serious cases where criminal prosecution would not be adequate, the Attorney General may, on the information of a member of the public, bring a 'relator' civil action for an injunction. A local authority may obtain an injunction to restrain it under Section 22 of the Local Government Act 1972.

It affects materially the comfort and convenience of a class of people[19], although it is not necessary that it should affect every member of the class. Examples of public nuisance are unauthorised obstructions of the highway, carrying on an offensive trade or keeping a disorderly house.

It is possible however that a public nuisance, whilst causing discomfort and inconvenience to a class of persons, may also particularly affect an individual, and any person who is particularly affected may sue for damages. Scaffolding erected without permission outside a shop to carry out repairs to the flat above will be a public nuisance in that it obstructs the pavement[20], but if the shopkeeper suffers loss of trade due to it, he can claim damages. For an individual to sue in public nuisance, the damage he suffers must be 'particular, direct and substantial'[21]. It is not necessary at all for a plaintiff in public nuisance to have an interest in land, as in private nuisance, and he may recover for personal injuries[22], whereas it is by no means certain to what extent it is possible to recover for personal injuries in private nuisance, which is primarily an interference with property rights[23].

Private nuisance

A private nuisance has been defined by Winfield as an 'unlawful interference with a person's use or enjoyment of land, or some right over or in connection with it'. It is essentially an infringement of proprietary rights, although it has been assumed that a person with such rights could recover for personal injuries.[23] The interference may take the form of actual physical damage[24] or, more frequently, interference with the enjoyment of land or rights attaching to it. In the former case, provided there is some substantial damage, the locality and the reasonableness or otherwise of the defendant's conduct are irrelevant, although both these factors are highly relevant to interference with enjoyment of land.

Nuisance arises from a state of affairs and an action will not lie for an isolated event[24]. However, an isolated event resulting from a state of affairs may still be nuisance[26].

Interference with land includes interference with rights in the land, such as easements or natural rights attaching to it. A person may therefore bring an action in nuisance for the obstruction of a right of way or a right of light, although the obstruction must be substantial. The degree of obstruction involved for a building erected to interfere with a right of light to a neighbouring window was discussed in *Colls* v *Home & Colonial Stores*[27]. In this type of nuisance, again factors such as the locality or reasonableness of the defendant's conduct are irrelevant, as it is the infringement of a right of the plaintiff's which is the essence of the action and not so much the commission of a wrong by the defendant[28].

Standards of liability in nuisance

A plaintiff in nuisance has two remedies available to him – an injunction to stop the nuisance, or threatened nuisance, and damages.

An injunction is an equitable remedy which the courts will usually only grant where damages are inadequate. An interim injunction can be obtained very quickly *'ex parte'* (by the presentation of evidence, usually in affidavit form, by the plaintiff only). The interim injunction will only be made for a limited period such as fourteen days until a full hearing *'inter partes'* (with representations from both plaintiff and defendant) can take place to decide if the injunction should be continued or not. An injunction will only be granted where the injury complained of is severe, and at this stage, the court are not so much concerned with the culpability of the defendant as with alleviating the hardship to the plaintiff. Where, however, the court is assessing a quantum of damages for nuisance, culpability and foreseeability are highly relevant.

As previously mentioned, they are particularly relevant too in those nuisances involving interference with comfort and convenience and less relevant where there is actual damage to property, as it is questionable whether it can ever be reasonable to damage a neighbour's property[29]. Winfield argues that it is probable that culpability is only relevant to this type of nuisance when the damage is unlikely and latent.

There are various factors which are to be taken into account in considering the reasonableness of the defendant's conduct:

(i) The nature of the locality

A plaintiff who lives in an industrial area must expect inconvenience, such as noise and fumes, from time to time. In *De Keyser's Royal Hotel (Limited)* v *Spicer Brothers (Limited) & Minter*[30] it was said that people who live in towns must expect the inconvenience of building operations near them at times. This has been aptly expressed by Thesiger L.J. in *Sturges* v *Bridgman*[31] when he said 'What would be a nuisance in Belgrave Square would not necessarily be so in Bermondsey'.

(i) The extent of the harm or interference

There are two construction cases which may be contrasted here – the De Keyser case[32] where pile-driving at night which caused serious inconvenience to the plaintiff's hotel guests was held to be excessive and an injunction was granted, and *Andreae* v *Selfridge & Co.*[33] where an hotel proprietor failed to obtain damages in nuisance for the noise and dust from demolition and rebuilding work which were legitimately carried out without undue inconvenience.

(iii) The utility of the defendant's conduct

Nuisance in effect regulates the law between neighbours and it is often necessary to balance their conflicting interests. Conduct of the defendant's which is beneficial and causes only minor inconvenience is obviously more tolerable than conduct which, however beneficial and short-lived, causes extreme disturbance affecting livelihood. In balancing conflicting interests, the test of reasonableness is applied to both the plaintiff and the defendant. It follows therefore that evidence of any malice on the defendant's part is highly relevant as it will negative reasonableness[34].

(iv) Abnormal sensitivity of the defendant's property

A defendant will not be liable in nuisance if damage is caused only because the defendant's property is unduly sensitive[35].

Who can sue for nuisance?

Any person whose land is affected may sue in nuisance. This obviously includes the freeholder of the land in possession. It also includes a tenant, and if the nuisance is likely to result in lasting damage, such as building so as to infringe a right of light or vibrations likely to damage a building, then the landlord who has the freehold reversion may also sue. A mere licensee, with no proprietary rights in the property, cannot sue however, and in the case of *Malone* v *Laskey*[23] a sub-tenant's wife was held not to have sufficient interest in the property to be able to maintain an action in nuisance. But in *Newcastle-under-Lyme Corporation* v *Wolstanton Limited*[36], where the Corporation's pipes and gas mains were damaged by mining operations affecting the subsoil, the Corporation's licence to lay pipes and drains was sufficient to enable them to recover damages in nuisance. This case may also be regarded as interference with a right in the nature of a servitude however.

Who can be sued in nuisance?

The person who creates the nuisance by some positive act is always liable for it, even if it subsequently becomes impossible for him to abate it as he no longer has entry to the land where it is.[37]

The occupier of the land from which it emanates will also be liable, and his liability generally covers the acts of persons lawfully on his land. He will be vicariously liable for the acts of his employee and for any infringement of strict liability or extra-hazardous acts of his independent contractor. Thus in two early cases the occupiers of land were held liable where construction work undertaken by their independent contractors resulted in undermining support to adjoining land or premises,[38] and in *Matania* v *National Provincial Bank*[39] the occupiers of the first floor of a building who had building work carried out were liable to the occupiers of other floors for the dust and noise from the operations of their independent contractors. Although there is strict liability for nuisance on a highway[40] there will not be liability in nuisance for the work of an independent contractor whom the occupier reasonably believes to be competent, carried out near the highway and which, through his negligence, results in injury to a user of the highway[41].

Where the nuisance is caused by a trespasser on the land, or by an act of nature, the occupier's liability will depend upon the extent to which he can be said to have 'adopted' the nuisance. Is it a nuisance of which he knew, or should have known, and did nothing about? This will depend in each case upon the circumstances and is illustrated as regards the act of a trespasser in the case of *Sedleigh-Denfield* v *O'Callaghan*[42] and an act of nature in the case of *Leakey* v *National Trust*[43].

A landlord who has let premises will not generally be liable as he is no longer in occupation, but there are exceptions to this principle. He will be liable if he has authorised the nuisance[44] or if he knew or ought to have known of it before he let the premises[45] or if the nuisance arises from a want of repair for which the landlord is liable. He will be liable either if he has expressly covenanted to repair in the lease or if it is a weekly tenancy where it would be unreasonable to expect the tenant to be responsible for structural repairs[46]. It should be noted that some statutes, such as Section 32 of the Housing Act 1961, imply obligations to repair on the part of the landlord. Under that section, which applies to leases for less than seven years, there is an implied covenant on the part of the landlord to repair the structure and exterior of the premises and to maintain installations for the supply of water, gas, electricity and drainage, and space and water heating. Section 4 of the Defective Premises Act 1972 makes the landlord liable for injury or damage to any person 'who might reasonably be expected to be affected by defects in the state of the premises', wherever he is liable for repairs, and the wording of this liability clearly covers nuisance to nearby occupiers.

Even where the tenant has covenanted to repair, the landlord may still be jointly liable with him for a nuisance arising from a defect in repair at the commencement of the tenancy[47].

Defences to nuisance

Apart from the general defences in tort such as contributory negligence, inevitable accident and consent of the plaintiff, the unforeseeable act of a stranger, or 'a secret unobservable operation of nature, such as subsidence under or near the foundations of the premises'[48] are also defences.

If a person has obtained a prescriptive right to carry on a nuisance by twenty years' uninterrupted use under the Prescription Act 1832, this will be a defence. The user must not be secretive however, and the prescriptive period will not start to run until it becomes known to the plaintiff and interferes with his enjoyment of his property[49].

A defence special to nuisance is statutory authority given to a public body to carry out certain works. Whether the statute amounts to a defence or not depends in each case upon the terms of the statute – whether the authority is mandatory or merely permissive, and whether a nuisance is an inevitable consequence of the work being carried out. Some statutes contain a 'nuisance clause' to the effect that nothing contained in the Act shall exonerate the undertakers from any action or proceedings for nuisance[50], but even this may not impose liability on a statutory undertaker if the statute is mandatory in its terms and nuisance is an inevitable consequence of the work.

It should be noted however that the following contentions by a defendant will not amount to a defence to nuisance:

(i) That the plaintiff came to the nuisance

It was no defence in one case where the plaintiff went to live near a tallow chandlery[51] nor in the case of *Sturges* v *Bridgman*[49] that the doctor built his surgery at the end of the garden near the defendant's bakery.

(ii) That the defendant's conduct is useful

Building operations, however useful, may still be a nuisance if not carried on reasonably[30].

(iii) That the defendant's act was only a nuisance because of similar acts by others.

For example, the defendant would still be liable for an accumulation of rubbish causing an obstruction notwithstanding that he had only contributed part of it, and that the part he had contributed would not have been a nuisance if others had not added to it.

3. THE RULE IN *RYLANDS* v *FLETCHER*

The origin of the Rule

The Rule is a tort of strict liability, which derives from the judgment of Mr Justice Blackburn in the case of *Rylands* v *Fletcher* in 1868[52], that a

person who for his own purposes brings on his lands and collects and keeps there anything likely to do mischief if it escapes, must keep it in at his peril, and, if he does not do so, is *prima facie* answerable for all the damage which is the natural consequence of its escape.

The case itself concerned water in quantity stored in a reservoir for use in the defendants' mill. The defendants had instructed civil engineers to build the reservoir, but, unknown to them, a disused shaft from the plaintiff's mine went under the land and this was not properly sealed off by the engineers. When the reservoir was filled, the water entered the shaft and flooded the plaintiff's mine in adjoining land.

The rule established a new head of liability for user of land, differing from trespass in that the encroachment was not a direct act by the defendants, and from nuisance in that the escape was an isolated event and not a state of affairs. There was no negligence on the part of the defendants, and in 1868 they could not be made vicariously liable for the negligence of their independent contractors. The statement of the Rule by Mr Justice Blackburn was modified by Lord Cairns' speech in the House of Lords however, whose decision in favour of the plaintiff was on the basis of the defendants' 'non-natural' use of the land. The meaning of 'non-natural' was later considered by Lord Moulton in *Rickards* v *Lothian*[53] to be 'some special use bringing with it increased danger to others, and must not merely be the ordinary use of the land or such a use as is proper for the general benefit of the community'. As Salmond points out however[54] the inherent dangerousness of the thing if it escapes introduces an element of foreseeability into the tort, and this in turn introduces an element of flexibility to the Rule in that the courts can decide what amounts to a 'non-natural' and inherently dangerous user. This flexibility is illustrated by changing social attitudes towards industrial use for instance. In the case of *Rainham Chemical Works Ltd* v *Belvedere Fish Guano Co.*[55] it was assumed that the manufacture of explosives in 1921 was a non-natural user of land, whereas in *Read* v *J. Lyons & Co. Ltd*[56] in 1947 the House of Lords expressed doubts as to this.

The Rule has been applied, among other things, to the escape of gas[57], electricity[58], colliery spoil[59], decayed wire rope[60], a chair-o-plane at a fairground[61], vibrations from building operations[62] and (*obiter*) to a flagpole at a fete[63]. The courts have refused to apply it to a fall of rocks from an outcrop on a hillside due to weathering[64], self-sown thistle seeds[65], to domestic water, gas and electricity installations[66] and to demolishing or erecting walls[67]. It is possible however that there would be liability nowadays in nuisance in some of these cases. The Royal Commission on Civil Liability and Compensation for Personal Injury[68] has recommended that a minister be empowered by statute to list dangerous things or activities for which liability should be strict for personal injury or death. As Winfield has pointed out[69], some Statutory Regulations, such as the Health and Safety at Work Regulations, already cover certain aspects of strict liability.

There must be an actual 'escape' from the defendant's land, and the plaintiff in *Read* v *J. Lyons & Co. Ltd*[56] failed on this ground. But given an escape, the occupier of adjoining land can recover damages not only for injury to the land, but also for personal injuries. It is questionable whether a non-occupier can recover for personal injuries[70]. Moreover, the defendant need not own and occupy the land and it is sufficient if he has some measure of control over the area from which the danger escapes. Thus in *Shiffman* v *Grand Priory etc.*[63] a flag pole which fell from the defendants' first aid tent was held to have 'escaped' from the tent of which the defendants were licensees. This is particularly relevant to services running under a highway, and a local authority have been held liable for the escape of sewage from a drain belonging to them[71]. The same principle has been applied to an escape of gas from a gas main under the highway[72] and electricity from cables[58] and in *Charing Cross Electricity Supply Co.* v *Hydraulic Power Co.*[73] where the defendant's water main burst in four places damaging the plaintiff's electricity cables, it was held still to apply even though the site of the plaintiff's injury (beneath the highway) was occupied by the plaintiff only as a licensee and the company had no proprietary interest in the soil.

The strictness of the Rule is modified by the exceptions to it, such as potentially dangerous things which are outside the scope of the Rule as they are held to relate to a natural user of the land, and the defences to it. Also there is a tendency in many torts nowadays for the courts to find liability only if there is some culpability, and this was the basis of the decision in *Northwestern Utilities Ltd* v *London Guarantee & Accident Co. Ltd*[72]. As Winfield points out[74] this is regrettable, as it is in just such cases, where negligence cannot be proved, that a plaintiff might need the protection of the Rule.

Defences to the Rule

(i) Consent of the plaintiff

Where the plaintiff expressly or impliedly consents to the source of danger on the defendant's land, this will be a defence to any action by him. Moreover, he will be taken to have consented impliedly where the source of danger is for the common benefit of himself and the defendant. This is well illustrated by the implied consent of tenants of the lower floors of a building to a water supply on the upper floors.

Consent will not be implied however where the installation is defective, or the defendant is negligent[75].

In *Dunne* v *North Western Gas Board*[76] the Court of Appeal took the view that the supply of services by nationalised industries did not amount to an accumulation for their own purposes, the purpose of the supply being for the benefit of the community, and there was no liability under the Rule therefore without some negligence on their part.

(ii) *Default of the plaintiff*

Where the plaintiff's damage is due entirely to his own default, he will not succeed in an action. Thus in *Dunn* v *Birmingham Canal Co.*[77] where the plaintiffs worked a mine under the defendant's canal, they had no cause of action when the water from the canal escaped and damaged the mine. In *Hoare & Co.* v *McAlpine*[62], however, it was said (*obiter*) that it would have been no defence to an action for damage to a building from vibrations that the building itself was very old.

(iii) *That the escape is due to the act of a stranger*

In *Rickards* v *Lothian*[53] where water escaped from a blocked washbasin in the defendant's premises to the plaintiff's premises on the floor below because a third person had maliciously turned a tap full on, the defendant was held not liable.

Who is within the definition of a stranger? Clearly a trespasser or an independent contractor would be, and a member of the occupier's family would not be. As for lawful visitors, the test is probably similar to that for nuisance and depends upon the degree of control which the occupier has over the person and the foreseeability of his causing harm. The foreseeability test was applied in *Northwestern Utilities* v *London Guarantee & Accident Co.*[72], introducing an element of culpability and bringing liability under the Rule nearer to the standard of liability in negligence.

(iv) *Act of God*

This applies where the escape is due to 'circumstances which no human foresight can provide against, and of which human prudence is not bound to recognise the possiblity'[78]. It is only the acts of a deity as evidenced in extreme natural phenomena, and it is thought that it would include earthquakes, tornadoes and lightning. The only English case is one of flooding due to an excessive and unprecedented rainfall[79], but later judges, having a more realistic opinion of English weather, have criticised this decision[80].

(v) Statutory authority

Where the dangerous accumulation is made under statutory authority, this may constitute a defence provided there has been no negligence. It will depend in each case upon the interpretation of the statute, and in particular, as to whether the statute imposes an obligation on the defendant (making it dubious that the accumulation is then 'for his own purposes') or whether it is merely permissive, allowing the accumulation. Thus in *Green* v *Chelsea Waterworks Co.*[81] where the defendants were under a statutory duty to maintain water in their water main at a high pressure, the statutory authority was a defence when the main burst and flooded the plaintiff's land, but in *Charing Cross Electricity Co.* v *Hydraulic Power Co.*[82], where the facts were similar but there was merely permissive authority to maintain a water supply under pressure, the statutory authority was no defence.

4. LIABILITY FOR DAMAGE DONE BY FIRE

Fire damage nowadays is amost invariably covered by insurance, so that claims in tort only become relevant where property is under-insured in times of high inflation, or in claims between insurance companies.

The subject requires consideration under two heads – the Fires Prevention (Metropolis) Act 1774 (which actually applies to the whole country) and under the common law.

(a) The Fires Prevention (Metropolis) Act 1774

This provides that there shall be no liaiblity for fires started by accident or by some unknown cause, but not for a fire started by negligence[83]. It was applied in *Collingwood* v *Home & Colonial Stores Ltd*[84]. It should be noted that the Act exonerates a defendant from liability only for the start of the fire and not for its spread. Thus in *Goldman* v *Hargrave*[85] a fire started when lightning struck a redgum tree on the defendant's land. The defendant had the tree felled, but then left the fire to burn itself out and took no steps to extinguish it. A freshening wind caused the fire to spread to the plaintiff's adjoining land, and the defendant was held liable for this. The distinction under the Act has often led the courts to consider separately liability for the start of a fire and for its spread in applying the common law rules also.

(b) Liability for fire at common law

The liability of an occupier for the start or spread of a fire arises basically in two ways:

(i) Where some non-natural user of the land creates a fire risk

This is sometimes considered to be an application of the general Rule in *Rylands* v *Fletcher*, but it differs from it in that it is the fire caused by the dangerous substance which escapes and not the substance itself. The fact that the exact cause of the fire is unknown will not bring it within the Act of 1774 and there is still liability, as illustrated by *Mason* v *Levy Auto Parts of England Ltd*[86] where the defendants had quantities of petrol and other inflammable materials on their land and were liable for the spread of a fire, the cause of which was unknown, to the plaintiff's adjoining land. The earlier case of *Musgrove* v *Pandelis*[87] had already found that a car with petrol in its tank fell within the principle of *Rylands* v *Fletcher*, although this has since been criticised, and with the increased use of cars nowadays, it would presumably be possible to argue that this is no longer a 'non-natural' user, as with the manufacture of explosives in *Read* v *J. Lyons & Co. Ltd*. There is no liability under this head for the ordinary domestic fire in a grate[88].

(ii) Where the fire is caused, or spreads, through negligence, nuisance or the wilful act of the occupier or persons for whom he is responsible

The occupier, as in *Rylands* v *Fletcher*, will be liable for the acts of everyone, except a stranger, whose acts may be foreseeable. He will be liable for their negligence[89] or for a nuisance caused by them[90] in starting the fire or in allowing it to spread[91].

In the case of *H.N. Emanual Ltd* v *GLC*[92] there was a liability where independent contractors had been expressly forbidden to light a fire to burn demolition rubbish, but nevertheless did so. Although the contractors were employed by the Minister of

Works, this was at the request of the Council, and it was said that the Council were in control of the site and could have foreseen that the contractors would burn rubbish.

Where the fire does not arise fron a non-natural user of the land and there is no other tort, the defendant will not be liable[93].

5. BREACH OF STATUTORY DUTY

In our industrial society, there is a vast body of legislation enacted with the intention of providing, as far as possible, for the safety and protection of individuals, particularly employees. The first Factory Act was passed for this purpose in 1844, and since then, legislation of this type has burgeoned. Detailed regulations affecting most employment situations have now been made under the Health and Safety at Work Etc. Act 1974, and those most directly affecting the construction industry are the Construction (Working Places) Regulations 1966.

Although the primary intention of Parliament in enacting such legislation is to protect an individual rather than to compensate him, the courts have frequently interpreted statutes as giving rise to a civil action in tort for a breach. In order to succeed in an action for breach of a statutory duty, a plaintiff must prove the following:

(i) That the statute was intended to protect the plaintiff's interest against a breach of duty by the defendant.

In deciding whether this was the intention, the court will have regard to the whole of the statute and to the pre-existing law. If the plaintiff is adequately protected without a statutory remedy (for example, by an action in negligence) then the court may refuse to find that the defendant's breach of statutory duty gives the plaintiff any further action[94].

The courts are reluctant to find that statutory duties imposed upon public bodies give rise to a claim for damages[95], although a notable exception has been claims for injuries resulting from dangerous highways[96].

Where the statute imposes a penalty for its breach, the presumption may be that its main aim was deterrent and that the fine imposed was intended to be an adequate retribution. This presumption is not conclusive however, as was shown by the early case of *Groves* v *Wimborne*[97], where a boy injured in a factory due to a breach of fencing regulations recovered £150 damages, although the statute imposed a penalty of only £100 and provided that all or part of the penalty might be applied in compensation. Conversely, a failure to impose a penalty for a breach raises a presumption that a civil action for damages will be available, as otherwise the statute would be virtually unenforceable.

The statute may protect the interests of a certain class of persons, such as certain employees, in which case it will be assumed that its breach will give rise to an action for damages. The plaintiff must then show however that he is within the class of persons for whose protection the statute was passed, and he may fail in his claim if he cannot show this[98].

Nevertheless, whether a breach of statutory duty gives rise to a civil action for damages or not finally depends upon the court's interpretation of the particular statute in each case. The rule of precedent applies of course, so that a previous interpretation will be followed in this respect in subsequent cases on the statute, and there are for example numerous cases under the Factories Acts. As Winfield has pointed out, however[99], the situation is hardly satisfactory as the courts are frequently required to deduce from a statute something which was never in Parliament's contemplation when the statute was passed, and Lord Denning has said: '(The Legislature) has left the courts with a guess-work puzzle. The dividing line between the pro-cases and the contra-cases is so blurred and so ill-defined that you might as well toss a coin to decide it'[100].

(ii) The plaintiff's injury was one which the statute was passed to prevent.

If the plaintiff's injury was caused in a way not envisaged by the statute, then he will not have any remedy for its breach. In *Nicholls v F. Austin (Leyton) Ltd*[101] the plaintiff, who was injured when struck by a piece of material from a machine on which she was working, was held not to have any action for breach of her employer's statutory duty to 'securely fence every dangerous part of any machinery'[102] as the object of such statutory duty was to 'keep the worker out, not to keep the machine or its product in'[103].

A case under the Building (Safety, Health & Welfare) Regulations 1948 where a similar point was taken is *Donaghey v Boulton & Paul Ltd*[104]. A workman was injured by falling through the roof of an aeroplane hangar, which his employers were constructing as subcontractors, when moving asbestos sheets. The subcontractors were uninsured and he therefore sued the main contractors for breach of their statutory regulations. It was held that Regulation 31(1) which required precautions to be taken to prevent a person working on a roof from slipping down or off a sloping roof, did not apply, although the contractors were found to be in breach of Regulation 31(3) which required a suitable support to be provided where work was in progress on roofs of fragile materials through which a person was liable to fall a distance of more than ten feet.

(iii) The plaintiff must show that his injury was caused by the defendant's breach of statutory duty.

If the defendant has complied with his statutory duties, for example by providing the requisite safety equipment for a job, and the plaintiff's injury is due to his own failure to use it, then the plaintiff will not succeed in an action against him. In *Ginty* v *Belmont Building Supplies Ltd*[105], the plaintiff was injured when he fell through a defective roof on which he was working. His employers were required by the Building Regulations 1948 to provide and use crawling boards for the work and they had in fact provided them. It was held that the plaintiff's injury was caused by his own failure to use the boards, and as there had not been any fault on the part of the employers which contributed to the accident, they were not liable. Even where the necessary safety equipment has not been provided, if there is evidence that the plaintiff would not in any event have used it, this may defeat the plaintiff's claim[106]

The nature of statutory liability

For a plaintiff to succeed in an action, all he needs to show is a breach of duty imposed by the statute. This may well be a strict duty imposed quite independently of any negligence or fault on the defendant's part, or an absolute duty which the defendant cannot evade by delegation. Even so, the courts have been prepared to apportion fault in cases of delegation of duties to the extent, as in *Ginty* v *Belmont Building Supplies Ltd*[105], where they have held that the employee was entirely to blame for his accident so that the employer was not liable at all. In *Boyle* v *Kodak Ltd*[107] the appellant fell about twenty feet from a ladder while painting an oil storage tank, the ladder having slipped sideways as it was not lashed to prevent this as it should have been under Regulation 29(4) of the Building (Safety, Health & Welfare) Regulations 1948. The Regulation imposed an absolute duty on both the employer and the employee. Although the employers had not been negligent, they had not taken sufficient steps to draw the employee's attention to the Regulation and were held to be liable for fifty per cent of his damage.

It is a completely separate tort deriving from the statute itself, so that unless the statute expressly provides that any remedy given by it excludes or is alternative to common law remedies, then the plaintiff may sue alternatively or additionally in any other tort such as negligence[108].

Defences to a claim for breach of statutory duty

(a) Plaintiff's contributory negligence

If the plaintiff has contributed to the accident by his own negligence, then damages will be reduced under the Law Reform (Contributory Negligence) Act 1945. Moreover, the court is entitled to come to the conclusion that the accident was entirely due to the plaintiff's own negligence and not to a breach by his employer of his statutory duty, in which case he will be 100 per cent contributorily liable and will in effect recover nothing[109].

(b) Volenti non fit injuria

This can never amount to a defence to the employer's own breach of statutory duty as he would always be able to avoid liability by pleading it[110], but he may plead it successfully as a defence to an action in which he is vicariously liable for the tort of another employee. In *Imperial Chemical Industries Ltd* v *Shatwell*[111] the plaintiff's brother did not carry out the correct procedure, required by statutory regulations, for testing a circuit for electric detonators in a quarry. The plaintiff himself was a party to this, however, and was held to be '*volens*' to his brother's tort, and the defence was also available to his employers whom he sued vicariously.

(c) Delegation

Although, as mentioned above, it may not be possible to delegate an absolute statutory duty, *Ginty* v *Belmont Building Supplies Ltd*[105] and *Boyle* v *Kodak Ltd*[107] (above) show that the courts are prepared to take a robust attitude to apportionment of blame for the accident in such cases.

In *Driver* v *William Willett (Contractors) Ltd & Another*[112], the employers, who were the 1st defendants, had consulted engineers, the 2nd defendants, on safety requirements on a building site, and they undertook the duties of a safety officer under Regulation 98 of the Building (Safety, Health & Welfare) Regulations 1948. The 2nd defendants failed to advise the 1st defendants about a hoist, which was used in an unsafe manner causing a scaffold board to fall from it, injuring the plaintiff. Both defendants were in breach of the Regulation, but damages were apportioned as to 40 per cent to the employers and 60 per cent to the engineers, and furthermore, the employers had a contractual claim against the engineers for any damages recovered against them by the plaintiff.

Remoteness of damage is not a defence to an action for breach of a statutory duty and the defendant will be liable, however unlikely and unforeseen an accident may be[113].

NOTES TO CHAPTER 6

1. *Winfield & Jolowicz*, 13th Ed. 359

2. (1765) 19 St. Tr. 1030

3. *Letang* v *Cooper* (1965) Q.B.232

4. (1848) 5 C.B.533

5. (1957) 2 Q.B.334

6. (1970) 1 W.L.R.411

7. As in *Hickman* v *Maisey* (1900) 1 Q.B.752, where the defendant wandered up and down the highway for the purpose of observing racehorse trials on adjoining land.

8. As in the *Six Carpenters' Case* (1610), where carpenters who had entered an inn for refreshment subsequently refused to pay for it, and it was held that they were not trespassers *ab initio* as this was an act of nonfeasance as opposed to misfeasance.

9. *Westripp* v *Baldock* (1938) 2 All.E.R.779
A jobbing builder stored ladders, planks and sand against a wall of the plaintiff's on adjoining property. The pointing on the wall was damaged by damp. Held – the defendant had committed a trespass and the plaintiff was entitled to the cost of repointing the wall.

10. *Hewlitt* v *Bickerton* (1947) 150 E.G.421
There is no doctrine whereby a person has a right to trespass on to the land of another to carry out repairs to his property.

11. The case of *Ward* v *Kirkland* (1967) Ch. 194 recognised that such a right could exist as an easement. In this case, the only way in which the plaintiff could reach the gutters of his property on a wall adjoining a farmyard belonging to the defendant was from the farmyard.

12. Law Commission Working Paper No. 78, 1980–81 on 'Rights of access to neighbouring land'.

13. (1839) 10 A & E 503

14. *Salmond and Heuston on Torts* 18th ed. 40.

15. A landlord could bring an action for trespass if permanent damage to the land were caused, as this would affect his freehold reversion whereby he would take possession again at the end of the lease.

16. As in *Williams Brothers Direct Supply Ltd* v *Raftery* (1958) 1 Q.B.159 where an intention to develop land in the future was held not to be inconsistent with use by the defendant as an allotment in the meantime, and so the plaintiff's right to recover possession was not barred, the defendant's occupation not being 'adverse'.

17. *Hemmings* v *Stoke Poges Golf Club* (1920) 1 K.B.720
The plaintiffs had let a cottage to the defendant and his wife whom they employed. The plaintiffs terminated their employment and served a notice to quit the cottage on the defendant, but the defendant did not leave. Several persons then entered the cottage and physically removed the defendant and his wife and furniture, using no more force than necessary. Held – the plaintiffs' right of re-entry was a defence to assault, battery and trespass.

18. *Woolleteron and Wilson Ltd* v *Richard Costain Ltd* (1970) 1 W.L.R.411
The plaintiffs alleged trespass to their airspace by an overhead crane used by the defendants on an adjoining building site. It was impractical to remove the crane, and without using it, the whole job would have had to be replanned. The defendants offered the plaintiffs damages of £250 for the right to continue the trespass until the job was finished, but the plaintiffs refused this. No actual damage had been caused to the plaintiff's land. The judge granted the plaintiffs an injunction, but exercised his discretion to postpone it for one year, thereby enabling the building operations to be finished. As damages had been offered by the defendants, the plaintiffs had a remedy other than mere nominal damages. This case has been criticised in *Charrington* v *Simons & Co. Ltd* (1971) 1 W.L.R.598, where an injunction suspended for three years was brought forward, but Winfield supports the decision.

19. Romer L.J. in *Attorney-General* v *P.Y.A. Quarries Ltd* (1957) 2 Q.B. at 184 said 'The sphere of the nuisance may be described generally as "the neighbourhood"; but the question whether the local community within that sphere comprises a sufficient number of persons to constitute a class of the public is a question of fact in every case. It is not necessary, in my judgment, to show that every member of the class has been injuriously affected; it is sufficient to show that a representative cross-section of the class has been so affected for an injunction to issue'.

20. But in *Harper* v *Haden & Sons Ltd* (1933) Ch.298 the defendants, who were tenants of the upper floors of a building, erected scaffolding in order to add another floor. The scaffolding, which obstructed the pavement and the plaintiff's greengrocery shop on the ground floor, was held not to be a public nuisance as it was not a wrongful obstruction, and the plaintiff had no legal remedy as it was temporary and reasonable in character.

21. Per Brett J. in *Benjamin* v *Storr* (1874) 30 L.T. 362.
The plaintiff, who had a coffee shop, sued successfully for the noise and smell of horse-drawn carts pulling up outside the defendant's neighbouring premises to collect and deliver goods, the defendant being an auctioneer.

22. *Mint* v *Good* (1951) 1 K.B.517
A boy walking along a public footpath was injured when a wall on adjoining property collapsed. He sued successfully for damages in nuisance. Weir points out that it is easier for a plaintiff to succeed in nuisance as he only has to show a dangerous state of affairs, and does not have to prove default by anyone, as in negligence. (Weir, *A Casebook on Tort*, 5th Ed. 174).

23. *Malone* v *Laskey* (1907) 2 K.B.141
A lavatory cistern became insecure and fell owing to vibrations caused by machinery on the defendant's neighbouring property. The sub-tenant's wife was injured. The court held that she could not sue in nuisance as she was not a person who had any proprietory interest in the property. The fact that she was suing for personal injuries was never specifically argued.

In *Cunard* v *Antifyre Ltd* (1933) K.B. at 557, however, Lord Talbot said 'We think that nuisance (we are speaking of private nuisance only) is correctly confined to injuries to property, whether to easements such as the obstruction of light or rights of way . . . or to other kinds of property, as by noise, noxious vapours, smoke or the like'.

24. *St Helen's Smelting Co.* v *Tipping* (1865) 12 L.T.776
Shrubs and trees on the plaintiff's estate were damaged by fumes from the defendant's factory a mile and a half away. Held – nuisance.

25. *Bolton* v *Stone* (1951) A.C.850
A cricket ball from a cricket field hit the plaintiff who was standing on the road outside her house. Oliver J at first instance decided that it could not amount to nuisance as there was evidence that it was a rare event (one witness said six times in twenty-eight years) for a ball to be hit outside the ground into the road.

This can be contrasted with *Miller* v *Jackson* (1977) A All.E.R. 338, where there was evidence that balls from an adjacent cricket ground were frequently hit into the plaintiff's garden – nuisance. Moreover, it was no defence that the plaintiff had bought the house knowing that the cricket ground was there, or that the cricket ground had been used for 70 years, as it is not possible to acquire a prescriptive right to exercise a nuisance until it becomes a nuisance.

26. *Spicer* v *Smee* (1946) 1 All.E.R.489
Defective electrical wiring in the defendant's adjoining bungalow caused a fire which destroyed the plaintiff's bungalow. The defective wiring was a state of affairs and therefore amounted to a nuisance.

27. *Colls* v *Home & Colonial Stores* (1904) A.C.179
To amount to an infringement of a right of light, a building must cause a 'substantial deprivation', making the premises uncomfortable or prevent-

ing business being carried on as before. The protection given by a right of light is for the light reasonably required. It is a 'fair working rule' that there will be no substantial injury where an angle of 45 degrees is left, particularly if the room receives light from other windows also (per Lord Lindley).

28. Per Lord Macnaghten in *Colls* v *Home & Colonial Stores.*

29. *Lord Westbury L.C. in St Helen's Smelting Co.* v *Tipping:* '. . . it is a very desirable thing to mark the difference between an action brought for a nuisance upon the ground that the alleged nuisance produces material injury to the property, and an action brought for nuisance on the ground that the thing alleged to be a nuisance is productive of sensible personal discomfort. . . . the latter must undoubtedly depend greatly on the circumstances of the place where the thing complained of actually occurs. But when an occupation is carried on by one person in the neighbourhood of another, and the result . . . is a material injury to the property, then there unquestionably arises a very different consideration.'

30. (1914) 30 T.L.R. 257

31. (1879) 11 Ch.D.852

32. *De Keyser's Royal Hotel (Limited)* v *Spicer Brothers (Limited) & Minter*
During the building work, the contractors used a steam pile-driving machine between 7.30 pm and 6.30 am. The plaintiffs were granted an injunction. Although city dwellers had to put up with some inconvenience, this was excessive. The building operations were not being conducted in a reasonable and proper manner.

33. *Andreae* v *Selfridge & Co.* (1938) Ch.1
The plaintiff, a hotel proprietor, claimed damages in nuisance for noise and dust from demolition and rebuilding work. Held – no action would lie if the building operations were reasonable. The defendant company should not be penalised for carrying out operations they were legitimately able to do if there was no undue inconvenience.

34. *Hollywood Silver Fox Farm Ltd* v *Emmett* (1936) 2 K.B.468
The defendant maliciously fired off guns near his boundary with the plaintiff's land where the plaintiff was breeding silver foxes to interrupt their breeding. Held – nuisance.

35. *Heath* v *Brighton (Mayor of)* (1908) L.T.718
Preacher in a church in Brighton sought an injunction to stop the noise from the defendant's electrical power station which distracted him. No evidence that it distracted or detracted from the numbers of the congregation and injunction refused.
  Bridlington Relay Ltd v *Yorkshire Electricity Board* (1965) 1 All.E.R.264
The defendants located an electricity cable near the plaintiff's television aerial, which caused interference on their transmissions. Held – not a nuisance, as the damage was due entirely to the sensitivity of the plaintiff's business.

36. (1947) Ch.92

37. *Fennell* v *Robson Excavations Pty Ltd* (1977) 2 N.S.W.L.R. 486

38. *Dalton* v *Angus* (infringement of natural right to support of land) and *Bower* v *Peate* (infringement of an easement of support acquired by twenty years' prescription).

39. (1936) 2 All.E.R. 633

40. *Tarry* v *Ashton* (1876) 1 Q.B.D.314
A lamp projecting from a wall over the highway was repaired by an independent contractor, but subsequently fell and injured a passer-by. Held – the owner was liable, as there is strict liability for the acts of an independent contractor for anything on the highway, and there was a continuing duty on the occupier to ensure safety after the contractor had gone.

41. *Salsbury* v *Woodland* (1970) Q.B.324
An owner employed a seemingly competent independent contractor to fell a tree in his garden. Owing to the negligence of the contractor, the tree fell on a telephone wire, which came down in the road and caused a pedestrian to be injured. Held – owner not liable. 'Near' the highway is not the same as 'on' the highway and no special risk in the work.

42. *Sedleigh-Denfield* v *O'Callaghan* (1940) A.C.880
A trespasser put a grating in a ditch on the defendant's land. This caused the plaintiff's land to flood three years later in a storm. Held – defendant liable as he should have removed the grating and had in effect 'adopted' it by failing to do so.

43. *Leakey* v *National Trust* (1980) Q.B.485
The plaintiffs lived in houses at the foot of a large mound owned by the National Trust. After an exceptionally dry summer, a large crack appeared in the mound. The plaintiffs informed the defendants, who did nothing. The soil subsequently fell from the mound on to the plaintiffs' houses damaging them. Held – defendants liable, nothwithstanding that the nuisance derived from a natural hazard.

44. *Harris* v *James* (1876) 45 L.J.Q.B.545
Landlord let field to tenant to quarry limestone. Held – liable with tenant for nuisance as he had authorised it.

45. *Gandy* v *Jubber* (1865) 5 B & S 78,485.
There was no liability in this case for a defective iron grating as it was not alleged that the grating was defective when the owner parted with possession of it. The court said there would have been liability however if there had been a tenancy (which they found there was not) and if the landlord had known of the defect when the property had been let.

46. *Mint* v *Good* (1951) 1 K.B.517
The plaintiff, on the highway, was injured by the collapse of the defendant's wall which was defective and a nuisance. Held – although the landlord had not covenanted to repair, this is implied as regards structural

repairs in a weekly tenancy, as to impose structural repairs on a weekly tenant would be unfair and excessive. The landlord was therefore liable for the wall in nuisance.

47. *Brew Bros Ltd* v *Snax (Ross) Ltd* (1970) 1 Q.B.612
Landlord let premises to tenant who was responsible under the terms of the lease for the repair of the drains. A year later, a wall abutting on to the plaintiff's land was bulging dangerously and had to be shored up, causing an obstruction for eighteen months. Held – the landlord was liable as well as the tenant as the defect existed when the premises were let.

48. *Wringe* v *Cohen* (1940) 1 K.B.229
British Road Services v *Slater* (1964) 1 All.E.R.816
The defendant was not liable in nuisance for a dangerous tree which he did not know and could not have realised was dangerous.
Noble v *Harrison* (1926) 2 K.B.332
A branch of the defendant's tree overhanging the highway and 30 feet above it snapped and fell on to the plaintiff's car. Held – not nuisance, since it was a latent defect, which inspection would not have revealed, which caused it to snap.

49. *Sturges* v *Bridgman* (1879) 11 Ch.D.852
A doctor built a surgery at the end of his garden where he was troubled by the noise and vibrations from a bakery which had been there for many years. Held – still nuisance. It was irrelevant that it was only a nuisance because the doctor had built his surgery there. Nor had the defendants obtained a prescriptive right to carry on the nuisance by twenty years' use as prescription does not start to run until the activity starts to be a nuisance.

50. *Midwood & Co. Ltd* v *Manchester Corporation* (1905) 2 K.B.597
The defendants were entitled to lay electrical mains by Order made under the Electric Lighting Acts 1882 & 1888, but clause 70 provided that nothing should exonerate them from any action for nuisance. A main fused, causing the bitumen on the cable to become volatilised into an inflammable gas. This accumulated and caused an explosion. Held – the defendants were liable in nuisance.

51. *Bliss* v *Hall* (1838) 4 Bing.N.C. 183

52. (1868) L.R. 3 H.L.330. The judgement of Blackburn J. was in the Court of Exchequer Chamber and the decision was affirmed by the House of Lords.

53. (1913) A.C.263

54. *Salmond & Heuston on Torts*, 18th Ed.

55. (1921) 2 A.C.465

56. (1947) A.C.146, per Lord Macmillan. The plaintiff was an inspector in the defendants' munitions factory who was injured by an exploding shell. Held – the defendants were not liable under *Rylands* v *Fletcher* as there was no escape from their premises.

57. *Batchellor* v *Tunbridge Wells Gas Co.* (1901) 84 L.T.765
The Gas Board were liable for the escape of gas from a gas main supplying two cottages.

58. *National Telephone Co.* v *Baker* (1893) 2 Ch.186
The electric current from cables laid by a tramway company caused interference on telephone wires. *Rylands* v *Fletcher* applied, but the defendants pleaded successfully the defence of statutory authority under which they operated the tramway.

59. *Attorney-General* v *Cory Bros. Ltd* (1921) 1 A.C.521
A landslide from a colliery tip went on to a road owned by the District Council.

60. *Firth* v *The Bowling Iron Company* (1878) 3 C.P.D.254
The plaintiff and the defendants were adjoining tenants of the same landlord, and the defendants were by the terms of their lease under an obligation to maintain the fence between the two properties. Their predecessors in title had done so by erecting a wire fence, and the defendants had replaced parts of the fence from time to time. Part of the old wire fence had rusted and dropped into the grass in the plaintiff's field, and was eaten by the plaintiff's cow which died as a result. Held – the defendants were liable, the rusty wire being a dangerous thing.

61. *Hale* v *Jennings Bros* (1938) 1 All.E.R.579
A chair-o-plane from the defendant's roundabout became detached and hit and injured the plaintiff, who was the tenant of a nearby stall. Evidence was given to show that persons riding on the roundabout could cause it to be dangerous by swinging the seat, so loosening the bolts which held it. Held – a chair-o-plane being a dangerous thing in itself, there was liability for its escape, notwithstanding that the escape was caused by some third person who had ridden in it swinging in it and causing it to become loose.

62. *Hoare & Co.* v *McAlpine* (1923) 1 Ch.167 Per Astbury J. *obiter*
The defendants had been served with a dangerous structure notice by the local authority in respect of their building and therefore had to carry out work on it. The plaintiffs alleged that the vibrations from the pile driving during the work caused damage to their building nearby. The defendants alleged that the vibrations only caused damage because the plaintiffs' building was old and therefore abnormally unstable. The judge found, as a fact, that the plaintiffs' building was not abnormally unstable, so that it was not necessary for him to go on to consider whether this would amount to a defence as part of the decision of the case. But *obiter*, he said it would not have been a defence.

63. *Shiffman* v *Order of St John* (1936) 1 All.E.R.557
The defendants undertook to be available for first-aid treatment at a fête and set up a tent for this purpose. A flagpole was erected with a flag on it indicating the whereabouts of the tent. This was insecurely held by its wire stays, and children at the fête were constantly around it. The defendants warned the children off it, but the children returned while the defendants were occupied in the tent, and their interference caused the flagpole to fall

and injure someone. Held – the defendants were liable in negligence for the insecurely erected flagpole, but would also have been liable under the Rule in *Rylands* v *Fletcher*. The flagpole, which could be easily caused to fall, was something exceptional and which was likely to cause harm if it did fall. The Rule is not limited to the escape of something from the defendant's own land on to the plaintiff's land, but applies to the escape from somewhere where the defendant is a licensee also, and the defendants were licensees of the first-aid tent. Note – the decision as regards *Rylands* v *Fletcher* is *obiter* as liability was in fact found in negligence, the defendants having been at fault.

64. *Pontardawe RDC* v *Moore-Gwyn* (1929) 1 Ch.656

65. *Giles* v *Walker* (1890) 24 Q.B.D.656
This should be contrasted with the case of *Crowhurst* v *Amersham Burial Board* (1878) 4 Ex.D.5, however, where the defendants planted a poisonous yew tree on their land, the branches of which protruded over the plaintiff's land. They were held liable under *Rylands* v *Fletcher* for the death of the plaintiff's horse after eating some of the leaves. Planting a poisonous yew tree was held not to be a natural user of the land.

66. Water – *Rickards* v *Lothian* – Note 53 above.
Gas pipes in à house or shop – *Miller* v *Addie & Sons (Collieries) Ltd* (1934) S.C.150
Electric wiring – *Collingwood* v *Home & Colonial Stores* (1936) 3 All.E.R.253

67. *Thomas & Evans Limited* v *Mid-Rhondda Co-operative Society Limited* (1941) 1 K.B.381
A wall was erected on the defendant's land on the bank of a river to prevent flooding. In the course of alterations and additions to the defendant's premises, parts of the wall were demolished. There was a heavy rainfall, as a result of which the river flooded through the gaps in the wall on to the plaintiff's land. Held – this was not within the Rule in *Rylands* v *Fletcher* as altering buildings was not a non-natural user of the land.

68. Cmnd. 7054 Vol.11 Ch.31

69. *Winfield & Jolowicz on Tort*, 12th Ed. 451

70. Doubts were expressed in the House of Lords in the case of *Read* v *J. Lyons & Co. Ltd* (Note 56 above) that damages for personal injuries could be recovered independently of occupation of land. Damages for personal injuries were recovered under the Rule in the case of *Hale* v *Jennings Bros* (Note 61 above), however, and in *Shiffman* v *Order of St John* (Note 63 above) the court considered that there would have been liability for personal injuries under the Rule.

71. *Smeaton* v *Ilford Corporation* (1954) 1 Ch.450.

72. *Northwestern Utilities Ltd* v *London Guarantee & Accident Co. Ltd* (1936) A.C.108 (Privy Council case on appeal from Canada).

The defendants were held liable for the escape of gas from their gas main under the highway into the basement of an hotel which was destroyed by fire as a result. The escape of the gas from a welded joint in the pipe was because the joint had been fractured when a storm sewer had been constructed under the main. The defence of act of a stranger failed in this case because, it was said, the defendants' undertaking (piping gas) was inherently hazardous, and they should have anticipated that the work on the storm sewer in the vicinity of their main might cause damage to it.

73. (1914) 3 K.B. 772

74. *Winfield & Jolowicz*, 18th Ed. 430

75. *Prosser* v *Levy* (1955) 1 W.L.R.1224
The defendants let the ground floor of certain premises to the plaintiffs. They subsequently let the upper floors to another tenant. On the second floor was a disused pipe which was still connected to the water main by a stop cock. This was turned on by one of the tenant's employees and the plaintiff's premises on the ground floor were flooded as a result. Held – the defendants were liable as they had been negligent in not taking precautions to stop the pipe and make it safe before letting the upper floors.

76. (1964) 2 Q.B.806
A leaking water main caused a sewer to collapse and fracture a gas main. Gas travelled along the sewer and there were a number of explosions at manholes. Held – the Gas Company was not liable. It had not collected gas for 'its own purposes' and had not been negligent at all.

77. (1872) L.R. 8 Q.B.42

78. Per Lord Westbury in *Tennent* v *Earl of Glasgow* (1864) 2 M(H.L.)22

79. *Nichols* v *Marsland* (1876) 2 Ex.D.1

80. *Greenock Corporation* v *Caledonian Railway* (1917) A.C.556, where the court declined to follow *Nichols* v *Marsland* and Lord Dunedin said 'It always comes to a question of fact whether such and such an occurrence was a *damnum fatale*'. This was a case on the Scottish equivalent of act of God.

81. (1894) 70 L.T.547

82. (1914) 3 K.B.772

83. *Filliter* v *Phippard* (1847) 11 Q.B.347

84. (1936) 3 All.E.R.253
A fire was started by an unknown defect in electrical wiring.

85. (1966) 2 All.E.R.989

86. (1967) 2 Q.B.530

87. (1919) 2 K.B.43
The petrol in the carburettor of a car in a garage caught fire. The chauffeur in charge of the car could easily have stopped it by turning off

the engine, but he failed to do so. The fire spread to the plaintiff's flat above. Held – (a) the defendant, who was a tenant of the garage below and employed the chauffeur was liable. A car with petrol in its tank was a dangerous thing and within the Rule in *Rylands* v *Fletcher* and the Fires Prevention (Metropolis) Act, 1774, did not apply to an action under *Rylands* v *Fletcher*; and (b) the fire which caused the damage was the fire which spread, and not the one 'accidentally begun', and it spread due to the chauffeur's incompetence.

88. *Sochaki* v *Sas* (1947) 1 All.E.R.344. A fire started from a domestic grate in a room which a lodger had left for a short time. Held – no liability for this.

89. *Balfour* v *Barty-King* (1957) 1 Q.B.496
The defendant employed a plumber to thaw frozen pipes in his attic. The plumber's mate used a blow lamp, although the pipes were lagged, and caused a fire. The fire spread to the plaintiff's neighbouring premises. Held – the defendant was liable for the negligence of his independent contractor in starting the fire.

90. *Spicer* v *Smee* (1946) 1 All.E.R.489
The owner of a bungalow was liable in negligence and nuisance for defective electric wiring installed by a contractor which caused a fire which spread to adjoining property.

91. *Musgrove* v *Pandelis* – see Note 87 above.

92. (1971) 2 All.E.R.835

93. *Doltis* v *Braithwaite & Sons* (1957) C.L.Y.2376
The defendants, installing a gas boiler on the second floor of the plaintiff's premises, lit a piece of paper to test the flue. The flue went down to a disused fireplace in the basement, where the plaintiffs had stored textile goods. Some of the fluff from these had gone up the flue, and ignited, causing a fire. Held – the defendants were not liable as they had not been negligent and *Rylands* v *Fletcher* did not apply as the user was natural and there was no escape.

94. *Phillips* v *Britannia Hygienic Laundry Co. Ltd* (1923) 2 K.B.832
A wheel came off the defendant's lorry and struck the plaintiff's van. The defendant, although not negligent, was guilty of a breach of the Construction and Use Regulations, which imposed an absolute duty and a fine for breach. It was held that they did not confer on the plaintiff any cause of action.

95. *Atkinson* v *Newcastle Waterworks Co* (1877) 2 ex.D.441
The Water Company were under a statutory duty to maintain water pressure in their pipes at a certain level, and because they failed to do so a fire on the plaintiff's property could not be extinguished. Held – the statute, which provided for a fine of £10 for its breach but not for compensation to any individual affected, conferred no right of action for its breach on the plaintiff.

96. *Griffiths* v *Liverpool Corporation* (1967) 1 Q.B.374
The plaintiff was able to recover damages for an injury sustained when he
fell over a flagstone, protruding half an inch above an adjoining flagstone,
the highway authority being under an absolute statutory duty to repair
imposed by the Highways (Miscellaneous Provisions) Act 1961.

97. (1898) 2 Q.B.402, a case on the Factory & Workshop Act 1878.

98. *Keating* v *Elvan Reinforced Concrete Co. Ltd & Another* (1968) 2
All.E.R.139
The local authority (2nd defendants) employed contractors (1st defendants) who excavated a trench in a street. The protective barriers were
removed by a third person and the plaintiff was injured when he fell into
the trench. Neither defendant had been negligent. The plaintiff sued the
2nd defendants for breach of Section 8(1) of the Public Utilities Street
Works Act 1950 that the local authority should secure that the street
should be fenced when broken up. The plaintiff failed because the statute
was intended to regulate relations between the highway authority and
contractors employed by them, and not to protect individuals.

99. *Winfield & Jolowicz on Tort*, 12th Edition. 167.

100. In *Ex parte Island Records* (1978) Ch.132.

101. (1946) A.C.493

102. Factory Act 1937, Section 14(1).

103. Per Lord Simonds in *Nicholls* v *F. Austin (Leyton) Ltd* (1946) A.C.
at 505

104. (1967) 2 All.E.R.1014

105. (1959) 1 All.E.R.414

106. *McWilliams* v *Sir William Arrol & Co. Ltd* (1962) 1 W.L.R.295
The plaintiff's husband, who was an experienced steel erector, was killed
when he fell from a tower. The Factories Act 1937 required his employers
to provide a safety belt, which was not available at the time. Evidence was
given however that it was highly unlikely that he would have worn a belt
even if one had been available, and the defendants were therefore held
not to be liable for his accident.

107. (1969) All.E.R.439

108. *Manchester Corporation* v *Markland* (1936) A.C.360
The Corporation, who were the water authority, failed to repair a burst
pipe and to remove water from it for three days, after which the water
froze and caused an accident. Held – they were liable in negligence as well
as for a breach of their statutory duty as the water authority.

109. *Jayes* v *IMI (Kynoch) Ltd* (1984) 81 L.S.Gaz.3180
Fencing was removed from a machine while it was being repaired. The
fitters had to start the machine in order to test it, and the plaintiff, who
was very experienced, tried to wipe some grease off its belt with a rag

while the machine was working and injured his finger. Held – he was 100 per cent contributorily negligent.

110. *Wheeler* v *New Merton Board Mill Ltd* (1933) 2 K.B.669
It was held to be no defence to a claim for breach of statutory fencing regulations that a workman had agreed to work on the machine while it was unfenced.

111. (1964) 2 All.E.R.999

112. (1969) 1 All.E.R.665

113. *Millard* v *Serck Tubes Ltd* (1969) 1 W.L.R.211

7. Property Law

1. THE DEFINITION OF LAND AND FIXTURES

The Latin phrase adopted into English law, '*cujus est solum, ejus est usque ad caelum et ad inferos*', means in effect that whoever owns the land also owns the air space above it and the ground below it. Because of this, a landowner can bring an action for trespass to the air space above his land[1] or the subsoil beneath it.

The right to support of land is a natural right, whereas the right to support of buildings can only be acquired as an easement. A landowner can bring an action for damages for interference with his right of support to land therefore without having to show that he has acquired it as an easement, whereas an action for an infringement of a right to support of buildings can only be maintained if it can be shown to exist as an easement.

Nevertheless there are nowadays many limitations on a landowner's absolute enjoyment of his rights over his airspace and subsoil. For example, the Civil Aviation Act allows for the flight of aeroplanes at a reasonable height over the land, and under the Coal Act 1938 coal under the land belongs to the National Coal Board. The right to erect buildings on the land and the use of the land may be restricted by the Town and Country Planning Acts. Neighbouring owners may have easements, such as rights of way or rights of light, over the land. There may be a restrictive covenant affecting the use of the land, for example, that it shall not be used for any manufacturing purposes. The statutory restrictions referred to are common to all land, but easements and restrictive covenants may, or may not, affect any particular plot of land, and we shall look at the effect of these where applicable later in this chapter.

Of more general practical importance perhaps is what precisely is included physically in the definition of 'land'. If you sell your house, is the purchaser entitled to insist that the sale includes items such as kitchen fitments and garden gnomes? Obviously a wise vendor and purchaser will agree during negotiations before contract exactly what items are to be included in the sale price and what are not. Unfortunately, not all vendors and purchasers are wise, and subsequent disagreements have given rise to litigation. The courts have decided that 'land' includes buildings and chattels which are 'fixtures'. What then is the test for deciding whether a chattel is a fixture or not?

The first test to be applied is that of annexation, that is, is the chattel physically attached to the land? If so, then it is *prima facie* a fixture. Examples would be central heating radiators, shelves, and light fittings. Conversely, if not attached to the land, a chattel will not be a fixture. A Dutch barn or a greenhouse[2] resting by its own weight on the land will not be a fixture.

This test is not conclusive, however, and there is a second test which may change the classification, namely, was the chattel affixed for the improvement of the land or building itself, or was it affixed for the better enjoyment of the chattel itself? Two cases clearly illustrate the application of this test. In *Leigh* v *Taylor*[3] a tapestry affixed to a wall was held to be still a chattel as the purpose of fixture was to enjoy the chattel, but in *D'Eyncourt* v *Gregory*[4] garden ornaments which were not affixed but were nevertheless part of the landscaping were held to be fixtures.

Apart from the everyday sale of land, it may also be important to determine whether a chattel has become a fixture or not on the termination of a lease or a mortgage. 'Tenant's fixtures'[5] may be removed by a tenant at the end of a lease but generally a mortgagor may not remove fixtures from the mortgaged property.

2. ESTATES IN LAND

English land law has its origins in English history and the manorial system and it is essential, even today, to look briefly at this to understand the meaning of an 'estate' in land.

Originally all land was owned by the king, and the king would allow the lord of the manor to have the land in return for certain services. The lord of the manor, in turn, allowed the inhabitants of the manor to have plots in return for services rendered to him. This was a medieval society before money became the predominant mode of barter, and the services rendered determined the type of 'tenure'. In a rural society, these were often agricultural services, but the influence of the Church was also evident in the spiritual tenures, where masses for the departed souls of the lord's family were payment for the land. The significance of this for modern land law however is that a person did not own the land itself, which was owned by the lord and ultimately by the king, but owned an 'estate' in the land. The extent of any interest in property is related to the time for which a person has it, and the duration of a person's interest in land is known as his 'estate'. There are two principal kinds of estate in land. They are:

(a) Freehold estates

These are estates of uncertain duration. The most obvious example of a freehold estate would be a life estate, as everyone's life is of indeterminate duration. The most common freehold estate, and the largest, however, is the fee simple, which is an estate which may be inherited by any heirs under a will or intestacy, and so may continue virtually for ever. Very occasionally, someone may die intestate (without having made a will) and without any heirs at all, in which case the land reverts to the Crown as '*bona vacanta*' – an interesting remnant of the old system of tenure whereby all land belonged to the crown. The property in an estate agent's window described as 'freehold' is land held in fee simple – saleable, deviseable and capable of being inherited by any heir.

(b) Leasehold estates

A person who has a fee simple in land, or freehold, may if he wishes carve out of it lesser interests. For example, X, who has a freehold interest in Blackacre, may grant a lease of Blackacre to Y for a certain number of years. Because the number of years is certain, Y will not have a freehold estate in Blackacre, but he has instead a leasehold estate.

A leasehold estate may be for any length of time – for one day or for 999 years. The essential requirement is that the term is for a fixed and definite duration[6] and the lessee must be given exclusive possession of the land.

Usually the grant of a leasehold estate is formally drawn up in a deed called a lease, with detailed provisions as to rent payable, covenants by the landlord and by the tenant and a proviso for re-entry by the landlord on breach of covenant by the tenant. Many periodic leases (weekly, monthly, yearly leases) are created verbally, however, and may even arise by implication of law where a person takes possession of the land and pays rent. There is extensive legislation protecting the rights of tenants.

3. INTERESTS IN LAND

(a) Easements

An easement is a right enjoyed by the owner for the time being of one piece of land over neighbouring land.

There are many common types of easements such as rights of light, rights of drainage and rights of support for buildings. The courts have also recognised many unusual rights as easements, however, such as the right to run telephone lines over neighbouring land and to fix a signboard or nail trees to a neighbouring wall. As Lord St Leonards said in *Dyce* v *Hay*[8] 'The class of easements is never closed'.

In order to qualify as an easement, a right must satisfy the four requirements laid down in *Re Ellenborough Park*[9]. They are:

(i)   there must be a dominant and a servient tenement;

(ii)   the two tenements must be separately owned;

(iii)   the easement must accommodate the dominant tenement, that is, it must be for the benefit of the land itself and not, for example, for the present owner's business interests, as in *Hill* v *Tupper*[10];

(iv)   it must be sufficiently definite to form the subject-matter of a grant. The flow of air to a ventilation shaft fulfils this requirement[11] but not a general flow of air to the sails of a windmill.[12]

Provided a right satisfies these four requirements then it may exist as an easement, and the courts have recognised as easements rights of storage and a right to enter onto adjacent land to carry out repairs to a flank wall[13]. The courts will generally be reluctant to impose expenditure on the owner of the servient tenement however, so that the easement of fencing[14] is an unusual one. Nor will they accept an easement which would be unduly restrictive of the servient owner's use of his land, and in one case they refused to recognise an easement for protection from weathering when an adjacent house was demolished[15]. It is possible however that this decision may not apply if it is a horizontal surface which is exposed when a roof is demolished[16].

In addition to showing that a right is capable of existing as an easement, a person seeking to claim it as such must show that he has acquired it in one of the ways recognised by the law for the acquisition of easements. These are:

(i) By express grant or reservation. Both of these are usually found in conveyances of houses in a housing estate development, where, for example, rights of drainage and light may be granted and reserved.

(ii) By implied grant. On the sale of part of a plot of land, if there is no express grant or reservation, it is sometimes possible to imply this. If it is the 'quasi-servient' part (the part over which the right is enjoyed) which is sold, then the owner of the 'quasi-dominant' part (the part which enjoys the right) retained may only claim easements of necessity, such as support to an upper flat, or intended easements, being those which the parties are presumed to have intended to grant in order to give efficacy to their transaction[17].

If the quasi-dominant tenement is sold off, however, in addition to easements of necessity and intended easements, the purchaser may claim as easements rights which were enjoyed with the land before the sale and which are continuous, apparent and reasonably necessary for the enjoyment of the land under the Rule in *Wheeldon* v *Burrows*[18], and also under Section 62 of the Law of Property Act 1925: 'all . . . privileges, easements, rights and advantages whatsoever appertaining . . . to the land'. This is a very widely drafted section, and although it will not elevate to the status of an easement a right which does not satisfy the four requirements of an easement, it may nevertheless result in a purchaser acquiring easements which a vendor did not intend him to have. The section should therefore be expressly excluded in the conveyance if it is not intended to give any easements to a purchaser.

(iii) Presumed grant, or prescription. An easement is acquired in this way when the law presumes a grant by reason of long user. In all forms of prescription, the user must be 'as of right', that is openly, without force and without permission. Common law prescription, which requires user since 1189[19] is usually defeated by showing that the right could not possibly have existed then[20]. The two other methods of prescription will usually be pleaded in the alternative. they are:

1. Lost modern grant. Twenty years' user raises a presumption (which can of course be defeated) that the claimant was given a grant at one time which he has carelessly mislaid.

2. Prescription under the Prescription Act 1832. This is a quite unnecessarily complex piece of legislation, but in broad outline a claimant for an easement other than light may have an absolute and indefeasible right after forty years user and a *prima facie* right after twenty years' user. In both cases the user must be 'next before action'. An easement of light becomes absolute and indefeasible after twenty years' enjoyment without written permission, and the enjoyment need not be as of right. In all cases of prescription under the Act, an interruption in the nature of some overt act or objection which subsists for

one year will stop the time from running. In the case of light, it would be necessary to physically erect a hoarding in order to obstruct the light to a window and so prevent the owner from acquiring an easement, which would obviously be impractical if the window was on a twelfth floor. It is therefore provided by the Rights of Light Act 1959 that a light obstruction notice may be registered with the local authority as a local land charge to prevent the prescriptive period from running. The owner of a plot overlooked by windows should therefore register such a notice if he intends to build at any time in the future.

The ways of acquiring an easement described above will give the claimant a legal easement if established. It is a legal right, which will endure through successive ownerships of both the dominant and servient tenements, and cannot be defeated, although it may be extinguished, either expressly by deed, or impliedly by abandonment with the intention of extinguishing it[21].

(iv) An equitable easement may be acquired by estoppel. Estoppel is an equitable doctrine whereby a person who makes a promise upon which the promisee acts to his detriment cannot subsequently retract it. The cases of *Ives (ER) Investment Ltd* v *High*[22] and *Crabb* v *Arun District Council*[23] illustrate the acquisition of rights like easements in this way.

(b) Restrictive covenants

'Covenant' is simply a legal word for agreement, and a restrictive covenant is one which in some way restricts the user of land. Such covenants almost invariably arise on the sale of part of a plot of land where the vendor, anxious to preserve the amenity value of the part which he retains, takes a covenant from the purchaser in the conveyance to him. Examples of covenants commonly found are not to build, or to build only private dwellinghouses to a certain density,[24] or not to cut down trees.

As between the original vendor and purchaser, such covenants are of course binding, and a breach would give the vendor an action for damages and possibly for an injunction to restrain the breach. There are complicated rules to determine whether or not the benefit and burden of such covenants will pass to the successors in title of the vendor and the purchaser.

The burden of the covenant will pass to the successor in title of the purchaser if the requirements of the Rule in *Tulk* v *Moxhay*[25] are satisfied. The Rule only applies however to negative covenants. A negative covenant is one which does not require the expenditure of money, as in the previous examples, but a covenant to maintain a boundary fence[26] or to repair would not be within the Rule as they are positive covenants. This gives rise to problems where blocks of flats are sold, and various conveyancing devices referred to below have been used to circumvent them. The other requirements for the Rule to apply are that the vendor must have owned land for the benefit of which the covenant was made, it must relate to the land itself and not to the vendor personally, and it must be registered if it is a covenant created after 1925, although the old doctrine of notice applies to covenants created before then[27]. Registration is at the Land Charges Register at Plymouth if the title to the land is unregistered and in the local Land Registry if registered.

If it is necessary to show that the burden of a covenant passes in equity, it may also be necessary to show that the benefit passes in equity. This may be done in one of three ways:

(i) By showing express assignment of the benefit of the covenant in each conveyance of the benefited land.

(ii) By annexation of the covenant to the land. This depends upon the wording of the covenant, which should make it clear that it is intended to pass with the land and each part of it. The case of *Federated Homes Ltd* v *Mill Lodge Properties Ltd*[28] is authority for the proposition that a covenant will in any event be annexed to the land by section 78, Law of Property Act 1925. This will not apply however if a clear intention against annexation is expressed in the conveyance[29].

(iii) A building scheme. In an estate development, it may be possible to make certain covenants, such as not to cut down trees or to keep 'open plan' landscaping, applicable to all plots on the estate and enforceable by successive owners against each other as a kind of 'local law'[30]. The requiremens of a building scheme were laid down in the case of *Elliston* v *Reacher*[31] although they have been relaxed to some extent in subsequent cases. They are:

1. the original purchasers of the plots must have derived title from a common vendor (but see *Re Dolphin's Conveyance*[32]);
2. before sale, the vendor must have laid out the estate in lots (but see *Baxter* v *Four Oaks Properties Ltd*[33]);
3. the restrictions imposed were intended to benefit all lots;
4. the original purchasers purchased on the understanding that the restrictions were to apply to all lots;
5. the scheme must have applied to a defined geographical area.

It is not necessary for the covenants to be contained in the conveyances to the original purchasers[34], and the vendor may reserve the right to waive or modify the covenants on any plots unsold for the time being.

Building schemes may apply to blocks of flats and to leasehold property as well as freehold.

One problem which may impede a proposed development is an old restrictive covenant on the title to the land which prevents building, or restricts the kind of property which may be built on it. How should this be dealt with?

Firstly, it is possible to apply to the court under Section 84 Law of Property Act 1925 for a declaration as to whether a restrictive covenant affects particular land or not and by whom it is enforceable. It should be remembered that many of these covenants were imposed last century and it is often unclear as to where the benefit and burden has passed.

Secondly, where a person who is entitled to the benefit of the covenant has acquiesced in its breach for a long time, they will be deemed to have waived it.

Thirdly, an application can be made to the Lands Tribunal under Section 84 as amended by Section 28, L.P.A. 1969 for the discharge or modification of the covenant. The grounds are that the person entitled to the benefit of the covenant has agreed to its discharge or modification, or will not be injured by it, or the covenant is obsolete due to changes in the neighbourhood, or it impedes the reasonable user of the land and monetary compensation would be adequate for its breach. With regard to the user of the land, the Lands Tribunal is to consider the development plan for the area and the results of any planning applications.

Finally, bearing in mind the antiquity of many covenants and the difficulty of establishing who is entitled to the benefit of them, a quicker and cheaper way of dealing with such a problem would probaby be to insure against any claim for breach arising in the future.

(c) Mortgages

A mortagage is a loan where property (usually land) is used as security, so that if the mortgagor (the borrower) defaults, the mortgagee (the lender) has certain rights of recourse against the property. Most people who buy their own homes require a mortgage in order to do so, and most home loans are made by building societies or banks. It may be possible to obtain a further mortgage for improvements or repairs to property too.

A mortgage will take the form of either a long lease of the property by the mortgagor to the mortgagee with a proviso for termination of the lease on repayment of the loan, or a charge designating certain property as security for the loan. Section 87, L.P.A. 1925 gives a mortgagee by way of charge the same 'protection, powers and remedies' as a mortgagee with a legal lease, so that there is no particular advantage in either form as far as a mortgagee is concerned, although a charge is a simpler form of mortgage and will be more appropriate where two or more properties are mortgaged, particularly if some are freehold and some are leasehold.

A mortgagee will require protection for his mortgage. In land with unregistered title, this is effected either by depositing the title deeds of the property with him, or he can register it at the Land Charges Register at Plymouth. A mortgage protected by the deposit of title deeds is not registrable however. In registered title, the Land Certificate is deposited with the local Land Registry, who issue a Charge Certificate in lieu with the mortgage entered in the Charges Register.

A mortgage is usually in the form of a deed executed by the borrower, but banks may be prepared to effect an informal mortgage by deposit of the title deeds or Land Certificate. They will usually ask a borrower to execute a memorandum under seal (by deed) as to the deposit, as a mortgage by deed gives the mortgagee certain rights under Section 105 L.P.A. on default of the mortgagor, such as sale and appointing a receiver of the property.

A building development will usually be financed by a mortgage which is payable in stages according to the stage which the development has reached. The mortgagee, usually a bank, will require a certificate by the architect at each stage certifying that the work has been completed to his satisfaction, before releasing the money. An architect under a building contract who is negligent in giving such a certificate is liable for damages, as in certifying he is acting as a valuer and not an arbitrator under the building contract[35]. As each house in a building development is completed and sold, it will be released from the security by the bank or other mortgagee when they receive the proceeds of sale towards repayment of the loan, so that a purchaser takes the house freed from the mortgage. If the title to the land is unregistered, the bank will join in the conveyance to the purchaser, but if it is registered title, all that is necessary is for the Land or Charge Certificate to be deposited with the Land Registry and a deed of release to be handed over to the purchaser on completion of the sale.

Sometimes a bank or other mortgagee is under an obligation to make further advances, as for instance in a building development when successive stages are reached. Under Section 94 L.P.A. they may be able to 'tack' these further advances on to their original advance and gain priority for payment for the further advances also over any intervening mortgage entered into by the mortgagor. To ensure that this right is available, it is preferable to expressly reserve it in the original mortgage deed.

4. THE CONVEYANCING PROCESS

The conveyancing process is in two stages – (a) pre-contract enquiries (b) contract to completion.

(a) Pre-contract

Pre-contract negotiations should always be made expressly 'subject to contract' which will mean that the transaction is not binding on either party until contracts are formally exchanged. This allows the purchaser time to make his pre-contract enquiries and arrange his mortgage.

A search with the local authority should be made to ascertain such matters as whether there are any road proposals which affect the property, the results of any planning applications made, whether the property is a listed building or there are any tree preservation or compulsory purchase orders.

'Preliminary enquiries' should be made of the vendor's solicitors which will disclose, among other things, any guarantees affecting the property, any disputes the vendor has had with regard to the property and whether any alterations requiring planning permission or Building Regulations approval have been made.

Once the purchaser, or his solicitor, is satisfied as to these enquiries, has seen any restrictive covenants or other rights affecting the land, and finance is arranged, it should be safe to exchange contracts and fix a date for completion. A deposit of ten per cent of the purchase price is paid on exchange of contracts, which is forfeited if the purchaser defaults. Completion is usually arranged for four weeks after exchange of contracts, but this can be varied to suit the parties.

(b) Contract to completion

After exchange of contracts, the formal conveyance (or transfer if the title is registered) is prepared and executed, and this, together with the title deeds, is exchanged for the balance of the purchase monies on completion. The purchaser will also make any requisitions on title, although in practice he will probably have satisfied himself as to the title before exchanging contracts and the requisitions at this stage are a formality. There are then certain pre-completion searches to be made which vary according to whether the title to the land is registered under the Land Registration Act 1925 or unregistered.

(i) Unregistered title

Title to the land is deduced by tracing ownership back to a disposition of the whole interest in the land at least fifteen years ago. The title deeds will consist of all those deeds and documents necessary to do this, although if the property is a plot which has been sold off from a larger plot, the sale to the purchaser may be the only deed, as the vendor will have kept the deeds with the plot he retains. The purchaser should, however, satisfy himself that a memorandum of the sale off was endorsed on the last conveyance which the vendor retains, as it has been known for a vendor to sell the same plot twice where this was not done[36]. In unregistered title, it is necessary to trace title back through each conveyance of the land, or if an owner has died, through his personal representatives, and if there have been a number of transactions, the process of deducing title can be quite laborious.

Before completion, a search should be made in the Land Charges Register at Plymouth where any charges under the Land Charges Act 1972 (replacing the L.C.A.1925) will be registered. The most important of these charges are restrictive covenants, estate contracts including options to purchase or contracts to sell the land, and mortgages not protected by the deposit of title deeds. There is also a Register of bankruptcy petitions. The official certificate of search will protect a purchaser against any adverse entries on the Register for twenty-one days, during which time he should complete the transaction.

(ii) Registered title

To avoid the laborious task of deducing title by tracing back ownership each time the land was conveyed, a completely new system of title was introduced by the Land Registration Act 1925 (L.R.A.). Under this Act local Land Registries are being set up, and on the first conveyance of the land after the date for compulsory registration is introduced for the area, the title must be registered with the local Land Registry.

Each property is given a title number and the owner (registered proprietor) is issued with a land certificate, which replaces the title deeds. The land certificate contains a copy of the filed plan and entries on the three registers at the Land Registry: 1. the property register, in which the property is described and indicated as freehold or leasehold; 2. the proprietorship register, with the name (or names) of the registered proprietor and the type of title which the Registrar has given (this is usually title absolute (the best title), but a squatter's title for instance would only be possessory); 3. the charges' register with entries of any mortgages, restrictive covenants or other rights affecting the property.

Title is then deduced to a purchaser by producing to him copies of the entries on the register. A transfer of the land in the title number is made on sale, and this automatically transfers the land to a purchaser subject to any entries on the register and any overriding interests. Overriding interests are set out in Section 70(1)(g), L.R.A. and enquiries will have been made of the vendor's solicitors as to these before exchange of contracts. Shortly before completion, a search is made of the register, which gives a purchaser twenty-one days' protection, during which nothing adverse to him will be registered. The transaction is then completed by the vendor's exchanging the transfer and land certificate for the balance of the purchase monies. The purchaser must then apply to register his name as registered proprietor within the twenty-one days' protection afforded to him by the search.

A mortgage in registered land is usually effected by a registered charge. This is a legal charge which is lodged with the Land Registry, and the Registrar will hold the land certificate and issue a charge certificate to the mortgagee instead. The charge will of course have to be discharged before any sale can be completed.

Conveyancing problems arising on building developments and conversions

The difficulty in English law of making the burden of repairing covenants, which are positive in nature, enforceable against subsequent purchasers of the property has already been referred to in the part of this chapter dealing with restrictive covenants. This presents a problem as regards the future maintenance of flats and private estates. The importance of it is that building societies will not advance money on flats unless satisfied that there are adequate arrangements for ensuring that repairs will be carried out to the whole building.

This can be achieved by letting the flats on long leases (often for 99 or 999 years) containing the necessary repairing covenants by the landlord and the tenants. The landlord usually covenants to maintain the common parts of the building and the tenants to maintain their respective flats. As the burden of covenants contained in leases passes to subsequent tenants and landlords, they are enforceable between future parties.

Unless there is a substantial rent, the landlord may not wish to keep the freehold reversion, and so a limited company can be set up in which it is compulsory for all the lessees to hold a share. In law, a limited company has a separate identity to that of its shareholders, so that the company, controlled by the lessee–shareholders, can enforce the covenants against any defaulting lessee and any lessee can enforce the landlord's covenants against the company.

A similar arrangement may be made where a building development is carried out and the purchasers are to remain responsible for the maintenance of private roads and landscaping.

On maisonettes and conversions involving only a few flats, however, it may be adequate for each purchaser to take the freehold and sign a deed of covenant as to repairs, undertaking not to sell to anyone without first obtaining their signature to the deed.

Alternatively, if there are only two maisonettes, it may be possible for each owner to take a long lease and a conveyance of the freehold reversion on the other maisonette. Each can then enforce the covenants in the lease against the other and his successors in title.

5. NEGOTIABLE INSTRUMENTS

In this section of the chapter, we are dealing with a type of property known as a 'chose in action'. Debts, patents and copyrights are also choses in action, as distinct from land and goods, which are tangible forms of property.

A chose in action is a right, enforceable by action, which is of some value. The document which gives entitlement to the right is not itself of any value, but the right is.

Some rights are assignable, that is, can be transferred without complying with the formalities laid down in Section 136 L.P.A. 1925 which applies to most types of choses in action, and they are said to be negotiable. For example, a bank note is transferred by delivery.

The largest class of negotiable instruments is bills of exchange, including cheques and bank notes. The law relating to bills of exchange was developed by merchants, and was largely their customs and usages incorporated into the common law, until it was codified in the Bills of Exchange Act 1882.

The definition of a bill of exchange contained in Section 3(1) of the Act is: 'An unconditional order in writing, addressed by one person to another, signed by the person giving it, requiring the person to whom it is addressed to pay on demand, or at a fixed or determinable future time, a sum certain in money to or to the order of a specified person or to bearer'.

A bill of exchange may be used under the following circumstances:

A, B and C are all traders. A owes money to B, and B agrees to accept payment from him by A transferring to him a debt which C owes to A.

Parties to a bill of exchange

The person who writes out the bill is the drawer, who requests the person to whom it is addressed (the drawee) to pay a fixed sum to the payee. In our example, A is the drawer, C the drawee and B the payee. The drawee to whom the bill is addressed incurs no liability on it until he accepts it, and until such time the drawer himself is liable on it. When the drawee accepts it, however, he becomes the acceptor and is primarily liable. The drawer is then only liable if he defaults. A bill should be presented for acceptance unless it is payable on demand, such as a cheque.

Negotiation of a bill

Usually a bill specifies the payee to whom, or to whose order, it is to be paid. It is then an 'order bill'. For the payee himself to transfer it, he must endorse it. Other bills, known as bearer bills, are transferable by delivery without endorsement, and Section 31 of the Act states 'A bill is negotiated when it is transferred in such a way as to constitute the transferee the holder of the bill'.

A person who endorses a bill and transfers it incurs liability on it as an endorser, that is, he is liable as a surety if the acceptor defaults. A person who gives value for a bill of exchange and takes it without notice of any irregulairty or defect in it is a 'holder in due course' and can sue on it in his own name, provided that he does not claim through a forged endorsement. An irregularity would be a discrepancy on the face of the bill or an apparent material alteration. A forged signature is wholly inoperative (Section 24), although sometimes an estoppel may operate to prevent a person from denying its validity[37].

A cheque is a bill of exchange drawn on a banker and payable on demand (Section 73, Bills of Exchange Act). All cheques are conditional payment, so that a creditor is not bound to accept payment of a debt by cheque. The debt is not paid until the cheque is honoured, and if the cheque is lost in the post, the drawer who posted it is liable for the loss unless the creditor specifically requested it to be posted[38].

A bank will not usually honour a cheque presented for payment over six months after it is drawn, or if it is not dated at all, although a holder of it may insert a date if it is undated.

A cheque may be crossed generally by drawing two transverse lines across the face of it. When so crossed, it may only be paid to a banker and may not be paid in cash by the paying bank on whom it is drawn. It may also be crossed specially, indicating a particular banker to whom it is to be paid.

If crossed 'not negotiable' it is still transferable, but the transferee cannot obtain a better title than the transferor had and is subject to any defects in his title[39]. Where a cheque is crossed 'account payee' or 'account payee only', the words have no statutory significance and do not affect the paying banker, but if the collecting banker credits the cheque to the account of someone other than the payee, he may lose his statutory protection under Section 4, Cheques Act 1957 (against an action for conversion by the true owner of the cheque) on the grounds of negligence.

Material alterations on a cheque must be initialled by the drawer. If they are not, neither he, nor the bank, nor any endorser, will be liable on it.

Section 1, Cheques Act 1957 protects a banker paying unendorsed or irregularly endorsed cheques and certain other instruments. However, outside the vast majority of cases where the apparent payee is paying it into his own account, banks, as a matter of practice, still require endorsement.

A cheque is stopped when the banker on whom it is drawn is instructed not to pay it, although one guaranteed by a cheque card cannot be stopped. If an oral instruction to stop a cheque is given, the bank usually require written confirmation. A cheque is also stopped if a bank receives notice of the customer's death, mental incapacity or bankruptcy, or the winding up of a company, or a court order. If the cheque is for more than the credit of the customer's account, or any overdraft which the bank have agreed he may have, the cheque will usually be returned marked 'refer to drawer'. If a bank wrongfully dishonours a cheque, it is a breach of mandate as regards the customer, who may also be able to claim in defamation.

A promissory note differs from a bill of exchange in that the drawer himself undertakes the obligation on it. It is incomplete until delivered to the payee or bearer.

An IOU is written evidence of a debt. It is not negotiable, but can be assigned by complying with the formalities of Section 136, L.P.A. 1925.

A banker's draft is an order to pay drawn by the bank upon itself and cannot be stopped by a customer of the bank.

6. OUTLINE PROCEDURE FOR DEBT COLLECTION

The courts dealing with the bulk of debt collections are the county courts where proceedings can be brought to recover debts of up to £5,000. For debts of over £5,000 proceedings must be in the High Court. For sums between £3,000 and £5,000 an action may be brought in either, but if less than £3,000 is recovered in the High Court, then costs may only be awarded on the lesser county court scale. The High Court will not usually award any costs on an action for less than £600.

It is probably better to instruct a solicitor for proceedings in the High Court, which are likely to be for a larger sum anyway, but most people who have the time should be able to take at least the initial steps in the county court themselves. The local county court staff will often assist, even though the action is in another court.

The action must be commenced in the county court for the area where the defendant resides or carries on business, or where the contract was made. It is usually better to choose the former as any enforcement proceedings will have to be there.

An action in the county court is commenced by completing a praecipe (form) for a default summons and sending this, together with two copies of the particulars of claim, to the court with the appropriate fee, calculated on a scale according to the amount claimed. The particulars of claim is a statement of the plaintiff's cause of action and usually a copy of an invoice or an estimate will suffice. The court then issues a plaint note with the number of the action, which has to be produced to the court in any future steps.

The summons and particulars of claim should identify the defendant as far as possible. If his (or her) full name is not known, then the initials and sex should be stated. Partners, or a sole trader trading under a name, should be sued individually and the words 'trading as' added.

When issuing the plaint note, the court also issues a summons which, although either the plaintiff or the court bailiff may serve personally, is usually better served by post in the first instance. A limited company should be served at its registered office, and if there is any doubt as to where this is, a search should be made in the Companies' Register.

If the defendant has not put in any defence to the claim after fourteen days, the plaintiff can sign judgment. The defendant may admit the debt and offer to pay by instalments, and if the offer is acceptable to the plaintiff, judgment may be signed on this basis. If not acceptable, then the matter will go before the registrar for disposal. If the defendant puts in a defence which is unrealistic, and the claim is for over £500, the plaintiff may apply to have the defence struck out and for summary judgment. If the claim is to be defended, it will go before the registrar for arbitration if it is for less than £500, and for trial before the judge (after a pre-trial review by the registrar) if for over £500.

Enforcement of judgment

An order for examination of the debtor can be obtained by post, although the court will be unable to issue a committal order on his failure to attend unless he is given travelling expenses to do so. The examination is to ascertain what assets he has and what he can afford to pay.

The most usual means of enforcement against businesses is to levy execution. The county court bailiffs may seize the defendant's goods, including stock, except for clothes, bedding and tools of trade. This does not include any goods which do not belong to the debtor, however – for example, his wife's jewellery or furniture on hire purchase.

If judgment is obtained for at least £15 and the defendant has defaulted on payment, an attachment of earnings order may be obtained whereby an employer deducts a sum from an employee's wages towards payment. This will only be worthwhile against someone in regular employment, and any fines or maintenance take priority. A search of the attachment of earnings index in the defendant's home county court will reveal whether there are any other orders with which the plaintiff's order will have to be shared. Basic living expenses for the debtor and his family will be 'protected earnings' and not available for the attachment order.

If the creditor is aware of money owed to the debtor, he may be able to obtain a garnishee order, which is then served on the person owing the money (the garnishee). It directs him to pay the money into court for the creditor. It is necessary to have the name and address of the garnishee and the amount of the debt owing. A debt will not be owing until an invoice has been delivered and, under a construction contract, an architect's or engineer's certificate has been given.

If the debtor has capital assets, such as land or shares, even jointly owned, then an application can be made for a charging order on these. This places a creditor in a much stronger position in the event of the debtor's bankruptcy, as he is then a secured creditor, the asset upon which the order is made being designated as security for his debt. Searches and enquiries should be made first, however, to ascertain whether there are any prior charges on the property, as it will only then be worthwhile if the asset is sufficient security for all the charges.

Where a debtor is running a business with a large cash turnover, such as a restaurant, it may be worthwhile to appoint a receiver to intercept the profits on behalf of the creditor.

Finally, if at least £750 is owed, the threat of bankruptcy may be sufficient to persuade the debtor to honour his obligation, particularly if he is a professional person or in business. A bankruptcy notice can be issued by the court and, if the debtor fails to comply with this, a bankruptcy petition can be presented. The dividend obtained by proving in a bankruptcy is not likely to be a very high proportion of the debt however, and the threat of bankruptcy is likely to be more effective than the reality. It should be noted however that certain threats or false representations may amount to the criminal act of harassment of debtors under Section 40 of the Administration of Justice Act 1970.

7. PATENTS AND COPYRIGHT

It is possible to protect an invention from being copied by applying for a patent, and this is usually done through a patent agent. An industrial design may be protected similarly by registration under the Registered Designs Act 1949, and works of art and literature are protected from copying under the provisions of the Copyright Act 1956. Patents, designs and copyright are all forms of property belonging to the person who created them, and the law protects them, so that an infringement of them gives the owner a claim for damages, or in some cases an injunction.

Most significant for the construction industry is the definition of 'artistic works' in Section 3(1) of the Copyright Act 1956, which specifically includes 'works of architecture, being either buildings or models for buildings'. A building is defined as 'any structure', but has been held to include the design and layout of a garden[40].

Not only is the building itself within the Act, but so are any architectural plans or designs, as Section 48 gives a wide definition of 'drawing', as 'any diagram, map, chart or plans'.

The copyright in the building and the plans will belong to the architect unless they were designed by him in the course of his employment, in which case they will belong to his employer. Work done by him independently outside his employment will belong to him, however, unless his contract of employment stipulates otherwise.

When an architect is employed to design a particular building, it will depend upon the contract with him as to whether the copyright in the plans and the building belong to him or to the client employing him. It will usually belong to the architect, and should the building be copied or the plans used again, it will be the architect who has a right to sue for damages. The matter of copyright in his plans is not always dealt with in the contract of employment with the architect, however, and the courts have had to decide retrospectively what the intention of the parties was. In *Blair* v *Osborn & Tomkins & Another*[41] an architect prepared plans for two clients for a pair of houses to be built at the bottom of their gardens. The R.I.B.A. Conditions of Engagement (then the 1962 Conditions) were used and it was provided that either side could terminate the employment at any time. Planning permission was obtained and the architect's fee was paid. The plans were then handed to a builder to whom the site was sold, and surveyors instructed by him made slight amendments to the plans and put their names on them. It was held by the Court of Appeal that the surveyors had infringed the architect's copyright in the plans by putting their name to them, but that as the clients had paid a full fee according to the Conditions of Engagement, there was an implied licence that the owner of the copyright would allow the plans to be used for building the houses, and the architect was given only nominal damages. Conversely, in *Stovin-Bradford* v *Volpoint Properties Ltd*[42], an architect agreed to draw up plans for a development company for the purpose of obtaining planning permission for the conversion of a building to a factory. He was to be paid on a time basis for the work and any out of pocket expenses, but the fee was nominal in comparison with the R.I.B.A. scale of fees. The architect withdrew from the project before it was started, but he was awarded damages for infringement of his copyright when part of his design was used in the subsequent construction of the factory, as no licence could be implied from the nominal fee paid to him to use the plans for anything other than obtaining planning permission.

As copyright is a form of property, it may be assigned in writing, signed by the person assigning it. It is possible to assign not only the copyright in existing plans and buildings, but also in future ones, so that a contract between a client and an architect could include such an assignment of future copyright.

Copyright exists for the lifetime of the architect and for fifty years thereafter, but the R.I.B.A.'s 'Memorandum of Agreement' provides that a client may use an architect's plans or drawings to complete a building if the architect dies or becomes incapacitated. Section 9(10) of the Copyright Act also allows the plans to be used to reconstruct a building. Section 9(9) of the Act allows the architect himself to reproduce parts of a building in later works, using the same plans and drawings, but not the whole of it.

The Act provides that it is not an infringement of copyright to take a photograph or make a drawing or painting of a building, or to include it in a film. It is an infringement of copyright in the plans to construct a building from a plan, and of copyright in the building to copy the building. Many buildings, such as semi-detached houses, will of course be similar, and the more unique a building or any particular feature of it is, the easier it will be to show an infringement of the copyright.

It may be possible for an architect to register a design for some particular feature, such as a fireplace, under the Registered Designs Act 1949, and registration will protect it from being copied for fifteen years. A design which is so registered is not excluded from the protection of the Copyright Act 1956.

Remedies for infringement of copyright

As previously mentioned, an owner of copyright may recover damages for its infringement. In the case of *Stovin-Bradford* v *Volpoint Properties Ltd*, the court assessed the damages at £500, being the fee which the architect could have obtained for the licence to use part of his plans.

It may also be possible to obtain an injunction to prevent an infringement of copyright, but by Section 17(4) of the Act, it will not be possible to obtain an injunction to prevent a building in breach of copyright which has been started from being completed, or to obtain an order for its demolition. In the case of *Hunter* v *Fitzroy Robinson*[43] where an injunction was sought to prevent plans drawn up by an architect from being used in the adaptation and reconstruction of an old building beside the river in Cambridge, the judge was not prepared to grant an injunction, bearing in mind the delay which this would cause to the work, and that if the infringement of copyright were proved, the architect would have a good claim for damages. Having decided that he would not grant an injunction, it was not necessary for him to consider whether Section 17(4) applied, but he intimated that he would have found it difficult to decide whether the laying of a floor slab and work on the skeleton of the building would have been within the section or not.

QUESTIONS

1. A building company is the owner of a plot of land with building potential at the rear of its depot. Some years ago, an office block was built with windows overlooking the plot.
   Advise the company;
   (a) as to how it can prevent the owners of the office block from acquiring rights of light to their windows.
   (b) as to the action it might take with regard to a restrictive covenant not to build upon the plot, imposed in an old conveyance of 1867, assuming that the character of the neighbourhood has changed since then.
   (Specimen paper)
2. (½ question) Explain the effect of:
    (i) crossing a cheque
    (ii) marking a cheque 'not negotiable'
   (iii) marking a cheque 'account payee only'
   (Specimen paper)
3. Discuss the nature and creation of easements.
   (1985 paper)
4. (a) Explain the difference between freehold and leasehold land.
   (b) A building developer has purchased a building which is subject to a restrictive covenant, imposed in a conveyance in 1960, that the building shall be used for residential purposes only. The other buildings in the area were formerly residences but are not used for commercial and industrial use.
      Advise the building developer of the action to be taken to allow him to use the building for industrial purposes.
   (1986 paper).

NOTES TO CHAPTER 7

1. *Woollerton & Wilson Ltd* v *Richard Costain Ltd* (1970) 2 All.E.R.483
In the course of building operations, a crane swung over the plaintiff's neighbouring factory from time to time. Held – this was a trespass. In this case, the defendants had offered a sum of damages (£250) to continue the trespass while finishing the building. This was refused by the plaintiffs. An injunction was therefore granted, but the judge exercised his discretion to postpone the injunction for a year to enable the defendants to complete

the building, as there was no other practicable way in which they could have completed it.

2. *H.E. Dibble Ltd v Moore* (1970) 2 Q.B.181
Greenhouses resting by their own weight on concrete were held not to be fixtures.

3. (1902) A.C.157

4. (1866) L.R.3. Eq.382

5. Fixtures added to the property by the tenant for trade, domestic or ornamental purposes.

6. *Lace v Chantler* (1944) K.B.368
A lease made for the duration of the war was held to be void as it was not for a fixed and definite period.

7. Occupational tenants are protected both as to tenure and rent by the Rent Acts and there is legislation affording similar protection to business tenants and agricultural tenants.

8. (1852) 1 Macq.305

9. (1956) Ch.131

10. (1863) 2 H & C 121
The lessee of the bank of a canal claimed the right to hire out pleasure boats as an easement and sought to prevent someone else from doing so. Held – such a right benefited the lessee's business interests and not the land itself, and so could not exist as an easement.

11. *Wong v Beaumont Property Trust Ltd* (1965) 1 Q.B.173

12. *Webb v Bird* (1862) 13 C.B.(NS) 841

13. *Wright v Macadam* (1949) 2 K.B.744

14. *Crow v Wood* (1971) 1 Q.B.77

15. *Phipps v Pears* (1965) 1 Q.B.76

16. This opinion was expressed in *Sedgwick Forbes Bland Payne Group Ltd v Regional Properties Ltd* (1978) 257 E.G.70. Under Section 29(5) of the Public Health Act 1961, a local authority can require anyone who demolishes a building to weatherproof any exposed surfaces of adjacent buildings.

17. *Wong v Beaumont Property Trust Ltd* (Note 11 above) is an example of this. A landlord let basement premises for use as a restaurant, but the Health Inspector refused to allow the use without a ventilation shaft. Held – the landlord was deemed to have intended to grant an easement for this, as otherwise the lease could not take effect.

18. (1878) 12 Ch.D.31

19. This is the date to which legal memory is deemed to go back.

20. For example, it would be impossible to claim a right of light to a window in a building erected after then.

21. *Moore* v *Rawson* (1824) 3 B & C 332
The plaintiff demolished a wall with windows with rights of light and built a stable with no windows. Fourteen years later, the defendant built on his adjacent land so that the rights of light would have been infringed had the windows still been there. Three years later, the plaintiff inserted a window in the stable wall where the previous windows had been and claimed a right of light to it. Held – his right of light no longer existed as he had shown an intention to abandon it.

22. (1967) 2 Q.B.379
The plaintiff, relying on the defendant's agreement to allow him access over the rear of the defendant's land, built a garage at the rear of his land which could only be reached across the defendant's land. Held – the defendant's successor in title was estopped from denying the right of access.

23. (1976) Ch.179
The plaintiffs were executors to the deceased, who had sold a plot of land fronting on to a main road by which he gained access to his factory at the rear, on the understanding that Arun District Council would give him access over a road built by them. Held – this was enforceable against the Council as he had acted to his detriment in reliance upon their agreement.

24. As in *Federated Homes Ltd* v *Mill Lodge Properties Ltd* (1980) 1 W.L.R.594.

25. (1848) 2 Ph.774

26. Although this may be circumvented as regards the maintenance of a fence by imposing an easement – see *Crow* v *Wood*, Note 14 above.

27. The Land Charges Act 1925 (L.C.A.) which came into force on 1st January 1926 provides that registration of certain equitable and other interests, including restrictive covenants, shall constitute notice of them. It applies to covenants created after 1st January 1926.

28. See Note 24 above for reference.
In 1971 planning permission had been granted for a certain number of houses on three plots of land (the 'red, green and blue' land). The plaintiff's predecessors in title had sold off the blue land, taking a covenant from the purchasers not to build to more than a stated density so as not the prejudice the planning permission for the number of houses to be erected on the red and green land retained. The plaintiffs, now owners of the red and green land, sought to restrain the defendants, owners of the blue land, from committing a breach of the covenant and so prejudicing their planning permission. The benefit of the covenant for the green land had passed to the plaintiffs by express assignment on each sale, but there was no such chain of assignments as regards the red land. Nor was the wording of the covenant sufficient to annex the benefit to the red land. Held – Section 78 L.P.A. would operate to do so, and the plaintiffs had the benefit of the covenant.

29. *Roake* v *Chadha* (1984) 1 W.L.R.40
A restrictive covenant in 1934 restricted building on land but was not to endure for the benefit of any future owner unless expressly assigned. There had not been a chain of express assignments of the benefit. Held – the benefit did not pass by annexation under Section 78 as this was expressly excluded.

30. Per Megarry J. in *Brunner* v *Greenslade* (1970) 3 All.E.R.833, 839.

31. (1908) 2 Ch.374

32. (1970) 2 All.E.R.664

33. (1965) Ch.816

34. *Baxter* v *Four Oaks Properties Ltd* where each purchaser signed a separate deed of covenant.

35. *Sutcliffe* v *Thackrah* (1974) A.C.727

36. *Re Seaview Gardens* (1967) 1 W.L.R.134
A company which owned land sold two plots to H in 1934. The title was not registered and no memorandum of the sale to H was endorsed on the conveyance to the company, as it should have been. In 1936 H sold one of the plots to the plaintiff. In 1964, the company sold the same plot again to the defendant, and compulsory registration of title having then been introduced for the area, the defendant registered himself as registered proprietor of the plot and started building on it. The plaintiff brought an action for rectification of the Register, but the court exercised its discretion to refuse this as the plaintiff had delayed bringing his action after he had learned of the defendant's building operations.

37. *Brown* v *Westminster Bank Limited* (1964) 2 Lloyd's Rep. 187
329 forged cheques payable to one A.C. were drawn on the plaintiff's account. The bank manager drew the plaintiff's attention to this, but the plaintiff satisfied him that the cheques were genuine. A new bank manager who was appointed drew the plaintiff's son's attention to the cheques and asked repeated questions about them. Held – the plaintiff was estopped from pleading the forgeries as the bank had acted to its detriment on the plaintiff's assurances to the manager.

38. *Pennington* v *Crossley & Sons (Limited)* (1897) 13 T.L.R.513
A cheque lost in the post will not be payment of a debt owed unless the sender was specifically requested to send it in the post. By a course of dealing for twenty years, carpet manufacturers had paid for wool by cheque which they posted. Held – a cheque lost in the post was not payment and they still owed the debt.

39. *Wilson & Meeson* v *Pickering* (1946) K.B.422
A partner in a firm signed a blank cheque which was crossed 'not negotiable' and handed it to a clerk to complete. The clerk filled in the defendant's name and a sum which she owed to the defendant and gave it to her. Held – the defendant had no better title to the cheque than the clerk from whom she took it, and the plaintiff could recover the sum paid on it.

40. *Vincent* v *Universal Housing & Co. Ltd* M.C.C.1930–31, 275
Copyright was recognised as existing in a garden designed with a lily pond,
steps, walls, flower beds and shrubberies.

41. (1971) 2 W.L.R.503

42. (1971) 3 W.L.R.257

43. (1977) 10 B.L.R.88

8. Highways

1. THE DEFINITION AND ORIGINS OF A HIGHWAY

There is no definition of a highway in the Highways Act 1980. The existence of a highway is established by reference to the common law, which requires evidence of dedication as a highway and acceptance of it by the public.

Dedication must be to the public generally and in perpetuity, although a restriction as to the type of traffic to use a way will not prevent it from being a highway. Dedication may be expressed in a formal document, or implied from user as of right by the public. There is no fixed period of user from which dedication will be presumed at common law and this will vary with the circumstances[1], but by Section 31 of the Highways Act 1980 dedication as a highway is presumed after twenty years' user unless there is evidence of a contrary intention. User as of right has much the same meaning as in the acquisition of easements by prescription and means open user, without secrecy or opposition, and not dependent upon permission.

Under Section 24 of the Highways Act, the Minister of Transport and local highway authorities are authorised to construct new highways, and Section 328 states that 'highway' means the whole or part of a highway, including a bridge or tunnel over, or through which, a highway passes. The Minister of Transport is responsible for the construction and maintenance of motorways and trunk roads, while county councils, whose duties are usually delegated to local authorities, are responsible for highways in their areas.

A carriageway is defined in Section 329 of the Act as a highway (other than a cycle track) for the passage of vehicles, and a footpath is a 'highway over which the public have a right of way on foot only, not being a footway'. A pavement along a highway is within the definition of a 'footway', which is 'a way comprised in a highway which also comprises a carriageway, being a way over which the public have a right of way on foot only'. A 'street' is defined by Section 329 to include 'any highway and any road, lane, footpath, square, court, alley or passage, whether a thoroughfare or not'. In *Robinson* v *Barton-Eccles Local Board*[2] Lord Selborne L.C. indicated that the statutory definition (then contained in the Highways Act 1959 but identical) was not comprehensive and should not be taken to change the ordinarily accepted meaning of a street as a road with houses along it.

2. THE MAINTENANCE OF HIGHWAYS AND STREETS

Highways maintainable at public expense are those which were in existence in 1835[3], trunk roads, and roads constructed or adopted by highway authorities[4]. Lists of streets maintainable at public expense are kept with local authorities and are open to inspection by the public.

Adoption of highways and streets

Under Section 37 of the Highways Act, a person may serve a notice on the local authority of his intention to dedicate a way as a highway. Unless the local authority considers that it will not be used sufficiently by the public to justify its maintenance at public expense (in which case they may seek an order of the magistrates' court to that effect) it will then certify that the way has been made up properly and has been dedicated. It becomes maintainable at public expense a year later provided it has been used as a highway during that time. Appeal lies to the magistrates' court against a local authority's refusal to issue a certificate.

Under Section 38 of the Act, a local authority may make an agreement with a person who intends to dedicate or construct a highway to maintain it at public expense. Section 38(6) provides that the agreement may include such provisions as to construction, payments and 'other relevant matters as the authority making the agreement think fit'. It is normal conveyancing practice for a developer to enter into an agreement with the local authority for the adoption of roads which he will construct, such an agreement being supported by a bond, before starting on the development, and a copy of the agreement and the bond is sent to solicitors acting for prospective purchasers along with the other conveyancing documents.

Adoption of private streets

A private street is one which is not a highway and over which the public has therefore no right of passage, or a highway not maintainable by a highway authority, but which has sufficient houses along it to bring it within the definition of a street. A local authority may, from time to time, resolve to carry out street works for sewering, levelling, paving, metalling, flagging, channelling, making good and lighting private streets (Section 205), and where they do so, the private street works code and advance payments code apply.

Private street works code

Where the local authority have passed a resolution (a 'domestic' resolution) to carry out street works in a private street, the proper officer of the authority (usually the surveyor) must prepare a specification of the works, with plans and sections, and an estimate and provisional apportionment of the cost between frontagers on to the street, showing how the apportionment is made and the reputed owner of the property by whom it is payable.

These are submitted to the local authority, which must then pass a second resolution (a 'resolution of approval'). The resolution and approved documents must be kept available for public inspection at the local authority's offices for one month, and publicised by an advertisement in a local newspaper and a notice in the street, in accordance with Section 205, informing the public where the resolution and the documents can be inspected. A notice to this effect must also be served on the owners of frontages on to the street who are liable to contribute to the cost of the street works, and the notice should inform each owner of the apportioned amount due from him.

The apportionment is basically according to the length of frontage on to the street, but allowances may be made for the benefit to be derived from the street works by any particular premises and work already done by any owners. Owners of premises which have no frontage on to the street at all but which nevertheless benefit from the works because they have 'access to it through a court, passage, or otherwise' may also be required to contribute. This does not include an owner whose premises front on to part of a street not to be made up but who has access to a part which is to be made up[5]. Property will be regarded as having a frontage on to a street even though a strip of land belonging to a developer[6] or a public footway[7] lies between the property and the street. Flats and maisonettes, where the property between the building and the street belongs to someone else, will not be regarded as fronting the street, however[8].

An owner served with a notice of apportionment may object within one month on grounds set out in Section 208. The grounds are: some defect in the procedure, that the street is not a private street, that the proposed works are insufficient or unreasonable, that the cost is excessive or that for a reason stated the apportionment is wrong. Thus in *Southgate Borough Council* v *Park Estates Ltd*[9] an objection was upheld as unreasonable where it was shown that a street which the local authority had resolved to make up would have to be re-opened subsequently for the installation of services. In *Bognor Regis Urban District Council* v *Boldero*[10], the plans approved by the local authority's second resolution were held to be 'insufficient' to carry out the works proposed by their first domestic resolution as the second resolution only concerned the making up of the road and not the sewering, which was included in the first resolution.

An objection is heard by the magistrates' court, which has power to quash or amend the resolution or its supporting documents in whole or in part, and has a wide discretion as to the costs of the objection.

Section 210 allows the local authority to amend the specification and apportionments, but due notice and publication must be given of any increase in cost. Under Section 236, a local authority may resolve to bear the whole or part of the cost of any street works, and an owner's expenses may be discharged or reduced accordingly.

When the street works have been completed, the proper officer makes a final apportionment, to which the owner upon whom it is served has one month to object. An objection may be on procedural grounds, or because the works vary unreasonably from the specifications and plans, or exceed the estimated cost by more than 15 per cent. The objection procedure is the same as for the original apportionment notice. When the final notice has been served, the apportioned costs, together with interest from the date of the final apportionment, are then recoverable from the owner. They become a charge on the property, which passes with it to any new owner, provided it is registered in the register of local land charges kept by the local authority. Registration operates as notice to any transferee of the land, who is therefore bound by it.

Once the street works have been completed, the street may then be adopted under the procedure set out in Section 228. The local authority must display a notice declaring the street to be a highway maintainable at public expense, and provided the majority of owners do not object, it is adopted as such one month later.

Objections are again heard by the magistrates' court.

Advance payments code

Where the advance payments code applies[11] the local authority may require payment for street works which could be executed under the private street works code. They may do this in advance, before work commences on any new building requiring approval under the Building Regulations, which has a frontage on to the street (Section 219(1)). The payment which may be required is the amount which would be recoverable if the street works were carried out. Alternatively, security such as a charge over the land, or a bond, may be accepted in lieu of payment.

It is an offence punishable with a fine to carry on work on a building in contravention of Section 219(1), but a person other than the owner who undertook the building work, reasonably believing that payment had been made or secured, has a defence (Section 219(3)).

The code is not applicable in eleven instances set out in Section 219(4) however[12], the most notable being where an agreement has been made under Section 38 with a person who undertakes to construct a street at his expense and subsequently to dedicate it as a highway.

Where payment has been made or security provided under the advance payments code by at least one frontager, then a majority of frontagers (numerically as persons or according to lengths of frontage) may serve a notice under Section 229 requiring the local authority to carry out street works under the private street works code and declare the street to be a highway maintainable at public expense.

Under Section 230, a local authority may serve a notice requiring frontagers to a private street to carry out repairs necessary to obviate a danger to traffic. If the danger exists in only part of the street, then the owners fronting that part alone may be served. Appeal lies to the magistrates' court. If the owners fail to carry out the work in the time specified, the local authority may carry out the work itself and recover the cost from the owners proportionately according to their frontages.

In these circumstances, it may be an advantage to the owners to follow the procedure set out in Section 230(5), whereby a majority of them (numerically as persons or according to rateable value) may serve a notice on the local authority requiring them to carry out the work under the private street works code, as the street may then be adopted under Section 22 and become a highway maintainable at the public expense on completion of the work.

3. IMPROVEMENT LINES AND BUILDING LINES

Improvement lines

A highway authority may be of the opinion that a street will need to be widened to take an increased volume of traffic at some future time. If the street is one which is maintainable at public expense, it may prescribe an improvement line for both sides, or one side, of the street. The effect of this is to prohibit any building or permanent excavation nearer to the centre line of the street than the improvement line unless the authority consents to this, although Section 73(3) expressly exempts statutory undertakers from this.

The authority's consent to a building which infringes the improvement line may be given, and if so, may be subject to conditions. Any such conditions, and the improvement line itself, bind any subsequent owners of the land affected provided they are registered as local land charges in the local land charges register kept by the local authority. It is an offence punishable with a fine to contravene the improvement line or any conditions attaching to consent which may have been given to a building which would infringe it.

Appeal against the imposition of an improvement line or against refusal of consent to build lies to the Crown Court, and any person whose property is injuriously affected by it may claim compensation from the authority, although compensation is not payable for any building erected after the date of deposit of the plan showing the improvement line, other than a building started before the date of deposit, or a building erected in pursuance of a contract to build made before that date. In *Westminster Bank* v *Beverley Borough Council*[13], the House of Lords upheld a decision of the Court of Appeal that it was not unlawful for a local authority to refuse planning permission, because they intended to widen a street, rather than prescribing an improvement line, although the effect of this was to deprive the applicant of the right to claim compensation for the improvement line.

'Building' is defined by Section 73(13) to include 'any erection however, and with whatever material it is constructed, and any part of the building, and "new building" includes any addition to an existing building'.

Building lines

An improvement line is prescribed where it is envisaged that a street will one day be widened, but no such possibility is necessary for a highway authority to prescribe a building frontage line under Section 74. They may do so for one or both sides of a highway maintainable at public expense. The effect is that no new building (defined as in section 73(13) for improvement lines) may be erected, or permanent excavation made, nearer to the centre of the highway than the building line, other than a boundary wall or fence, without the authority's consent. Such consent may be subject to conditions, and the building line and any conditions attaching to consent to infringe it are binding on subsequent owners of the land affected if registered as local land charges in the register of local land charges kept by the local authority. It is an offence punishable with a fine to infringe the building line or any conditions attaching to consent.

There is no right of appeal against the prescribing of a building line, but a person injuriously affected by it may claim compensation from the authority within six months of receiving notice of it. No compensation is payable for buildings erected after the date notice of the building line was received except for buildings finished after that date or built in pursuance of a contract to build made before that date.

Statutory undertakers are exempt from the section.

The procedure for imposing improvement and building lines

The procedure for imposing improvement and building lines is laid down in Schedule 9 to the Act. If a Minister or County Council impose a line, they must first consult the local authority. A plan, signed by the proper officer of the authority, must be deposited at the local authority's offices for one month, and notice of this given to owners, lessees or occupiers of land affected, together with notice of their rights of appeal or objection. Any objections within six weeks must be considered by the local authority, and then they prescribe the line by resolution. Within a further six weeks, they must then prepare a sealed and authenticated plan showing the position of the line, and give notice to all owners, lessees or occupiers of land affected as to where this may be inspected.

If an improvement or building line is revoked, which must also be done by resolution, notice must similarly be given to all persons affected.

4. OBSTRUCTION OF HIGHWAYS AND BUILDING OPERATIONS

Section 130 of the Highways Act imposes on highway authorities a duty to protect the rights of the public to use highways and 'roadside waste', being land along the edge of a highway and between the highway and boundary fences. There is a presumption (rebuttable by evidence) that the public have a right to use roadside waste.

A local authority has a power to assert the rights of the public to use any highway within its area for which it is not the highway authority, and thus to prevent the obstruction of any such highway or roadside waste and reinstatement of it[14], claiming the expenses of this from the person responsible.

Section 131 makes it an offence punishable with a fine for a person without lawful authority or excuse to damage the surface of a highway by excavating, removing soil or turf, depositing anything on the highway or lighting a fire within fifty feet of its centre. Lawful authority justifying damage would be the exercise of statutory powers by statutory undertakers. Lawful excuse is clearly wider than lawful authority, but would not include ignorance of the statutory offence.

Under Section 133, a highway authority may repair any damage to the footway of a street maintainable at public expense caused by work done on adjoining land, and the cost of such repair is recoverable from the owner of the adjoining land or the person causing the damage.

Section 137 makes it an offence punishable with a fine to wilfully obstruct free passage along a highway without lawful authority or excuse. Lord Russell said[15] that 'wilfully' means that 'the act is done deliberately and intentionally, not by accident or inadvertence'.

In *Dunn* v *Holt*[16] it was said that what amounts to obstruction of free passage is a matter of degree and must depend upon the particular circumstances of each case. In *C. Gabriel* v *Enfield London Borough Coundil*[17], a skip deposited on the highway was held to constitute an obstruction.

Section 139 makes provision, however, for a builder's skip to be deposited on a highway where the permission of the highway authority has been obtained. Permission may be granted unconditionally or conditionally, and in particular, conditions may be imposed relating to the size and siting of the skip, its visibility to traffic, the lighting and guarding of it, the care of its contents and its ultimate removal. In any event, the skip must be marked with the owner's name and telephone number or address, lighted at night and removed as soon as practicable after it is filled. It is an offence punishable with a fine not to comply with these conditions and any others imposed by the highway authority, but under section 139(6), a person who shows that he himself took all due care and that the commission of the offence was due to the act or default of another person has a defence[18]. The section specifically provides that permission to deposit a skip under the section shall not authorise the commission of a nuisance or danger on the highway.

Section 140 provides that a highway authority, or a constable in uniform, may require a skip to be removed or repositioned, or may themselves remove or reposition a skip, recovering the expenses of doing so from the owner. The owner of a skip includes the person in possession of it under a hire purchase agreement, or a person who hires it for more than a month (Section 139(11)).

Where building operations are carried out in or near a street, the owner of the land on which work is being done is guilty of an offence punishable with a fine under Section 168 if an accident occurs which could give rise to serious injury to a person in the street. It is a defence, however, to show that he took all possible precautions to avoid risk to persons in the street, or that the offence was caused by the act or default of another person, such as a building contractor carrying out the operations or presumably even a mischievous third person who removed a safety barrier. Such other person is then guilty of an offence under the section. Building operations are widely defined in Section 168(5) to mean 'the construction, structural alteration, repair or maintenance of a building (including re-pointing, external redecoration and external cleaning), the demolition of a building, the preparation for, and laying the foundations of, an intended building and the erection or dismantling of cranes or scaffolding'.

Where it is intended to erect any scaffolding or structure, for the purposes of building or demolition work, which obstructs a highway, Section 169 provides that a licence in writing must first be obtained from the highway authority. The authority are under a duty to issue a licence on application, however, unless they consider that the structure would cause unreasonable obstruction of the highway, or that an alternative structure suitable for the work would cause less obstruction to the highway. The licence may be subject to conditions. Appeal lies to a magistrates' court against refusal to issue a licence or any conditions attached to it. The licensee must in any event ensure that the structure is adequately lit at night and must comply with any directions as to traffic signs required by the authority. He must also comply with any reasonable requests from statutory undertakers to ensure access to and protection of their apparatus. It is an offence punishable with a fine to erect a structure without a licence, or to fail to comply with any of the terms of a licence.

Under Section 170, it is an offence punishable with a fine to mix or deposit on a highway cement or mortar 'or any other substance which is likely to stick to the surface of the highway . . . or likely to solidify in the drains or sewers' unless it is mixed or deposited on a plate or receptacle which prevents contact with the drains or highway.

Section 171 allows a person to temporarily deposit rubbish or building materials in a street, or to make a temporary excavation, with the consent of the highway authority. Consent may be given subject to such conditions as the highway authority thinks fit, such as a condition to ensure access to and the safety of the property of statutory undertakers, and appeal lies to a magistrates' court against refusal of consent or conditions imposed. Any obstruction or excavation must be properly fenced and lit at night, and any written directions of the highway authority as to traffic signs must be complied with. The highway authority (or the local authority if the street is not a highway) may require the obstruction to be removed or the excavation to be filled, and the person causing it must not allow it to remain any longer than is necessary. It is an offence punishable with a fine to contravene the section, and the highway authority (or local authority) may itself remove the obstruction or fill in the excavation and recover the expenses of doing so from the person responsible for it.

Section 172 requires a person who proposes to erect, demolish, repair or alter a building in a street or court to first erect a close boarded hoarding to the satisfaction of the local authority, unless the local authority dispenses with the requirement. If the local authority so require, he must provide a covered platform and handrail for pedestrians outside the hoarding, which should be maintained and lit at night. Appeal against the requirement of a hoarding, or conditions attaching to consent to it, lies to a magistrates' court. Contravention of the section is an offence punishable with a fine, and constitutes a fresh offence for every day the unlicensed hoarding remains in position.

Section 173 requires any hoardings to be securely fixed to the satisfaction of the local authority.

QUESTIONS

1. See first question under Chapter 6.
2. Outline the statutory provisions a contractor needs to observe when carrying out operations to a building which is adjacent to a highway.
   (1985 paper).
3. (a) Explain the legal provisions available to a building contractor to secure the temporary closure of a highway whilst building operations are carried out.
   (b) Describe the legal powers available to a highway authority to secure that a developer will complete the construction of new streets to a residential development.
   (1986 paper)

NOTES TO CHAPTER 8

1. *Woodyer* v *Haddon* (1813) 5 Taunt. 125

2. (1883) 8 App.Cas.798

3. Before 1835, the inhabitants of a parish were bound to maintain any highway within the parish. The Highways Act 1835 changed this as regards highways subsequently created, by providing that they should not automatically be maintained by the parishioners, but only if adopted.

4. Section 36, Highways Act 1980.

5. *Chatterton* v *Glanford Rural Council* (1915) 3 K.B.707

6. *Warwickshire County Council* v *Adkins* (1967)

7. *Ware Urban District Council* v *Gaunt* (1960)

8. *Buckinghamshire County Council* v *Trigg* (1963) 1 W.L.R.155

9. (1954) 1 All.E.R.520

10. (1962) 2 Q.B.448

11. Section 204(2) provides that the advance payments code applies:
'(a) in all outer London boroughs;
(b) in all areas in counties in which the advance payments code in the Highways Act 1959 (which is replaced by the advance payments code in this Act) was in force immediately before 1st April 1974; and
(c) in any parish or community in which the advance payments code in the Highways Act 1959 was, after 1st April 1974, adopted in accordance with Schedule 15 to this Act'.

12. Section 219(4) provides that the Section shall not apply:
'(a) where the owner of the land on which the building is to be erected will be exempt, by virtue of a provision in the private street works code, from

liability to expenses incurred in respect of street works in the private street in question;

(b) where the building proposed to be erected will be situated in the curtilage of, and be appurtenant to, an existing building;

(c) where the building is proposed to be erected in a parish or community and plans for the building were deposited with the district council or, according to the date of deposit, the rural distirct council before the date on which the New Streets Act 1951, or the advance payments code (either in this Act or in the Highways Act 1959) was applied in the parish or community or, as the case may require, in the part of the parish or community in which the building is to be erected;

(d) where an agreement has been made by any person with the street works authority under Section 38 above providing for the carrying out at the expense of that person of street works in the whole of the street or a part of the street comprising the whole of the part on which the frontage of the building will be, and for securing that the street or the part thereof, on completion of the works, will become a highway maintainable at the public expense;

(e) where the street works authority, being satisfied that the whole of the street or such part thereof as aforesaid is not, and is not likely within a reasonable time to be, substantially built-up or in so unsatisfactory a condition as to justify the use of powers under the private street works code for securing the carrying out of street works in the street or part thereof, by notice exempt the building from this section;

(f) where the street works authority, being satisfied that the street is not, and is not likely within a reasonable time to become, joined to a highway maintainable at the public expense, by notice exempt the building from this section;

(g) where the whole street, being less than 100 yards in length, or a part of the street not less than 100 yards in length and comprising the whole of the part on which the frontage of the building will be, was on the material date built-up to such an extent that the aggregate length of the frontages of the buildings on both sides of the street or part consituted at least one half of the aggregate length of all the frontages on both sides of the street or part;

(h) where (in a case not falling within paragraph (g) above) the street works authority, being satisfied that the whole of the street was on the material date substantially built-up, by notice exempt the building from this section:

(i) where the building is proposed to be erected on land belonging to, or in the possession of

(i) the British Railways Board, the London Transport Executive, the National Freight Corporation (as far as included in this paragraph by paragraph 15(a) of Schedule 23 to this Act) or any wholly-owned subsidiary (within the meaning of the Transport Act 1968) or joint subsidiary (within the meaning of section 51(5) of that Act) of any of those bodies;

(ii) the council of a county, district or London borough, the Greater London Council or the Common Council;

(iii) the Commission for the New Towns or a new town development corporation;

(j) where the building is to be erected by a company the objects of which include the provision of industrial premises for use by persons other than the company, being a company the constitution of which prohibits the distribution of the profits of the company to its members, and the cost of the building is to be defrayed wholly or mainly by a government department;

(k) where the street works authority, being satisfied –

(i) that more than three quarters of the aggregate length of all the frontages on both sides of the street, or a part of the street not less than 100 yards in length and comprising the whole of the part on which the frontage of the building will be, consists, or is at some future time likely to consist, of the frontages of industrial premises, and

(ii) that their powers under the private street works code are not likely to be exercised in relation to the street, or to that part of it, as the case may be, within a reasonable time'.

13. (1971) A.C.503

14. *Louth District Council* v *West* (1896) 65 L.J.Q.B.535
The defendant cut a straight ditch in the roadside waste between his land and the highway, and filled in an irregular ditch. The local authority filled in the ditch cut by the defendant and reinstated the original ditch. Held – they were able to recover the expenses of this from the defendant.

15. In *R* v *Senior* (1899) 1 Q.B.290

16. (1904) 74 L.J.K.B.341
Obstruction is a matter of degree in every case. A truck 2 feet 8 inches wide placed opposite a house in a carriageway 30 feet wide for several hours, to remove dust from the house, was held not to be wilful obstruction within Section 54(6) Metropolitan Police Act 1839. Although it might well be inconvenient, there was no evidence that anyone was prevented from passing along the street.

17. (1971) L.G.R.382
The appellants let out skips. Their driver deposited a skip on a highway without having obtained authority under the Highways Act. The hirer signed a form acknowledging that the appellant's driver was 'agent of the customer' for the deposit of the skip. Held – the appellants were liable. They could not avoid liability by the conditions on the form signed by the customer. The criminal act of depositing the skip was that of the appellants' driver.

A contrary decision to this however was the case of *Derrick* v *Cornhill* (1970) Crim. L.R.467. The defendant there hired a hopper on terms that he would obtain the necessary permit and see to its lighting. Held that he was liable even though he was not present when the hopper was delivered and was not responsible for its siting.

18. *Lambeth London Borough Council* v *Saunders* (1974) R.T.R.3190
The owners of a skip hired it out on conditions set out on the back of a printed form. The face of the form stated that the hirer was responsible for lighting the skip according to permits issued by the local authority, but

the hirer did not light it. The owners were prosecuted. Held – defence under Section 32(4)(6) of the Highways Act 1971, that the commission of the offence was due to the act or default of another person, and that he should have taken all reasonable precautions, applied, and owners were not guilty.

9. Definition and Terms of a Contract for the Sale of Goods

1. DEFINITION

Contracts for the sale of goods are goverened by the Sale of Goods Act 1979 which re-enacts an earlier Act of 1893 as amended by subsequent legislation.[1]

The purpose of the original Act was to incorporate various terms, for example as to the quality of goods, their delivery and risk, into a contract where the parties themselves had failed to deal expressly with such matters, but the Act did not apply where the contract terms as agreed between the parties covered these matters. This is largely true of the 1979 Act, but certain legislation, such as the Misrepresenttion Act 1967 and the Unfair Contract Terms Act 1977, limit the freedom of contracting parties as to the inclusion of certain terms such as exemption clauses in a contract for the sale of goods.

The Act only applies to a contract for the sale of goods, defined by Section 2(1) as 'a contract by which the seller transfers or agrees to transfer the property in goods to the buyer for a money consideration, called the price'. Although the definition distinguishes between a sale (where the property in the goods passes under the contract to the buyer) and an agreement for sale (where the property is to be transferred in the future), both are within the definition and are therefore governed by the Act.

'Goods' are defined by Section 61 of the Act as 'all personal chattels other than things in action[2] and money'. A coin sold for its intrinsic value was nevertheless held to be within the definition of 'goods'[3]. Crops and 'things attached to or forming part of the land which are agreed to be severed before sale or under the contract of sale' are expressly included within the definition of goods.

Difficulties may sometimes arise in distinguishing a contract for the sale of goods from other types of contract, and in particular the courts have distinguished the following contracts:

(a) Contracts for the sale of materials forming part of the land itself (other than crops) such as sand or gravel from a pit

Such a contract is not a contract for the sale of goods unless the material has already been severed from the land. Thus in the case of *Morgan* v *Russell*[4] a contract for the sale of cinder and slag lying on the land, but not in identifiable heaps, was held not to be a contract for the sale of goods.

(b) Contracts of exchange

Because the definition requires a 'money consideration', a contract of exchange is not within it. A contract for part-exchange and part money consideration (commonly used in the motor trade) will still be a contract for the sale of goods, however[5].

(c) Contracts for materials and labour

A contract involving the use of skill and labour in the production of an article will not be a contract for the sale of goods if the skill and labour involved are the real substance of the contract and the materials supplied are incidental to it. Thus in *Young & Marten* v *McManus Childs*[6] a sub-contract where the sub-contractor undertook to tile a roof was not a contract for the sale of goods even though the terms of the contract required him to supply the tiles. On the other hand, a contract to make and supply a ship's propellors was a contract for the sale of goods[7]. The distinction is not always easy to make but it may nevertheless be important as liability for defective goods may attach irrespective of any negligence, whereas liability under a contract for labour may depend upon proof of negligence.

(d) Contracts of credit sale, conditional sale and hire purchase

A credit sale is a contract under which payment for goods is to be made by instalments and is within the definition of a contract for the sale of goods. Property usually passes to the purchaser as soon as the contract is made. A conditional sale is a contract under which property in the goods remains with the seller and only passes to the purchaser when the condition (usually payment of the price by instalments) has been fulfilled. A hire purchase contract is a contract to hire goods with an option to purchase them on completion of payment of the hire instalments. The distinction between a hire purchase agreement and a conditional sale is artifical as it is always contemplated that the hirer will eventually become the purchaser of the goods, and the law relating to conditional sales has been largely assimilated to that relating to hire purchase agreements, for example, as to the capacity of a hirer or purchaser under a conditional sale agreement to pass a good title to the goods under Section 9 of the Factors Act 1889 or Section 25, Sale of Goods Act. All three types of contract fall within some of the provisions of the Consumer Credit Act 1974, and in both forms of contract the 'purchaser' will not be able to pass a good title to a third person until the specified instalments have been paid.

(e) Contracts of agency

Where an agent sells or buys for a principal, the contract is made with the principal and not with the agent. It may not always be clear, however, whether a person is acting as an agent for the sale or purchase, or whether he is himself a 'middle man' who is buying and re-selling. A person who receives goods under a 'sale or return' agreement may be only an agent, but will be a purchaser if he himself has an option to purchase the goods. The distinction may become important if it is necessary to decide whether property has passed to him or not, or whether payment to him will discharge the ultimate purchaser's obligations.

2. TERMS OF A CONTRACT

A breach of an express or implied term of a contract will give rise to a claim for damages, but will only give the injured party the right to repudiate the contract if it is a condition. A condition is such a vital part of the contract that it can be said to 'go to the root of the contract'. In most commercial contracts, a delivery date is presumed to be 'of the essence' and a condition of the contract, unless the buyer waives this or unless the contract provides otherwise.

A breach of a term which results in a substantial performance of the contract, although not exactly as stipulated, is a breach of a warranty and will not give rise to a right to repudiate, although the injured party will be able to claim damages. An example of this would be where the goods are not exactly as contracted for but are near enough to the contract description to be marketable[8].

In deciding whether or not a particular term 'goes to the root of the contract' the courts are seeking to apply a subjective test, namely, do the parties themselves regard this term as being so fundamental that a breach of it effectively renders the contract worthless? Certain terms (such as the delivery date) are presumed to be fundamentally important, but it is open to the parties to stipulate in the contract that any particular term is to be regarded as fundamentally important so that its breach will give rise to a right to repudiate, when it effectively becomes a condition of the contract.

Terms implied in a contract for the sale of goods

Sections 12–15 of the Sale of Goods Act incorporate certain conditions and warranties into a contract for the sale of goods. It will be apparent from above that the implied terms under Sections 12–15 of the Sale of Goods Act 1979 apply only if they are not negatived or varied by any express terms so far as the parties are free to negative or vary them[9]. It should be noted that although most of the cases are prior to the 1979 Act, they were decided on essentially similar sections in the 1893 Act to those which the new sections replace, and are therefore likely to be still applicable.

Section 12. Implied terms as to title

S.12(1) 'In a contract of sale . . . there is an implied condition on the part of the seller that in the case of a sale he has a right to sell the goods, and in the case of an agreement to sell he will have such a right at the time when the property is to pass.

(2) In a contract of sale . . . there is also an implied warranty that

(a) the goods are free, and will remain free until the time when the property is to pass, from any charge or encumbrance not disclosed or known to the buyer before the contract is made, and

(b) the buyer will enjoy quiet possession of the goods except so far as it may be disturbed by the owner or other person entitled to the benefit of any charge or encumbrance so disclosed or known'.

Section 12(1) clearly covers the situation where the seller has no right to sell the goods, as in *Rowland* v *Divall*[10] where a purchaser who bought a car which did not belong to the vendor but belonged to a third person was able to recover the full price of the car from the vendor when it was returned to its original owner.

If the seller's defect in title is remedied before the buyer repudiates the contract, however, then this 'feeds' the buyer's title and he no longer has a right to repudiate[11].

Section 12(2) amounts to a warranty for quiet enjoyment of the goods and covers any undisclosed liens on them. It is wider than this however and covers also any interference with the buyer's unfettered enjoyment of the goods. In *Niblett Ltd* v *Confectioners' Materials Co.*[12], the sale of tins of milk which infringed Nestlé's trademark and could not therefore be resold without changing their labels, was held to amount to a breach of the warranty and also to a breach of the condition that the sellers had the right to sell the goods. In the more recent case of *Microbeads* v *Vinhurst Roads Markings*[13], a road marking machine was sold which the inventors subsequently patented. It was held that the condition as to the right to sell in Section 12(1) relates to the time of the sale, and as at that time the patent had not been taken out, the condition had not been broken. It was nevertheless still a breach of warranty for quiet enjoyment within Section 12(2)(b) as that subsection specifically covers future quiet enjoyment, in the words 'the buyer will enjoy . . .'.

Section 13. Implied condition on sale of goods by description

S.13(1) 'Where there is a contract for the sale of goods by description, there is an implied condition that the goods will correspond with the description.

(2) If the sale is by sample as well as by description it is not sufficient that the bulk of the goods corresponds with the sample if the goods do not also correspond with the description.

(3) A sale of goods is not prevented from being a sale by description by reason only that, being exposed for sale or hire, they are selected by the buyer'.

A sale of goods by description clearly covers the situation where the buyer has never had the opportunity to inspect the goods, as where, for example, the goods are to be purchased or manufactured by the seller.

S.13(3) expressly includes the situation where the buyer selects the goods himself, for example from a supermarket shelf, in the definition of a sale by description. In the Australian case of *Grant* v *Australian Knitting Mills Ltd*[14], a sale of 'woollen underwear' was held to be a sale by description although the buyer was able to inspect what he bought. Most manufactured goods are sold, at least partly, by description and Atiyah expresses the view that a sale not by description probably only occurs where the purchaser makes it clear that he wishes to buy that particular unique article[15].

Descriptive words are words which identify the goods, and there may be a breach of the condition even if the description is only slightly erroneous. Thus in *Arcos Ltd* v *E.A. Ronaasen & Son*[16], 95 per cent of the staves sold for use in manufacturing cement barrels were not exactly half an inch thick (as the remaining 5 per cent were) but were less than nine-sixteenths of an inch. They were nevertheless held not to comply with their description. Lord Atkin said 'If the written contract specifies conditions of weight, measurement and the like, those conditions must be complied with. A ton does not mean about a ton, or a yard about a yard. Still less when you descend to minute measurements does half an inch mean about half an inch. If the seller wants a margin he must and in my experience does stipulate for it . . .'.[17]

In *Re Moore & Co. Ltd & Landauer & Co. Ltd*[18] a description of the packaging of the goods was held to be within the section, but this has been doubted by Lord Wilberforce in a subsequent case[19] and will probably now only apply if the manner of packaging is expressed to be of sufficient importance to amount to a condition of the contract.

Descriptions as to quality, as distinct from identity, do not generally have to be so strictly complied with and in *Cehave* v *Brenner (Hansa Nord)*[8] the sale of fruit pellets 'in good condition' was held not to be a breach of Section 13 where one third of the pellets, although not 'in good condition', were still marketable. It may even be that a trade description will be accepted as accurate by the court although the description does not accurately describe the goods themselves[20], and the tendency is for the courts to take the view that descriptive words will not amount to a condition within Section 13 unless they are of vital importance to the nature of the contract.

Goods complying with their description but not suitable for their purpose will not amount to a breach of Section 13[21] unless the description implies certain qualities essential to the contract. If the sale is in the course of a business, however, this may amount to a breach of Section 14.

Section 13(2) specifically includes a sale by sample within the implied condition as to description, and in *Nichol* v *Godts*[22] 'foreign refined rape oil' bought by sample, which did in fact comply with the sample as to quality, was nevertheless held to be in breach of the implied condition as to its description.

Section 14. Conditions as to merchantable quality and fitness for purpose

S.14(2) 'Where the seller sells goods in the course of a business, there is an implied condition that the goods supplied under the contract are of merchantable quality, except that there is no such condition –

(a) as regards defects specifically drawn to the buyer's attention before the contract is made; or

(b) if the buyer examines the goods before the contract is made, as regards defects which that examination ought to reveal.

S.14(3) Where the seller sells goods in the course of a business and the buyer, expressly or by implication, makes known to the seller . . . any particular purpose for which the goods are being bought, there is an implied condition that the goods supplied under the contract are reasonably fit for that purpose, whether or not that is a purpose for which such goods are commonly supplied, except where the circumstances show that the buyer does not rely, or that it is unreasonable for him to rely, on the skill or judgment of the seller'.

It should be noted that both subsections only apply where the goods are sold 'in the course of a business'. 'Business' is defined by Section 61(1) of the Act as including 'a profession and the activities of any government department . . . or local or public authority'. A sale is still in the course of business if the goods are of a type with which the seller's business is concerned even though he does not normally sell them[23]. A sale by an agent will be deemed to be in the course of business unless he makes it clear to the buyer that his principal is a private individual.

'Merchantable quality'

By Section 14(6), goods are defined as being of merchantable quality 'if they are as fit for the purpose or purposes for which goods of that kind are commonly bought as it is reasonable to expect having regard to any description applied to them, the price (if relevant) and all the other relevant circumstances'.

The description of the goods is crucial in deciding whether the buyer was reasonable in assuming that they were fit for his purpose. Thus 'animal feeding stuff' would be wide enough to cover all animals whereas 'pet food' or 'poultry feed' would not. It does not indicate that the goods are of a good or fair quality but that they are marketable goods of that description. The price may reflect the quality which the buyer can expect. Thus a second hand car may be expected to have defects which a new one would not have. Even a second hand car would not be of merchantable quality however if it was not fit to drive at all[24]. The exclusions from the section of defects drawn to the buyer's attention and defects which he ought to have discovered on examination of the goods[25] are more likely to apply to second hand goods. Although the Unfair Contract Terms Act negatives any limitation on a sale to a consumer[26], goods supplied to a business may be supplied specifically subject to a limitation, provided the limitation is reasonable. This has given rise to difficulties in building contracts where exclusion clauses have been included in contracts with subcontractors, but the main contractors have remained liable to the employers, and is particularly unfair where the contractors are bound to accept a contract with a nominated subcontractor or supplier[27]. The position has now been remedied by a provision in the 1980/84 edition of the J.C.T. Contract that the building owner may not nominate a subcontractor or supplier who will not accept the warranties.

Section 14(3) requires that the buyer place some reliance upon the seller's 'skill or judgment'. Where goods are purchased by a trade name therefore, the condition will not apply. Where both the seller and the buyer are in the same trade, the presumption will be against the buyer relying upon the seller's skill or judgment, but a partial reliance will invoke the condition as to that part of the contract where the buyer has relied upon the seller's skill. In *Cammell Laird & Co. Ltd* v *Manganese Bronze and Brass Co. Ltd*[28] a ship's propellers were to be supplied to a specification drawn up by the buyer, but the specification did not include details as to the thickness of the materials required other than along the 'medial lines'. It was held that the buyer had relied upon the seller's expertise in these matters, and the propellers being inadequate in these respects amounted to a breach of the condition in Section 14(3).

The fact that no amount of skill on the seller's part could have discovered a latent defect is irrelevant if the goods are nevertheless unfit for the purpose for which they are sold[29]. The purpose for which the goods are required may be obvious and implicit, as in *Priest* v *Last*[30] (a hot water bottle), but where the goods are required for an unusual purpose, the seller will not be liable unless that purpose is made known to him. Moreover, specialised knowledge making the goods unfit for their purpose will not be imputed to the seller.[31]

The wording of Section 14(3) ('goods supplied under the contract') includes not only the goods sold but the containers in which they are delivered[32].

In the case of both merchantable quality and fitness for purpose, minor defects will probably not amount to a breach of the conditions, although the buyer may be able to recover damages. The goods should probably remain in a merchantable quality or fit for their purpose for a reasonable time after their delivery[33].

Section 15. Conditions applicable to a sale by sample

S.15(1) 'A contract for sale is a contract for sale by sample where there is an express or implied term to that effect in the contract.

(2) In the case of a contract for sale by sample there is an implied condition –
(a) that the bulk will correspond with the sample in quality;
(b) that the buyer will have a reasonable opportunity of comparing the bulk with the sample;
(c) that the goods will be free from any defect, rendering them unmerchantable, which would not be apparent on reasonable examination of the sample'.

The fact that a sample is available for inspection will not of itself make it a sale by sample, and it will only be a sale by sample if there is an express or implied intention that it should be so. Generally a written contract should include a clause to this effect, but where goods are identifiable only by reference to a sample, then it will be deemed to be a sale by sample[34].

There is a breach of the condition in S.15(2)(a) even though the goods can very easily be made to comply with the sample[35].

The conditions implied by Sections 13 and 14 still apply to a sale by sample, but there will be no liability for such defects, which would have been discoverable by a proper inspection of the sample.

3. EXEMPTION CLAUSES

An exemption clause is a clause in a contract excluding or limiting a party's liability.

A preliminary point for consideration is whether any such clause is a term of the contract or not. In order to be a term of the contract, it must be incorporated into it at the time the contract is made. Thus a condition limiting liability on a receipt for the purchase price is unlikely to be a term, as usually payment is made and a receipt given after the contract has been made. In order to incorporate the terms of a notice into a contract, the notice must be displayed where the contract is made[36] and must clearly cover the circumstances of that contract[37].

Moreover, the clause will be ineffective, even though adequately incorporated, if negatived by a subsequent oral statement[38] or if misrepresented as to its effect[39].

Under the doctrine of privity of contract, the terms of a contract bind only the parties to it, and only they may enforce it. It follows that a third party will not be bound by an exemption clause in a contract to which he was not a party. Thus on a sale of manufactured goods a consumer will not be bound by the terms of a contract of purchase between the manufacturer and the wholesaler, and may still be able to sue the manufacturer in the tort of negligence.

With regard to contracts for the sale of goods, Section 55(1) of the Act provides that implied rights or obligations of the parties may be 'negatived' or varied by express agreement, or by the course of dealing between the parties, or by 'such usage as binds both parties to the contract'.

Any 'express agreement' between the parties to exclude or limit liability will be restrictively construed by the courts, that is, construed as narrowly as possible against the party seeking to exclude liability (almost invariably the seller). Thus in *Andrews Bros Ltd* v *Singer & Co. Ltd*[40] the purchaser entered into a contract to buy a 'new' Singer car. The contract excluded liability for implied conditions or warranties. The car was not new at all, and the court held that the purchaser could rescind the contract. The description of the car as 'new' was an express condition of the contract and was not therefore included in the clause exempting the seller from liability for breach of implied conditions.

To establish a course of dealing between the parties, the seller must show a number of previous transactions which are consistently identical (except perhaps for very minor variations). The terms of these transactions may then be deemed to be incorporated into a subsequent transaction[41].

Usage binding on the parties would be the terms implied in dealings in any particular trade.

In addition to the above, the validity of an exemption clause is now also governed by the Unfair Contract Terms Act 1977, and Section 55(1) expressly make the effectiveness of any variation of implied terms subject to this Act. Section 13 of the Unfair Contract Terms Act gives a very wide definition of an exemption clause, which, in addition to a total exclusion of liability, includes a restriction of the buyer's remedies and the time during which he may enforce them, any conditions attaching to the enforcement, and a restriction as to the extent of the seller's liability. Sometimes the parties may expressly agree upon an appropriate sum as compensation for a breach (other than for a breach of the implied terms), and provided the sum is a genuine attempt to assess the loss resulting from the breach and not a penalty clause, this will still be valid and will not amount to an exemption clause under Section 13. The clause is likely to be regarded as a penalty and void if the sum payable under it is out of proportion to the possible loss caused by the breach of contract.

The Unfair Contract Terms Act may now be considered specifically in its application to contracts for the sale of goods as regards the following exemption clauses:

(a) Exemptions of the implied terms under Sections 12 to 15 of the Sale of Goods Act

Where the buyer is a consumer

Section 6 of the Unfair Contract Terms Act provides that on a sale to a consumer, the seller cannot exempt himself from liability for breach of the terms implied by these sections.

Under Section 12, a buyer is a consumer if:

'(i)   he neither makes the contract in the course of a business nor holds himself out as doing so; and

(ii)   the other party does make the contract in the course of a business; and

(iii)   . . . the goods . . . are of a type ordinarily supplied for private use or consumption.'

The burden of proof that a party is not dealing as a consumer is on the seller except in sales by auction or competitive tender, where a buyer will 'not in any circumstances' be deemed to be a consumer. Clearly any purchases of goods for, or in the course of a business, will not be consumer purchases, but a purchase by a limited company which took over the contract as purchaser from an individual who owned the company was held to be a consumer purchase[42]. The sale of goods by a private individual will never be a consumer deal.

Where the buyer is not a consumer

In these circumstances, the seller may not exempt himself from the implied condition as to title in Section 12, but he may exempt himself from the implied terms in Sections 13, 14 and 15 in so far as the exemption is reasonable having regard to the circumstances 'which were, or ought reasonably to have been, known to or in the contemplation of the parties when the contract was made'. The burden of proof of reasonableness is on the party claiming the benefit of the exclusion clause, and Schedule 2 of the Unfair

Contract Terms Act gives 'guidelines' to assist, together with all other circumstances, in determining the reasonableness or otherwise of such a clause. These include the relative bargaining strength of the parties, alternative opportunities for purchasing the goods, any inducement to the purchaser to contract with the seller, and whether the goods were a specialised order for the customer. Where the exemption clause relates to some particular condition, it may be relevant to consider whether, when the contract was made, it was reasonable to expect the condition to be complied with, or whether the customer should have known of the condition through some particular trade usage or previous course of dealing, as in *Kendall* v *Lillico*[41]. Section 11(4) provides that in determining the reasonablness of a clause limiting financial liability, account shall be taken in particular of the resources which the seller would have had available to him to meet the possible liability, and to what extent he would have been able to insure against such liability.

There are two contrasting cases on the 'reasonableness' test applied to exemption clauses, both decided on reasonable reliance upon an exemption clause under the Supply of Goods (Implied Terms) Act 1973 (the test for which is considered to be similar to the test under the present Act which replaces it), and both concerning the sale of seeds. In *R.W. Green Ltd* v *Cade Bros Farm*[43] a provision that the buyers should give notice of any defects within three days of delivery was held to be unreasonable, although the exclusion clause as a whole, which limited the seller's liability to the cost of the seed and not to any consequential loss of harvest, was found to be reasonable and valid. This was because the clause had been approved by negotiating bodies on behalf of both seed merchants and farmers, the presence of the virus which caused the failure of the potato crop was not attributable to any fault on the part of the sellers, and the buyers could have purchased seed certified by the Ministry of Agriculture at a higher price. In *George Mitchell Ltd* v *Finney Lock Seeds Ltd*[44] where a similar exemption clause limited the seller's liability to the cost of the seed and excluded liability for failure of the crop, the wrong seeds were delivered and the crop failed. The exemption clause did not pass the test of reasonableness, however, as it was one inserted unilaterally into catalogues by the seed dealers and not negotiated with the farmers, the error was due to the fault of the seed dealers which the farmers could not have discovered before sowing the crop, and although it might have been difficult for the farmers to insure against crop failure, it would not have been difficult for the seed dealers to insure against such an error.

A wide exclusion clause was considered in the case of *Rees*

Hough Ltd v *Redland Reinforced Plastics Ltd*[45]. Tunnelling contractors ordered concrete pre-cast jacking pipes which were supplied on the suppliers' written standard terms excluding liability in tort, a liability under Section 14, and for any defects not notified within three months. The pipes cracked after being laid. It was held that the defendants had failed to show that the exemption clause was reasonable and they were liable under Section 14.

(b) Other exemption clauses

A contract may contain an exemption clause exluding liability for breach of other express or implied terms, for example, as to the date or place of delivery. Section 3 of the Unfair Contract Terms Act, which applies where the sale is in the course of business and the buyer is either a consumer, or buys on the seller's written terms of contract, provides that such a clause will only be valid if reasonable. Although the guidelines in Schedule 2 are not specifically referred to as a test of reasonableness here, it is considered that the courts would be likely to take them into account in practice, and the burden of proving the reasonableness of the clause is on the seller[45]. Under Section 3(2) of the Act, the test of reasonableness is applied to any exemption clause under which the seller exempts himself from, or restricts his liability for any breach, or claims to be entitled:

'(i)   to render a contractual performance substantially different from that which was reasonably expected of him or
(ii)   in respect of the whole or any part of his contractual obligation, to render no performance at all'.

It should be noted however that even if the clause passes the test of reasonableness under Section 3(2), the buyer may still have a remedy under the implied terms as to the state of the goods if Section 6 applies, in misrepresentation if Section 8 applies (see below), and in tort if Section 2 applies (see below).

(c) Exemptions from liability for negligence

Section 5 of the Unfair Contract Terms Act provides that a manufacturer cannot exclude his liability in negligence to an ultimate consumer of his goods. As regards a person selling directly to a consumer (a trader or a manufacturer through a catalogue or door-to-door salesman), Section 2 provides that liability for death or personal injuries through negligence cannot be excluded, and liability for other loss can only be excluded in so far as such exclusion is reasonable. The section only applies to a person selling in the course of a business.

(d) Exemptions for misrepresentation

By Section 8 of the Unfair Contract Terms Act, any exemption for misrepresentation in the course of a business dealing is only valid in so far as it is reasonable.

QUESTIONS

1. (½ question) Explain the important terms which should be included in a contract for the purchase of materials from a supplier who has been nominated under the JCT Standard Form of Building Contract (1980 Edition) Private with Quantities.
   (Specimen paper)

2. (a) Outline the principal provisions in the Sale of Goods Act 1979 which are of importance to a buyer in a builder's office.

   (b) A supplier of concrete units has in his contract of supply the following term: 'In the event of any of our goods proving to be defective our liability shall be limited to either replacement of the goods or payment of their value; in no circumstances whatsoever will we be liable for any consequential loss as a result of any defect to the goods supplied'.

   A number of concrete units fixed in a building have been found to be defective. Their removal has caused damage to plasterwork and decorations and loss of the use of the building.

   Consider the effectiveness of this term in the event of the supplier being sued.
   (1985 paper)

NOTES TO CHAPTER 9

1. The Misrepresentation Act 1967, Supply of Goods (Implied Terms) Act 1973, Consumer Credit act 1974, Unfair Contract Terms Act 1977.

2. Choses in action are dealt with in Chapter 6.

3. *Moss* v *Hancock* (1899) 2 Q.B.111

4. (1909) 1 K.B.357

5. *Dawson (G.J.) (Clapham) Ltd* v *Dutfield* (1936) 2 All.E.R.232
A contract for the purchase of two lorries worth £475, to be paid for by
trading in two lorries worth £250 and the balance in cash, was a contract
for the sale of goods.

6. (1969) 1 A.C.454

7. *Cammell Laird & Co. Ltd* v *Manganese Bronze & Brass Co. Ltd* (1934)
A.C.402

8. *Cehave* v *Bremer etc. The Hansa Nord* (1976) Q.B.44
About one third of fruit pellets delivered under a contract did not comply
with the contractual requirement that they should be 'in good condition'.
They were still fit for making cattle food, however (the purpose for which
they were bought), and the term had not been expressly made a condition
of the contract. It was held therefore to amount only to a breach of
warranty entitling the buyer to damages.

9. See statutory restrictions on exemption clauses in Section 3 of this
chapter.

10. (1923) 2 K.B.500

11. *Butterworth* v *Kingsway Motors Ltd* (1954) 1 W.L.R.1786
A car which was the subject of a hire purchase agreement was sold by the
hirer A to B, who resold to C, who resold again to Kingsway Motors, who
resold to Butterworth. Butterworth discovered that he was not the owner
and repudiated the sale, claiming the purchase price from Kingsway
Motors. A then completed the hire purchase payments, making good her
title, which fed B's, C's and Kingsway Motors' titles, but not Butterworth's as he had repudiated the contract before Kingsway Motors' title
was perfected.
    Note that this decision would be different to-day because of the
provisions of Part III of the Hire Purchase Act 1964 relating to private
purchases of motor cars.

12. (1921) 1 W.L.R.218

13. (1975) 1 W.L.R.218

14. (1936) A.C.85

15. Atiyah, *The Sale of Goods*, 7th ed.

16. (1933) A.C.470 at p.479

17. (1933) A.C.

18. (1921) 2 K.B.519
Tinned pears, half of which were packed in boxes containing 24 tins
instead of 30 tins as contracted for, were held not to comply with their
description.

19. *Reardon Smith Lines* v *Hansen Tangen* (1976) 1 W.L.R.989

20. *Peter Darlington Partners Ltd* v *Gosho Co. Ltd* (1964) 1 Lloyd's Rep.149
A seller under a contract for the sale of canary seed, 'pure basis', was held not to be in breach on delivering 98 per cent pure seed, as 100 per cent pure seed was unknown in the trade, and 'pure seed' meant 'the best known quality', viz, 98 per cent pure.

21. *Christopher Hill Ltd* v *Ashington Piggeries Ltd* (1969) 3 All.E.R.1496
The sellers contracted to sell 'Norwegian herring meal fair average quality for the season . . .' The preservative used reacted with the herring meal to create a chemical poisonous to mink. The fact that the herring meal became unfit for the purpose for which it was bought did not amount to a breach of S.13, as it still complied with the contract description of 'Norwegian herring meal' and preservative.

22. (1854) 10 Exch. 191

23. *London Borough of Havering* v *Stevenson* (1970) 3 All.E.R. 609
The defendant, who was in business as a car hirer, sold a car. The sale was held to be in the course of his business, even though his business was to hire and not to sell cars.

24. *Crowther* v *Shannon* (1975) 1 W.L.R.30
A second hand Jaguar car, the engine of which seized up and had to be replaced three weeks after its sale, was held not to be reasonably fit for its purpose, namely, to be driven.

25. *Thornett & Fehr* v *Beers & Son* (1919) 1 K.B.486
Buyers, who were in a hurry, examined barrels of glue without looking inside the barrels, although the sellers offered this facility. Held – they had no cause of action under S.14.
Note. The wording of this subsection has been changed in the 1979 Act from 'such' examination to 'that' examination, inferring an examination which the buyer actually makes rather than one which he ought to have made, so that the circumstances of this particular case might be decided differently now.

26. See Section 3 of this chapter.

27. *Young & Maten Ltd* v *McManus Childs Ltd* (1969) 1 A.C.454
Builders employed subcontractors to do roofing, specifying particular tiles to be used made only by one manufacturer. The tiles were defective and cracked in frost but the exclusion clause in the contract with the manufacturers exempted them from liability. The subcontractors were still held liable to the builders however as they had been free to make whatever contract they saw fit with the manufacturer.

In *Gloucestershire County Council* v *Richardson* (1969) 1 A.C.489, however, the architect for the Council, by whom the builders were employed, nominated suppliers for concrete columns which were defective and authorised acceptance of their tender, so that the subcontractors had no right to object either to the suppliers or to the terms of the subcontract with them. The subcontract contained an exclusion clause excluding liability under Section 14 unless notified within twenty-four hours of delivery. The builders were not liable to the Council for the defects in the columns. The case was distinguished from *Young & Marten Ltd* v *McManus Childs Ltd* on the ground that the subcontractor had no freedom as to the terms of the contract.

28. (1934) A.C.402

29. *Frost* v *Aylesbury Dairy Co. Ltd* (1905) 1 K.B.608
Milk contaminated with typhoid bacteria was sold. It was no defence that the sellers had taken all reasonable care.

30. (1903) 2 K.B.148

31. *Teheran – European Corporation* v *Belton Ltd* (1968) 2 Q.B.545
Tractors purchased for re-sale in Persia were in breach of Persian regulations. But as the buyer had more knowledge of the Persian market than the seller, it was held that he had relied upon his own knowledge rather than the seller's and was not therefore within the section.

32. *Geddling* v *Marsh* (1920) 1 K.B.668
The seller was liable for a defective bottle in which mineral water was sold.

33. As to merchantable quality, this was applied in *Mash & Murrell* v *Joseph I. Emmanuel* (1961) 1 All.E.R.485
Potatoes were sold in Cyprus which were bad when they arrived in Liverpool. Lord Diplock said that goods must be in 'such a state that they could endure the normal journey and be in a merchantable condition on arrival'.

As to fitness for purpose, see *Crowther* v *Shannon*, Note 24 above.

34. *Cameron & Co.* v *Slutzkin Property Ltd* (1923) 32 c.L.R.81
A written contract for the sale of 'No.2475 39/40 white voile' was nevertheless held to be a sale by sample as it was not otherwise identifiable.

35. *E. & S. Ruben Ltd* v *Faire Bros Ltd* (1949) 1 K.B.254
Linatex was crinkly and did not conform with the sample, which was soft, but could easily be made to conform by the simple process of heating. It was held to be a breach of the Section. (S.15(1)(c).

36. *Olley* v *Marlborough Court Ltd* (1949) 1 K.B.532
The plaintiff booked into a hotel and later saw a notice in her room disclaiming responsibility for guests' property. Held – the notice was ineffective as she did not see it until after the contract was made at the reception desk.

37. *D. & M. Trailers (Halifax) Ltd* v *Stirling* (1978) R.T.R.468
Notices in auction rooms included an exemption clause and stated this also applied to sales by private treaty. The plaintiff returned after an auction and purchased by private treaty a tractor which had not been sold. Held – the exemption clause was not incorporated into the sale as it was a separate transaction.

38. *Harling* v *Eddy* (1951) 2 K.B.739
A catalogue at a cattle auction contained an exemption clause stating that
no warranty was given in respect of any animal. The auctioneer
subsequently orally guaranteed a heifer offered for sale at the auction.
Held – the oral guarantee overrode the exemption.

39. *Curtis* v *Chemical Cleaning and Dyeing Co. Ltd* (1951) 1 K.B.805
The plaintiff signed a receipt for a wedding dress which she left to be
dry-cleaned. The shop assistant said that the terms of the receipt
exempted the company from liability for damage to beads and sequins,
but in fact the exemption clause was wider. Held – the defendants were
liable for damage (other than to the beads and sequins) as the exemption
clause had been misrepresented to the plaintiff.

40. (1934) 1 K.B.17

41. *Kendall (Henry) & Sons* v *William Lillico & Sons Ltd* (1969) 2 a.C.31
A sold note, given to the buyers of animal food after the contract was
made, contained an exemption clause. Although this was not incorporated into this particular transaction, there had been over a hundred
similar transactions between the parties during the previous three years.
Held by the House of Lords – the exemption clause was binding on the
buyers, even though they were not aware of its terms.

42. *Rasbora Ltd* v *J.C.L. Marine Ltd* (1977) 1 Lloyds Rep.645
Mr Atkinson contracted to purchase a boat from boat builders, the
contract containing a clause 'Any implied condition or warranty is
expressly excluded, and the company shall not be liable for any loss,
damage, expense or injury howsoever arising, except as accepted under
the terms of the warranty certificate'. The warranty certificate provided
that the company would replace items which were defective due to faulty
materials or workmanship. Rasbora Ltd was a private company in which
Mr Atkinson owned all the shares, and for tax reasons, the company was
substituted as purchaser. Held – although the sale became a sale to a
limited company, it was still in reality a sale to a consumer, and the
implied condition in Section 14 as to merchantable quality applied. The
defendants were liable when the boat sank shortly after delivery. The
court also expressed the opinion that even had it not been a consumer
sale, the clause would not have been a fair and reasonable exclusion.

43. (1978) 2 Lloyds Rep.602

44. (1983) 3 W.L.R.163

45. (1984) 134 N.L.J.706

10. The Passing of Property and Risk Under a Contract for the Sale of Goods

1. PROPERTY IN GOODS

The significance of property in goods

For various reasons it may be necessary to decide whether the property in goods has passed to the buyer. Property, in this context, means ownership of the goods, and may become separated from the physical possession of them, so that the seller retains possession although property has passed to the buyer or the buyer obtains possession while property is still vested in the seller.

Firstly, if either the seller or the buyer becomes bankrupt, his trustee in bankruptcy may only be able to claim the goods if they are his property. Similarly, the liquidator of a limited company cannot usually claim goods unless they belong to the company.

Secondly, the general rule is that a party can only pass a title in the goods to a third person if he has a title himself. This rule is subject to many exceptions however, such as Sections 24 and 25 of the Sale of Goods Act, whereby a seller or buyer in possession may pass a good title to a *bona fide* purchaser without notice of the seller's lack of title.

Thirdly, risk will usually (although not always) attach to whoever has property in the goods, and this party will have the right to sue any third person, such as a carrier, who damages the goods.

Finally, the general rule is that the seller cannot sue the buyer for the price until the property in the goods has passed.

The passing of property in the goods

The overriding rule as to the passing of property in the goods is the intention of the parties at the time the contract was made. This is to be ascertained from 'the terms of the contract, the conduct of the parties, and the circumstances of the case' (S.17(2)). The relevant time is when the contract was made, and a subsequent intention will not change this[1], although in shop purchases probably no property passes until payment is acutally made or a mode of payment agreed upon[2]. Diplock L.J. has said '. . . in modern times very little is needed to give rise to the inference that property in specific goods is to pass only on delivery or payment'[3].

Specific goods are defined by Section 61 as 'goods identified and agreed upon at the time a contract of sale is made'. Usually they will be goods which belong to, or are in the possession of, the seller, but goods which belong to, or are in the possession of a third person may still be specific goods[4]. Goods which are not identified and agreed upon at the time the contract is made are unascertained goods. This will include all future goods, which are to be manufactured or acquired by the seller after the contract is made, and also goods which have not been appropriated to the contract. For example, 'five tons of aggregate' or '10,000 bricks' will be unascertained goods until the seller segregates these from other aggregate or bricks in his yard. Although Section 17 is stated to apply to 'specific or ascertained goods', the principle also applies to unascertained goods, subject to the proviso that the property in unascertained goods can never usually pass until the goods become ascertained. (A specimen order form for the purchase of building materials is reproduced on p.197.)

It may not always be possible to determine from the contract the intention of the parties as to the passing of property, however, or it may well be a matter which they have not even considered. In these circumstances, the five Rules set out in Section 18 of the Act apply to assist in ascertaining their intention. The Rules distinguish between specific and unascertained goods.

Rule 1

'Where there is an unconditional contract for the sale of specific goods, in a deliverable state, the property in the goods passes to the buyer when the contract is made, and it is immaterial whether the time of payment or the time of delivery or both be postponed'.

The relevant time for the applicaton of this Rule is when the contract is made[1], and any subsequent agreement to postpone delivery or payment will be ineffective as the property in the goods will already have passed. It is possible however that such an agreement at the time the contract is made may evince an intention that property should not pass until a later date when delivery or payment is made, and as the Rule only applies in the absence of any intention to be deduced from the contract, such an intention would displace it.

In the case of *Underwood Ltd* v *Burgh Castle Brick & Cement Syndicate*[5], a heavy engine which was cemented to the floor was held not to be in a deliverable state. Where there is a contract to install and fit goods, as in a building contract, the property in the goods will not usually pass to the purchaser until they are installed, as this is usually the inference as to the parties' intention[6]. If, however, there are in effect two separate contracts, for the sale of goods and for their subsequent installation, then Rule 1 will apply in the absence of any contrary intention[7].

Rule 2

'Where there is a contract for the sale of specific goods and the seller is bound to do something to the goods, for the purpose of putting them into a deliverable state, the property does not pass until the thing is done, and the buyer has notice that it has been done'.

Rule 3

'Where there is a contract for the sale of specific goods in a deliverable state, but the seller is bound to weigh, measure, test or do some other act or thing with reference to the goods for the purpose of ascertaining the price, the property does not pass until the act or thing is done and the buyer has notice that it has been done'.

Both of these Rules deal with conditional contracts for the sale of goods, but only cover the two particular conditions stated. It is probable that Section 17 (that property passes when the parties intend it to) would have the same effect however where the contract is subject to other conditions, such as the seller to repair the goods, as it may well be possible to infer that the parties did not intend the property to pass until the condition was fulfilled.

In both Rules, it is the seller who has to fulfil the condition. Thus in *Nanka Bruce* v *Commonwealth Trust Ltd*[8], where cocoa was sold and it was agreed that a sub-purchaser from the original purchaser would weigh the cocoa in order to ascertain the price due from the purchaser to the seller, this was held to be outside the scope of the Rule and the property had therefore passed to the purchaser.

It is probable that Rule 3 does not apply to the situation where the seller merely has to look up the price of the goods in a catalogue, so that the passing of property there would be determined under Section 17 and would depend upon whether the goods had been delivered or not, or whether the sale was dependent upon the price being acceptable to the buyer.

Rule 4

'When goods are delivered to the buyer on approval or on sale or return or other similar terms the property in the goods passes to the buyer:
>   (a) when he signifies his approval or acceptance to the seller or does any other act adopting the transaction;
>   (b) if he does not signify his approval or acceptance to the seller but retains the goods without giving notice of rejection, then if a time has been fixed for the return of the goods, on expiration of that time and, if no time has been fixed, on the expiration of a reasonable time'.

An 'act adopting the transaction' is any act by the buyer which makes it impossible for him to return the goods. This includes pledging or reselling the goods, or reselling under a similar sale or return contract where the time limits are inconsistent with his being able to return the goods to the seller within the time limits stipulated by him – for example, where A sells to B on sale or return within a week and B resells to C with a sale or return period which extends beyond the week stipulated in his contract with A. Some extraneous event, beyond the buyer's control, which makes it impossible for him to return the goods within the stipulated time limit, will not result in property passing to the buyer, however. Thus in *Re Ferrier*[9] where goods were seized by execution creditors of the buyer and retained by them until after the time limit for their return, it was held that property had not passed to the buyer.

Because the Rules only apply in the absence of any contrary intention, a provision that property shall not pass until the seller has been paid displaces the Rules and effectively protects the seller from a resale by the buyer passing property to some third party[10].

Rule 5

'(1) Where there is a contract for the sale of unascertained or future goods by description, and goods of that description and in a deliverable state are unconditionally appropriated to the contract, either by the seller with the assent of the buyer, or by the buyer with the assent of the seller, the property in the goods then passes to the buyer, and the assent may be express or implied, and may be given either before or after the appropriation is made.

(2) Where, in pursuance of the contract, the seller delivers the goods to the buyer or to a carrier or other bailee or custodier (whether named by the buyer or not) for the purpose of transmission to the buyer, and does not reserve the right of disposal, he is taken to have unconditionally appropriated the goods to the contract'.

Part (2) of this Rule contains specific examples of appropriation, and would include goods in the possession of a warehouseman which become appropriated when he accepts a delivery note from the seller and sets the goods aside for delivery to the buyer.

As has already been mentioned, the property in unascertained or future goods can never pass until the goods become ascertained (Section 16). Where the sale is of goods from a bulk, even delivery to a carrier will not make the goods ascertained if they are not segregated from goods to be delivered to other customers; in *Healy* v *Howlett & Sons*[11] boxes of fish in the course of transit by rail were not ascertained because they were in transit with other boxes to be delivered to other customers and it could not therefore be said which boxes were to be delivered to the buyer.

To be sufficient for the Rule to apply, an appropriation by the seller must be irrevocable. Thus in *Carlos Federspiel & Co. S.A.* v *Charles Twigg & Co. Ltd*[12], goods which had been packed and labelled at the seller's premises were nevertheless held not to have been unconditionally appropriated. Pearson J. gave as a reason in that case that 'A mere setting apart or selection by the seller of the goods which he expects to use in the performance of the contract is not enough. If that is all, he can change his mind and use those goods in performance of some other contract and use some other goods in performance of his contract'.

Where the contract is for the sale of future goods to be manufactured by the seller, there is a presumption that no property in the goods shall pass to the buyer until the goods are completed. On a large contract, there may be provision for payment by instalments, but this does not displace the presumption unless there is a provision to the contrary. In *Re Blyth Shipbuilding Co.*[13] a contract to build a ship provided that on payment of the first instalment the ship and all materials appropriated to it should become the property of the buyer. The sellers became bankrupt before completion, and it was held that property in the incomplete ship passed to the buyer and could not be claimed by the seller's trustee in bankruptcy, but materials lying around in the shipyard for use on the ship had not passed to the buyer as they had not been sufficiently appropriated to the contract.

There must be an assent to the appropriation by the other party, but the assent may be express or implied. In *Pignataro* v *Gilroy & Son*[14] the sellers set aside some bags of rice for collection by the buyer and sent him a delivery note to enable him to collect it. The buyer did nothing at all for a month, and this was held to be an implied assent to the sellers' appropriation.

Effect of a reservation by the vendor of rights over the goods

Section 19 states: 'Where there is a contract for the sale of specific goods or where goods are subsequently appropriated to the contract, the seller may, by the terms of the contract or appropriation, reserve the right of disposal of the goods until certain conditions are fulfilled; and in such a case, notwithstanding the delivery of the goods to the buyer, or to a carrier . . . for the purpose of transmission to the buyer, the property in the goods does not pass to the buyer until the conditions imposed by the seller are fulfilled.'

The most usual condition is that no property in the goods shall pass until payment is made. Thus in *Re Shipton Anderson & Co. Ltd* and *Harrison Bros & Co. Ltd*[15] the stipulation 'payment cash within seven days against transfer order' was held to be a reservation which prevented property from passing, so that when the wheat which was the subject of the contract was requisitioned, the contract was discharged by frustration.

In *Aluminium Industries B.V.* v *Romalpa Aluminium Ltd*[16], foil was delivered by the sellers to the buyers for use in their manufacturing process. The contract of sale provided that ownership in the foil would only pass to the buyers when they had made payment in full and that the seller's claim to property in foil not paid for attached to any manufactured goods in which it had been used or the proceeds of sale of the foil or goods, so that the purchasers became fiduciaries and held the foil or proceeds in trust for the sellers until payment was made to them. The buyers became insolvent and went into liquidation. It was held that any moneys received by them for foil sold were held by them on trust for the sellers, as property was not intended to pass until payment was made, and the contract established a fiduciary relationship which enabled the sellers to trace the goods into the proceeds of sale[17].

Each case however depends upon the precise construction of the particular contract and the circumstances of the claim, and a case where there was held not to be any fiduciary relationship and the sellers were unable to trace goods used in a manufacturing process was *Borden (UK) Ltd* v *Scottish Timber Products Ltd*[18].

The transfer of risk

Section 20(1) states: 'Unless otherwise agreed, the goods remain at the seller's risk until the property in them is transferred to the buyer, but when the property in them is transferred to the buyer, the goods are at the buyer's risk whether delivery has been made or not.

(2) But where delivery has been delayed through fault of either buyer or seller the goods are at the risk of the party at fault as regards any loss which might not have occurred but for such fault.

(3) Nothing in this section shall affect the duties or liabilities of either seller or buyer as a bailee or custodier of the goods of the other party'.

As mentioned earlier, one of the reasons for establishing when property in the goods passes is the general rule that risk passes with it. The seller is therefore liable for any loss or damage to the goods before property passes, and the buyer afterwards.

It is irrelevant as regards risk who has physical possession of the goods, except that Section 20(3) imposes on the party in possession (seller or buyer) a duty to take reasonable care of the goods, and such party is liable for any loss or damage caused by his negligence.

Section 20(1) makes the general rule stated therein subject to any contrary agreement between the parties. A contrary agreement is invariably expressed in hire purchase agreements where the hirer undertakes to insure the goods even though no property passes to him until all instalments due have been paid. It may also be inferred from the particular circumstances, and in *Stern Ltd* v *Vickers Ltd*[19] a contrary agreement was inferred. In that case, 120,000 gallons of white spirit, stored within a total quantity of 200,000 gallons in tanks belonging to a third person, was sold to the buyers and the buyers were given a delivery note enabling them to collect it. Until they did collect it, the spirit was to remain stored with the other spirit in the tanks, free of charge to the buyers. The buyers did not collect it and the spirit deteriorated. It was held that the delivery note giving the buyers access to the spirit was evidence that the parties intended the buyers to be responsible for it, and risk passed to them, even though the goods were still unascertained and property had not passed.

Section 20(2) makes a further exception to the general rule in

Section 20(1). It was applied in the case of *Demby Hamilton & Co. Ltd* v *Barden*[20] where apple juice deteriorated when the buyer delayed in taking delivery of it. The buyer, being at fault, was held liable. The subsection only applies, however, to loss or damage caused by the fault of the party delaying delivery, and loss due to any other cause will not be within the scope of the subsection.

A further provision dealing with the risk of deterioration of goods in transit is contained in Section 33, dealt with below.

2. LIABILITY FOR THE CARRIAGE OF GOODS

It depends upon the terms of the contract whether the seller is to deliver the goods or the buyer to collect them. In the absence of any express term, the presumption is that the buyer will collect the goods from the seller's place of business, or from the premises of some third person if the goods are specific goods known by both parties at the date of the contract to be at those premises.

If the seller does agree to deliver the goods, then he must do so within a reasonable time, and he discharges the duty if he hands over the goods to someone whom he reasonably believes to be authorised to accept them.

Goods handed over by the seller to a carrier are unconditionally appropriated to the contract, unless they are handed over in bulk with other goods for other customers and there has been no segregation[21], or the seller reserves a right of disposal under Section 19 (see above).

Delivery to a carrier is usually performance of the seller's obligation to deliver. The general rule in Section 20 as to risk passing with property in the goods applies, but if the seller agrees to deliver the goods at his own risk, then the risk is on him until delivery, even though property has passed to the buyer, subject to the provision in Section 33 that the buyer must bear 'any risk of deterioration in the goods necessarily incident to the course of transit'. This appears to place responsibility on the seller for accidental damage or loss, and on the buyer for natural deterioration of the goods in the course of transit. However, it will be recalled that the judges have expressed opinions that the condition as to merchantable quality implied by Section 14 is one which should apply for a reasonable time after delivery of the goods, and the seller may still be liable if the goods do not fulfil this condition on arrival[22].

If the seller is arranging for carriage of the goods, Section 32(2) requires him to make a reasonable contract with the carrier, having regard to the nature of the goods and the circumstances. If he does not do so, the buyer may refuse to accept delivery of the goods or claim damages for any loss. In *Thomas Young & Sons Ltd* v *Hobson & Partners*[23], the plaintiffs were shipbreakers who sold two engines to the defendants. They arranged for carriage by rail at the owner's risk. The engines were damaged and the buyers refused to accept delivery of them. The Court of Appeal held that even if property in the goods had passed under Section 18 as they were in a deliverable state, the buyers were justified in refusing the goods as the sellers had not made a reasonable contract with the carriers as required by Section 32(2).

If goods are to be delivered 'at owner's risk', there is an obligation on the seller to make the best possible contract with the carrier.

The carrier's liability

The carrier is not liable for any inherent defect in the goods, or their packaging, which causes deterioration during carriage. He is liable however for any damage caused by his own negligence, or which his negligence has contributed to. The onus of proof is on the carrier to show that the damage was due to an inherent quality of the goods, or alternatively to show the proportion of damage due to this and the proportion due to his fault. If he is unable to do this, he may be responsible for the whole loss.

It may be possible, under certain circumstances, for a carrier's sub-contractor to rely upon an exclusion clause in the seller's contract with the carrier[24].

Even though the seller may not have reserved a right of disposal of goods under Section 19, he may have a lien on goods for their price, although property in the goods has passed to the buyer, or, if property is still with the seller, a right of retention. Subject to the limitations in Section 47[25], he may stop the goods in transit if the buyer has become insolvent. By Section 61(4), the buyer is insolvent 'if he has either ceased to pay his debts in the ordinary course of business or he cannot pay his debts as they become due'. Goods are in the course of transit where they are deliverd to an independent carrier to deliver to the buyer, but not when they are given to the buyer's carrier. Transit ceases when the buyer takes delivery of the goods, or the independent carrier acknowledges that he holds the goods on behalf of the buyer. The seller may stop goods which are still in transit by re-taking possession of them, or by giving notice to the carrier of his claim. The notice must allow the carrier a reasonable time to intercept the goods.

The carrier also has a lien on the goods for the cost of carriage, and this takes precedence over the seller's right of stoppage in transit. He may therefore refuse to redeliver the goods to the seller until his costs are paid.

If the buyer is entitled to reject the goods for a breach of condition (as distinct from a breach of warranty which will probably only allow him to claim damages) the cost of redelivering the goods to the seller is the seller's responsibility. If the seller does not collect the goods for redelivery within a reasonable time, then the buyer may charge him for storage of the goods[26].

QUESTIONS

1. A contractor received through the post a leaflet and a sample of stone tiling from a firm at some distance away and ordered thirty square metres for a job on which he proposed to start work in a month's time. The leaflet said that the firm would deliver to anywhere in the United Kingdom within two weeks. Two weeks later, twenty square metres were delivered, but the tiling was not the same shade as the sample. The contractor is now ready to start work on the job and the remainder of the order has not been delivered.

    Advise the contractor.

    (Specimen paper)

2. A contractor was visited in his office by a representative of a door manufacturing company. The representative showed his samples and stated that delivery could be made anywhere in the country. The contractor examined the samples and placed two orders. One was for delivery to the office and the other to a site some distance away. The goods delivered to the office were inferior to the standard of the samples. The goods delivered to the site were up to standard but part of the order was missing. Consequently the site work is delayed.

    Advise the contractor on his legal position.

    (1986 paper)

Opposite: Specimen order form for the purchase of building materials.

PAYMENT WILL ONLY BE MADE IF THIS ORDER No.　　／　　／
IS QUOTED IN FULL; INVOICES WITHOUT THIS INFORMATION WILL BE RETURNED

TO ....

FROM

DATE............　............... 19 ....

Tel ....　Telex: ....

SUPPLIER'S CODE..............................

HEAD OFFICE:　　　　　　Telephone:　　　Telex:

OUR REF:　　　　　YOUR REF:　　　　　　　INDENT No.　　MATERIAL CODE

PLEASE SUPPLY TO US AT:

Your prices shall remain firm until ....

CARRIAGE:

TERMS:

DELIVERY PERIOD:　　　　　　　　　　　　　　for and on behalf of

1. ADVICE NOTES must be sent DIRECTLY TO SITE unless otherwise instructed.
2. ALL INVOICES must be sent to THE ADDRESS FROM WHICH YOU RECEIVED THIS ORDER unless specifically instructed otherwise. Invoices to be sent (original only) quickly following delivery of supplies and separately for each order number. Regular supplies of an extended period to be invoiced weekly.
3. STATEMENTS are essential before payment is made and must be submitted as early as possible following month of delivery to
4. NO VARIATION to the terms of this order will be accepted unless we issue a revised order.
5. ADDITIONAL SUPPLIES may only be made beyond those covered by this order if authorised by an addendum order. QUANTITIES IN EXCESS of those stated on this order will not be paid for unless an official order has been issued.
6. DRAWINGS AND SPECIFICATIONS are as mentioned hereon or enclosed herewith—items supplied under this order shall comply therewith.
7. ALL ITEMS SUPPLIED under this order must be to the satisfaction of the Local/Employing Authority and ourselves.
8. INSPECTION in your works prior to despatch of the items to be supplied shall be permitted, any such inspection shall not imply approval and shall be without prejudice to Conditions 6 and 7 above.
9. BRITISH STANDARD SPECIFICATIONS and CODES OF PRACTICE—the quality of items supplied to be in accordance therewith in the absence of any alternative provisions requiring higher standards.
10. SIZE OF CONSIGNMENTS AND SITE PROGRAMME—deliveries shall be made to suit our requirements.
11. The Supplier will observe the provisions of the Health and Safety at Work etc. Act 1974 and all Regulations and Codes approved under the Act.
12. This Order is subject to and in accordance with the terms and conditions of the Permanent contract of Purchase or the Conditions of Purchase set out overleaf.

Should you have any queries regarding invoice/s for these goods, please quote order number and site name in any correspondence.

Registration　　　　　　Registered Office

NOTES TO CHAPTER 10

1. *Dennant* v *Skinner & Collom* (1948) 2 K.B.164
A van was purchased at an auction sale and on handing over his cheque, the buyer signed a statement acknowledging that no property in the van should pass to him until the cheque was honoured. Held – this was ineffective as a contract is made at an auction when the hammer falls and a subsequent intention as to the passing of property is irrelevant.

2. Lord Parker C.J. said in *Lacis* v *Cashmarts* (1970) 2 Q.B.407
'. . . in supermarket sales, it is the intention of the parties that no property in the goods should pass until payment is made'.

3. In *Ward (R.V.) Ltd* v *Bignall* (1967) 1 Q.B. 534

4. *Varley* v *Whipp* (1900) 1 Q.B.513
The seller agreed to sell to the buyer a second-hand reaping machine which he intended to acquire from someone else.

5. (1922) 1 K.B.343

6. *Aristoc Industries Pty Ltd* v *R.A. Wenham (Builders) Pty Ltd* (1965) N.S.W.R.581
Contractors building a lecture hall sub-contracted with Aristoc for the supply and installation of 301 'varsity model lecture theatre seats', which Aristoc delivered to the site but were unable to install as the building had not progressed sufficiently. The contractors then had financial problems and assigned the contract to the defendants, who refused to allow Aristoc to remove the seats. Held – the contract was not a contract for the sale of goods but for work and labour, and therfore property in the goods did not pass until they were installed.

7. *Pritchett & Gold & Electrical Power Storage Co Ltd* v *Currie* (1916) 2 Ch.515
The defendant company contracted to install electrical equipment at the premises of C and subcontracted with the plaintiffs to install a storage battery there. The battery was sent by the plaintiffs by rail and the defendants collected it and took it to C's premises where they installed it as the plaintiffs did not proceed with the work. Held – the delivery of the battery was an unconditional appropriation to the contract of goods in a deliverable state under Rule 5 and property therefore passed to the defendant company. The company was in liquidation and the liquidators were entitled to the money for the battery, paid into court by C, and not the plaintiff company.

8. (1926) A.C.77

9. (1944) Ch.195

10. Unless the buyer is a mercantile agent under the Factors Act 1889, when he can pass a good title to a sub-purchaser.

11. (1917) 1 K.B.337

12. (1975) Lloyd's Rep.255

13. (1926) Ch.494

14. (1919) 1 K.B.459

15. (1915) 3 K.B.676

16. (1976) 1 W.L.R.676

17. Tracing is an equitable remedy which enables a beneficiary under a trust to claim trust property from anyone other than a purchaser for value and in good faith. Its application in commercial transactions has been criticised (see *Modern Law Review* (1980) Vol.43,489).

18. (1979) 3 All.E.R.961
The sellers supplied resin to the buyers for use in the manufacture of chipboard. The contract provided that property should not pass to the buyers until payment was made. The buyers became insolvent and the sellers claimed to be entitled to trace any resin supplied by them into manufactured chipboard or the proceeds of sale of chipboard. Held – the effect of the reservation of title was to reserve rights in unused resin, but once it had been used in the manufacturing process, then it became untraceable. The sellers were aware that the resin supplied by them would be used within approximately two days after delivery, and there was therefore never any intention that it should be recoverable and there was no fiduciary relationship between the parties as to the resin.

19. (1923) 1 K.B.78

20. (1949) 1 All.E.R.435

21. *Healy* v *Howlett & Sons* – see Note 11 above.

22. *Mash & Murrel Ltd* v *Joseph I. Emanuel Ltd* (1961) 1 All.E.R.485
Potatoes loaded on to a ship in Cyprus were not in merchantable quality when the ship arrived in Liverpool. Held – that there was a breach of the condition implied by Section 14 as the potatoes should have been in such a condition that they were able to survive the journey and to remain in merchantable quality on arrival.

23. (1949) 65 T.L.R.365

24. Lord Reid said in *Midland Silicones Ltd* v *Scruttons Ltd* (1962) A.C.474 that this would be contrary to the general rule of privity of contract, but might be possible if certain conditions were satisfied. The case concerned a claim by stevedores to be able to rely upon an exemption clause in a contract with carriers, but might possibly apply to other more general contracts of carriage.

25. Section 47 provides –
'(1) Subject to this Act, the unpaid seller's right of lien or retention or stoppage in transit is not affected by any sale, or other disposition of the goods which the buyer may have made, unless the seller has assented to it. (2)Where a document of title to goods has been lawfully transferred to

any person as buyer or owner of the goods, and that person transfers the document to a person who takes it in good faith and for valuable consideration, then –

    (a) if the last-mentioned transfer was by way of sale the unpaid seller's right of lien or retention or stoppage in transit is defeated; and

    (b) if the last-mentioned transfer was made by way of pledge or other disposition for value, the unpaid seller's right of lien or retention or stoppage in transit can only be exercised subject to the rights of the transferee'.

26. *Kolfor Plant Ltd* v *Tilbury Plant Ltd* (1977) 121 S.J.390

Under a contract for the sale of a diesel generator, it was to be delivered to customers of the buyers on 6 February, and at the latest on 7 February. It was not delivered until 8 February and the buyers rejected it and claimed the cost of carriage from their customers' premises to their own and safe storage. Held – as time was of the essence of the contract, they could reject it, and costs of carriage and storage were recoverable as damages for breach of contract.

11. The Contract of Employment
Richard Howells

1. INTRODUCTION

(a) The basic obligations under the contract

Readers should be familiar with the law relating to the formation of a valid contract of employment, and also with the special significance accorded by English law to the distinction between a contract of employment and a contract for the supply of services.

Of equal importance is the significance given by the common law to the 'set' of mutual obligations arising under the contract that together makes up the complex relationship of employer and employee. These obligations, which may be found in either the 'express' or the 'implied' terms of the contract, vary in importance from the fundamental to the marginal. Apart from the terms which are peculiar to the individual contract, and which must, of necessity, be set out expressly in the contract (for example, duties or remuneration), there is a range of important obligations that go to make up the employment relationship and which will be implied into any contract of employment, except to the extent that they are expressly excluded[1]. Arguably, some, such as duty to safeguard the employee, cannot be excluded. The most frequently encountered obligations arising in this way include, on the part of the employer, the duties to provide work, or in the alternative, to pay wages[2], to treat the employee with trust and confidence[3] and to take reasonable care for the safety of the employee. This latter obligation is discussed below at p. 205.

Entitlement to holiday and sick pay, in the absence of express provision, gives rise to difficulty[4]. However, the written statement of terms and conditions of employment that every employer must furnish to his employees (see p. 209) must include any terms relating to sick and holiday pay.

The most important duties of the employee include the duty to obey all lawful orders relating to the discharge of his duties under the contract[5], to discharge his contractual duties with all due care and skill[6], to act in good faith towards the employer (including observing confidentiality towards the employer's business), not to impede the employer's business and not to compete with the employer's business[7].

(b) Variation of the contract of employment

Contracts of employment may only be varied by the mutual agreement of the employer and the employee: a unilateral variation of a term of the contract by one party, which is not acquiesced in by the other party, amounts in law to a repudiation of an existing contract. On the other hand, a unilateral variation which is accepted without protest by the other (for example, a worker continuing in employment after agreed wages are reduced by the employer) is regarded in law as a consensual variation of the terms of the contract.

However, at common law, a contract of employment may be terminated by reasonable notice; thus, an employer might succeed in varying the terms of a contract of employment by giving appropriate notice to terminate, followed by an offer of fresh employment on the varied terms. The coming into force of the Employment Protection legislation has rendered the concept of termination followed by an offer of fresh employment on new terms, or of unilateral variation, unrealistic in most situations, as under the Employment Protection Consolidation Act 1978 a termination of the contract by the employer or an attempt at unilateral variation of the contract by the employer, which is not accepted by the employee, amounts to a dismissal or a repudiation on the part of the former, which may entitle the latter to seek a statutory remedy under the Unfair Dismissals Code. In this particular circumstance, an Industrial Tribunal may hold that the employee has been 'unfairly' dismissed, and entitled to compensation under the provisions of the code (see below at p. 210). For present purposes, it is enough to appreciate that this statutory concept severely limits, in many instances, the employer's practical power to vary contracts unilaterally, either by simply changing the terms or by purporting to terminate the contract and offering fresh employment on the basis of new terms.

Where an employer is forced to make changes in the employment conditions of his employees by changed circumstances (for example, the closing down of a school in response to falling numbers of children to be educated) an employee who refused to accept changes in his terms of employment involved in his transfer to another school might find himself without remedy under either the common law or the Employment Protection legislation. At common law, the employer's obligation would be limited to a period of notice to terminate in accordance with the terms of the contract, followed by an offer of fresh employment: under the legislation, an employee who unreasonably refused to accept necessary changes in his contract of employment runs the risk of an Industrial Tribunal ruling that, owing to his unreasonable conduct, his subsequent dismissal was 'fair' (see below at p. 211).

It should be noted that mechanisms for variation of contract otherwise than by agreement may be built into the contract. These may either be express, for example, that the employee will work at X, or at any other location which the employer may nominate in the future; or the contract may make some express reference to some collective agreement that the remuneration shall be such sum as is agreed from time to time between the Y trade union and the employer[8]. In either case, the contract may be varied in this manner without express or implied acquiescence by the employee concerned.

More difficult is the situation where the contract may not expressly incorporate the terms of a collective agreement in this way, but it is claimed that, by custom and practice, its terms are followed in arriving at the conditions of a particular employee's contract[9].

Under Section 1 of the Employment Protection Consolidation Act 1978, every employee is entitled to a written statement of the terms of his employment. A supplementary statement must be issued if there is any variation in these terms (Section 4). It must be appreciated that these statutory requirements do not alter the basic principles as to the variation of a contract discussed above: thus the issue of a varied statement by an employer can only be evidence of a pre-existing agreement to vary the terms, and if issued without the prior agreement of the employee, is merely an attempt unilaterally to alter the terms of the existing contract.

(c) Termination of the contract of employment

At common law, contracts of employment may be terminated in one of the following ways: by agreement, performance, notice, frustration and breach. A contract may be terminated at any time by the express agreement of employer and employee. A contract for a fixed period of time, or for the completion of a specific task, will be terminated by the completion of the task, or the expiry of the time.

Perhaps the most common method of termination of the contract is by notice. The necessary period of notice may be expressed in the contract; otherwise, it will be implied by the court. In the absence of express contractual provision to the contrary, all contracts of employment are terminable by reasonable notice[10].

Termination without notice (summary dismissal or summary resignation) may be either 'lawful' or 'wrongful'. Lawful dismissal (or resignation) might arise in response to a fundamental breach of the contract on the part of the other party; otherwise summary termination of the relationship might amount to a wrongful dismissal or resignation, with a remedy in damages available to the injured party. This remedy would normally be limited to the amount of wages payable during the period of notice by which the contract might have been lawfully terminated: in the case of a wrongful resignation, the damages might relate to the loss to the employer suffered by the employee's leaving without notice – but in practice such damage is difficult to substantiate[11].

In wrongful dismissal, no remedy is normally available for loss other than wages in lieu of notice, but recent cases seem to indicate some movement away from this strict doctrine[12].

In practice, claims of wrongful dismissal at common law are most significant in the cases of fixed term contracts and contracts involving a long period of notice. Minimum periods of notice are now laid down by statute (Employment Protection Consolidation Act, Section 49), involving a basic period of one week's notice for up to two years' continuous employment, up to a maximum of twelve weeks after twelve years' continuous employment. The same statutory provision requires an employee to offer a minimum of one week's notice to terminate; but, of course, he may be bound under his individual contract of employment to offer more.

The term 'self dismissal' is frequently used in employment matters, containing the implication that the conduct of an employee is so gross as to bring the contract to an end of itself. This concept has now been clarified by the Court of Appeal[13]. It appears that it is not possible to frame a contract of employment that, if an employee breaches a certain term, he will be deemed to have dismissed himself; the correct analysis is that an employer may certainly stipulate that breach of a given term will be regarded as a fundamental breach, but this will not, of itself, terminate the contract; the basic contract rule must be followed, that the 'innocent' party must elect either to treat the contract as broken, or to exercise the right to sue upon the breach, as the case may be.

Thus there can be no 'constructive resignation' as opposed to the statutory concept of 'constructive dismissal' discussed below.

Readers will be familiar with the doctrine of frustration of contract; this doctrine has little practical relevance to contracts of employment except where the continuing existence of a contract of employment is in dispute. Examples are alleged frustration due to protracted illness[14] and alleged frustration owing to the imposition of a sentence of imprisonment upon the employee.

However, at common law the main significance would be in respect of contracts not susceptible of termination by reasonable notice; but wholly different considerations arise with respect to contracts of employment subject to the Unfair Dismissals Code (discussed below at p. 210).

A contract may be terminated as a consequence of a breach of fundamental term by one party, which entitles the other party to bring the contract to an end. A breach of a minor term of a contract does not entitle the wronged party to treat the contract as terminated in this way, but only to seek a remedy in damages. An important question in contract of employment litigation is which actions would be regarded as fundamental breaches for this purpose. For example, any failure to obey lawful orders was formerly regarded as repudiatory conduct entitling the employer to terminate; this harsh view is somewhat softened by a tendency in some recent cases to consider the employee's conduct in terms of intention to continue to be bound by the employment relationship[15]. Lateness and repeated absences from work give rise to difficulty in applying this type of analysis; however, owing to the coming into force of the Unfair Dismissal Code, such issues are more likely to be resolved in the Tribunals than in the courts nowadays.

2. THE EMPLOYER'S DUTY OF CARE FOR THE SAFETY OF HIS EMPLOYEES

The employer's duty to take reasonable care for the safety of his employees while at work is perhaps the most important of his implied obligations under the contract of employment. In practice, as the duty may be expressed in tortious as well as in contractual terms, it is advantageous to bring a claim purely as an action in tort. Insurance against this liability has been made compulsory under the Employer's Liability (Compulsory Insurance) Act 1969.

The duty is one of 'reasonable care' rather than an 'insurance against risk' standard. Thus an employer cannot be expected to foresee dangers beyond the then-current state of knowledge, nor to take precautions that are not commercially available at the relevant time[16]. An employer's duty is limited to the state of knowledge, equipment and practice current at the time when the cause of action arises[17].

The employer's duty is 'personal' in that it is not discharged by the appointment of competent technicians and managers, for whose negligence the employer remains liable: the duty is also 'personal' to the individual employee, in that it is his needs, and not the needs of employees generally, which must be taken into consideration[18].

The duty is primarily owed to the employees of the employer; however, circumstances may arise in which the employer may find himself liable for the safety of contractors and their workmen working on his premises, particularly in situations where both his own employees and contractors are working together on one integrated task[19]. Although the duty is nowadays seen as part of a unified duty of care, it is nevertheless still helpful in employment situations to follow the division into three component parts set out by the House of Lords in *Wilson & Clyde Coal Co.* v *English*[20]: (i) safe plant, machinery and equipment necessary for the work; (ii) adequate numbers of competent and fully trained fellow workers; (iii) an integrated and safe system of working into which men and equipment are co-ordinated.

(i) Safe equipment

This obligation renders the employer responsible for the consequences of defective, unsafe or badly maintained equipment. Since the passing of the Employers' Liability (Defective Equipment) Act 1969, it is no longer open to an employer to assert that the defect in equipment was due to the sole fault of a third party (that is, the supplier of the equipment)[21].

(ii) Competent staff

This obligation places great emphasis on training and discipline. The employer is usually vicariously liable for the negligence of his employees one to another within the course of their employment: he is liable under this heading where employees are not so much negligent as untrained for the duties assigned to them, or not allocated in sufficient numbers for the safe discharge of their duties. The employer may further be liable where employees are guilty of skylarking with, or making assaults upon, their fellow employees. Such actions may well be outside the course of their employment, but still constitute conduct that a careful employer would seek to identify and bring under control by his hiring and disciplinary policies[22].

(iii) Safe system

The duty to organise and, in certain eventualities, seek to enforce, a safe system of working is a fundamental component of an employer's duties. It is the employer's duty to plan the work in advance, to provide all the necessary equipment, including safety equipment, and to take positive steps to see to it that the laid-down system is adhered to by the employees concerned. To be acceptable, the system must be one that reasonably balances the risks to the employees against the economic and technical costs of compliance with the specified precautions. Provided that the balance is fairly struck the employer is not necessarily at fault if an element of risk remains and an employee is injured. Thus an employer could not be heard to say that the cost of eye protection was 'uneconomic' in a process that imposed serious risk of eye injury: in some other situation, he might well succeed on the argument that some precaution would render the process uneconomic, and lead to the closure of the factory. But even in the latter instance, it would not be acceptable to carry on with a hazardous system that imposed a known risk to the life of an employee[23].

Considerable difficulty may arise where a safe system is laid down and the specified safety precautions provided, but the employee fails to follow the system or to use the safety equipment. At the minimum, an employer must ensure that an employee is familiar with the details of the system and the availability and use of the equipment[24]. But the danger may be great, or its nature insidious; in such cases, the employer may be under a duty to go a very long way towards enforcing the system and the use of the protective devices[25].

Breach of statutory duty

A claim for damages for injury at work may also be based upon evidence of a breach of 'statutory duty' by an employer. Such actions are increasingly common nowadays, due to the increase in the volume of statutory safety duties imposed for the benefit of employees at work. (For example, Factories Act 1961, Construction (General Provisions) Regulations 1961). To succeed, the plaintiff in such an action must prove:

    (i)   the statutory duty is imposed on the defendant for the benefit and protection of the plaintiff, or more usually, of employees of the class to which the plaintiff belongs;

(ii)   breach of that duty by the employer;

(iii)   damage to the plaintiff directly resulting from that breach.

In practice, the evidence necessary to succeed in a 'breach of statutory duty' claim is frequently less difficult to compile than that necessary to establish breach of a duty of 'reasonable care' in a common law claim[26].

Claims for damages

A claim for damages based upon an employer's duty of care must be brought in the Queens Bench Division of the High Court within three years of the date when the cause of action arose, or of the date when the plaintiff had knowledge of the injury, under the Limitation Act 1980.

The onus of proof of negligence of the employer is placed upon the claimant: the employer is entitled to rebut this claim by introducing evidence that he did, in all the circumstances, what was reasonable to protect the safety of the claimant while at work.

Defences to the action include:

(i)   Contributory negligence.

If the employer can establish that the injury suffered by the claimant arose partly from the fault of the claimant, the damages payable may be reduced proportionately to the relative degrees of fault of the parties under the Law Reform (Contributory Negligence) Act 1945[27].

(ii)   Voluntary assumption of risk.

The essence of this defence is that the employee had voluntarily agreed to run the particular risk which resulted in his injury. This defence is only relevant where the 'risk' relates to the alleged neglect by the employer of some precaution: as the employer does not guarantee the safety of the work activity, there can in any event be no liability at common law for risk outside the ambit of the employer's duties of care. Thus the 'risk' referred to in the defence is better referred to as 'risk from breach of duty'. It is not easy, even where the defence does apply, to produce evidence that the employee has expressly agreed to run the risk of his employer's neglect; mere evidence of knowledge of the 'risk' on the part of the complainant certainly will not amount to evidence of agreement to accept the risk[28]. In fact, the defence has rarely proved successful in a work situation in recent years[29].

3. EMPLOYMENT PROTECTION LEGISLATION

Since the passing of a number of recent acts (the Employment Protection Act 1975, the Employment Protection (Consolidation) Act 1978, the Employment Acts 1980 and 1982) the common law contract of employment must be read subject to the rights and duties set out in this extensive code of legislation. Much of the content of the code lies outside the scope of this chapter. The following provisions relate directly to the basic contract of employment, and should be understood by the student.

(i) The duty imposed upon employers in Sections 1–6 of the Employment Protection (Consolidation) Act 1978 (E.P.C.A.) to issue a written statement containing certain particulars of the employment contract to all their employees within thirteen weeks of the commencement of employment;

(ii) The right, contained in Sections 49–52, E.P.C.A., of all employees who have been continuously employed for one month or more to a minimum period of notice. The notice will vary from a minimum of one week to a maximum of twelve weeks for those employees who have been continuously employed for twelve years or more.

The minimum notice required of an employee who has been continuously employed for one month or more under the same statutory provisions is one week in all cases;

(iii) The right of an employee who has been continuously employed for a period of not less than two years not to be 'unfairly dismissed' by his employer. This important right, given by Part V of E.P.C.A., is discussed below at pp. 210–213;

(iv) The right of an employee who has been continuously employed for a minimum period of two years to receive a 'redundancy payment' from his employer if he is dismissed, and his dismissal is adjudged to be due to 'redundancy'. This right, contained in E.P.C.A. Part VI, is discussed below at pp. 214–219;

(v) The right of every employee who has been continuously employed for a minimum period of six months to a written statement from his employer of the reasons for his dismissal by that employer (E.P.C.A., Section 53). This statement of reason is admissible either in proceedings arising from an alleged breach of the contract of employment at common law, or in proceedings before an Industrial Tribunal alleging unfair dismissal or other complaint.

4. UNFAIR DISMISSAL

A novel remedy against arbitrary dismissal is created by Part V of the Employment Protection (Consolidation) Act which, in Section 54, gives to employees the right not to be unfairly dismissed. For the purposes of this statutory remedy, 'dismissal' is defined in Section 55(2) as a situation where:

> '(a) the contract under which he is employed by the employer is terminated by the employer, whether it is so terminated by notice or without notice, or
>
> (b) where under the contract he is employed for a fixed term that term expires without being renewed under the same contract, or
>
> (c) the employee terminates the contract, with or without notice, in circumstances such that he is entitled to terminate it without notice by reason of the employer's conduct'.

The employee must show that he has been dismissed within the meaning of Section 55. This burden is in most instances not an unduly heavy one. It should be noted that it is not necessary to establish that the employer's conduct would amount to a breach of contract at common law; there is no need to show that the dismissal was 'wrongful' in any legal sense. A legal novelty is the concept of 'constructive' dismissal set out in Section 55(2)(c). After some uncertainty, the law was clarified by the Court of Appeal in *Western Excavating Co* v *Sharpe*[30](before the employee can himself terminate the contract, he must have suffered conduct from the employer which would itself amount to a fundamental breach of the employment contract; behaviour that might be described as 'unreasonable' would not suffice to trigger off the remedy).

Once the dismissal has been established, the burden then passes to the employer to establish, if he is able, the 'fairness' of the dismissal. For this purpose, he first has to show that the principal reason for the dismissal was one of the causes set out in Section 57, as follows:

> (a) related to the capability or qualifications of the employee for performing the work of the kind which he was employed by the employer to do; or
>
> (b) related to the conduct of the employee;
>
> (c) was that the employee was redundant;
>
> (d) was that the employee could not continue to work in the position which he held without contravention (either on his part or on that of his employer) of a duty or restriction imposed by or under an enactment.

In addition to the specific causes listed above, the employer can also take advantage of Section 57(1)(b), namely '. . . some other substantial reason of a kind such as to justify the dismissal of an employee holding the position which the employee held . . .'

This latter clause has been widely interpreted by the Tribunals to include matters such as sound commercial reasons and business necessity[31].

All dismissals for what are regarded as 'inadmissible' reasons are deemed automatically unfair: these are

  (a) dismissals relating to trade union membership or activity, which are protected by Section 58;

  (b) redundancy, where the complainant has been selected for redundancy for an inadmissible reason (Section 59);

  (c) dismissal on the grounds of pregnancy (Section 60).

In all other cases, the Tribunal must address itself to all the circumstances surrounding the dismissal, to determine its fairness within the statutory formula, considering whether 'in the circumstances (including the size and administrative resources of the employer's undertaking) the employer acted reasonably or unreasonably in treating it as a sufficient reason for dismissing the employee; and the question shall be determined in accordance with equity and the substantial merits of the case'. (Section 57(3)).

The statute does not state upon whom the onus of proof of fairness is placed, merely indicating that the determination of the Tribunal must depend upon its assessment of the reasonableness of the employer's conduct in dismissing for the stated reason. Two of the main areas in which the question of the reasonableness of the employer's conduct has been crucial have been in regard to (a) procedural fairness and (b) the appropriateness of the employer's reasons to the situation as established.

Procedural fairness

This area has proved as important as the substantive law. The Tribunals have regard to the employer's disciplinary procedures and to the ACAS 'Code of Practice on Disciplinary Practice and Procedures in Employment' when determining whether a dismissal has been fairly carried out. Procedural fairness is clearly important in all dismissals, but may be crucial in those instances where the facts may be in dispute, the employees are not represented, or issues such as previous conduct may have an important bearing on the case[32].

Fairness of response

This consideration might include somewhat intangible matters such as the reasonableness of the sanction of dismissal as measured against the employee's conduct or previous employment record, or the extent to which the employer has canvassed other options open to him before coming down in favour of dismissal. The axiom that employment policies and practices, when applied to disciplinary areas, should be 'remedial rather than punitive' gives an excellent light upon the attitudes of the Tribunal when weighing up the fairness of a dismissal as against some other action in a particular situation[33].

Excluded cases

(a) Under current law, an employee with less than two years' continuous service with an employer in full time employment (that is, more than sixteen hours per week) will be excluded.

(b) Employees who have reached normal retiring age[34].

(c) Employees dismissed in connection with a lockout, strike or other industrial action. Such a dismissal may not be adjudicated by a Tribunal unless it is shown that the dismissals were 'selective' in the sense that 'one or more of the relevant employees of the same employer (that is, those on strike) had not been dismissed . . .' (Section 62(2))[35].

(d) Certain dismissals relating to trade union membership (Section 58(3)).

In this instance, the basic principle is simple enough; namely that, where a union membership agreement (popularly, a 'closed shop') is in force, a dismissal of an employee for non-membership of the union or unions concerned shall be regarded as fair and excluded from the jurisdiction of the Tribunal. This basic principle has been overlaid with a number of complex safeguards of employees' rights, which fall outside the purview of this chapter.

Failure to permit a woman to return to work after childbirth is regarded as a dismissal for the purposes of Part V; while in this situation the respective rights of the woman and her employer are set out in Sections 56 and 56A. Similarly, an 'unfair' selection for redundancy (see p. 218) will be regarded as an unfair dismissal for the purposes of Part V (Section 59).

Remedies for unfair dismissal

A person claiming that he has been unfairly dismissed must put his case to an Industrial Tribunal within a period of three months from the effective date of termination of his contract of employment, or within a 'reasonable period' when the Tribunal is satisfied that it was not reasonably practicable to present it within the normal period (Section 67). Where the Tribunal finds that the complaint was well founded, it may award the complainant one (or more) of the following remedies (Section 68):

(a) an order for reinstatement or re-engagement of the complainant by his employer (these terms are defined for the purposes of Part V in Sections 69(2) and (4) respectively);

(b) an award of compensation calculated in accordance with Sections 72–75.

The compensation award consists of three component parts:

(a) a basic award, varying in accordance with the length of service, age, and rate of pay of the complainant, with a current maximum of £4,560 (Section 73);

(b) a compensatory award, being such amount as the Tribunal considers just and equitable in all the circumstances having regard to the loss sustained by the complainant in consequence of the dismissal, insofar as that is attributable to the action taken by the employer. The current maximum is £8,000 (Section 74);

(c) a special award not exceeding £21,000. This sum, which may be reduced in the light of the complainant's own conduct, is only payable in the following circumstances:

(i) the complainant was dismissed for the 'inadmissible reason' of trade union membership or activity; or

(ii) the complainant had been selected for redundancy for the same 'inadmissible reason'; or

(iii) the Tribunal had recommended the reinstatement or re-engagement of the complainant and the employer had refused to do so, or alternatively, had not satisfied the Tribunal that it was not reasonably practicable[36] to do so (Section 75).

It should be noted that, despite the use of the word 'order' in Section 69 relating to reinstatement or re-engagement, the only sanction against an employer who refuses to comply with such an order is the 'special award' discussed above.

5. COMPENSATION FOR DISMISSAL ON THE GROUNDS OF REDUNDANCY

The redundancy payments scheme is distinct from the unfair dismissals code already discussed. However, dismissal for the purposes of entitlement to a redundancy payment is defined in Section 83 in the same terms as 'unfair' dismissal is defined in Section 55. The contract of employment may also be terminated for redundancy purposes by the death, dissolution or liquidation of the employer.

Where a dismissal has been established, there is a statutory presumption that it is by reason of redundancy (Section 91) leaving it to the employer to establish, if he can, that the dismissal was due to some other cause.

Thus, if a factory is closed by a strike and does not reopen afterwards, the employer may be able to establish that the consequent dismissals of his employees were by reason of the strike and therefore not by reason of redundancy. In that situation, no compensation payments would be due to the former employees under the redundancy payments scheme[37].

Where an employer has given notice to terminate a contract of employment, but before the ending of the contract makes an offer to the employee either (a) to renew the contract under terms which do not differ from the previous contract, or (b) to re-employ the employee under a new contract which, although differing in terms from the old contract, constitutes 'suitable employment' for that employee, the latter will not be entitled to a redundancy payment if he is deemed to have 'unreasonably refused' that offer (Section 82).

Where the terms of the new contract differ from that of the old, the employee is entitled under Section 84 to a trial period of four weeks in the new employment: but again, if he 'unreasonably terminates' the employment during that period, his rights to any redundancy payment are lost.

Redundancy situations

If, and only if, the dismissal is wholly or mainly attributable to redundancy as defined below, will any question of entitlement to a payment arise. Section 81 sets out three redundancy situations, as follows:

'(i)   the fact that his employer has ceased, or intends to cease, to carry on the business for the purposes of which the employee was employed by him, or

(ii)   has ceased, or intends to cease, to carry on that business in the place where the employee was employed by him, or

(iii)   the fact that the requirements of that business for employees to carry out work of a particular kind in the place where he was so employed, has ceased or diminished or are expected to cease or diminish'.

Of the three basic redundancy situations, cessation of the business is the most straightforward. The second situation may give rise to more difficulty, as it consists of either a straightforward dismissal on redundancy grounds, or of what is, in effect, an attempt to transfer employees between work locations. The success of the latter depends in many instances upon the exact terms of the individual employee's contract of employment. If the contract requires the worker to be 'mobile', a refusal to transfer between sites may involve him in a breach of his contract sufficient to justify a 'fair' dismissal, and therefore not a dismissal on the grounds of redundancy[38]. Where there is no such contractual provision, such a transfer requirement may constitute an offer of alternative 'suitable employment'; but this could be a hotly contested issue before the Tribunal[39]. Where the move between sites can be regarded as marginal, a Tribunal may decide that, even without a contractual mobility clause, the employer cannot be said to have broken the contract by requiring a move to a nearby, and equally convenient, location; in such circumstances, again, a subsequent dismissal of a non-co-operating employee might be held to be for 'cause' and not for redundancy[40].

Where an employer wishes to transfer, rather than dismiss, an employee, if the enforced transfer could be regarded as a significant breach of the contract, the employee might resign and claim that he had been 'constructively' dismissed in a redundancy situation in accordance with Section 83(2)(c).

The third type of redundancy situation presents the greatest difficulties in practice. The problem is essentially the employer's reduced need for a particular type of labour, whether due to a declining market, automation, or reorganisation of the work. But a mere re-shuffle of workers between day and night work, or between shifts, cannot amount to a redundancy situation unless it amounts, overall, to a reduced demand for labour[41].

Similarly, reorganisation of a process may call for qualities of adaptability which the existing staff do not possess. Whether this situation would be regarded by a Tribunal as a redundancy situation, or as a situation in which the staff who cannot adapt may be fairly dismissed as 'incompetent', is frequently finely balanced[42].

Redundancy in layoff and short time situations

Where an employee has been 'laid off' (that is, not provided with work) or put on 'short time' (that is, unable to earn less than one half of a week's pay) for four or more consecutive weeks, he may claim a redundancy payment. This right applies only (a) where the qualifying period of four weeks is consecutive, or (b) where it is not consecutive, but consists of at least three weeks' consecutive layoff or short time, and a further three weeks within a total period of thirteen weeks. But no employee may claim a redundancy payment in a layoff or short time situation under these provisions unless he first terminates his contract by one or more weeks' notice, as required under his contract (Sections 82, 84, 94).

Transfer of undertakings

Where a business changes hands, and the new owner offers to renew the old employment contracts or to re-engage the old employees under a new contract, no redundancy situation can arise unless an employee has reasonable grounds not to enter into a new contract with the new employer (Sections 82, 84, 94). Also, in that situation, continuity of employment for redundancy purposes is preserved. For these provisions to operate, there must be a complete transfer of the business, and nothing less will suffice. If there is a mere purchase of the physical assets of a business, a redundancy situation would arise[43].

Transfers of business are also subject to the Transfer of Undertakings (Protection of Employment) Regulations 1981. Under these Regulations, a sale of a business does not terminate the contracts of the employees concerned, but merely transfers the existing contracts to the new employer, thus securing continuity of employment for both redundancy and employment protection purposes. The new employer may, however, terminate the contract of any of his new employees for 'economic, technical or organisational reasons' without being required to make a payment in respect of unfair dismissal – but would still be required to compensate for redundancy on the basis of the combined length of service with the old and new employers of the employee concerned.

Excluded cases

   (a) employees with less than two years' continuous service with the employer ending at the relevant date;

(b) employees under eighteen, or who have reached normal retiring age;

(c) employees who are not of good conduct, in the sense that the employment has been terminated fairly for cause by the employer;

(d) where an employee has unreasonably refused suitable alternative employment, discussed above;

(e) employees who ordinarily work outside Great Britain;

(f) employees who work fewer than sixteen hours a week, or who have not worked eight hours a week for a minimum of five years.

Redundancy payments

Claims for redundancy payments must be made in writing to the employer within six months of the 'relevant date'. This term is defined in Section 90 to include, in the case of a contract terminated by notice, the date on which the notice expires; in the case of a contract terminated without notice, it is the date on which the termination takes effect. The six months' limitation period may be extended by up to a further six months by a Tribunal, if it considers it 'just and equitable' to do so.

Any disputes over the right to, or the amount of, a redundancy payment, will be determined by a Tribunal.

The amount of a redundancy payment varies according to the age, period of continuous employment, and rate of pay of the claimant. At the present time, only the first £152 per week of pay may be taken into account, so that the present maximum payment, according to the statutory formula, is £4,650.

Redundancy payments are made by employers, who are entitled to a rebate from a publicly maintained Redundancy Fund of 35 per cent (since October 1986, such rebates have only been available to firms with fewer than ten employees). In addition, where awards of redundancy payments cannot be collected by the claimant (for example, because of the bankruptcy of the former employer) the whole claim may be met out of the Redundancy Fund.

The Secretary of State for Employment, as custodian of the Fund, may be represented before the Tribunal dealing with a claim in order to ensure that awards are in fact made only to claimants who are legally 'redundant' within the statutory formula.

Relationship of redundancy to unfair dismissal

Although Section 57(2)(c) gives redundnacy as one of the reasons which might enable a dismissal to be regarded as fair, it does not follow that all dismissals on this particular ground are automatically fair. For example, in the difficult third category of redundancy referred to above, the mechanism by which the employer has identified those who are to be made redundant in an undoubted redundancy situation may be stigmatised as 'unfair selection' for redundancy by a Tribunal. The 'unfairness' may be identified in a lack of consultation (although it might reasonably be argued in many instances that consultation would have made no difference, as in *B.U.S.M.* v *Clarke*[44]), or in failure to consider alternative strategies, such as the possibility of re-deployment in some other employment capacity, of the individuals concerned, as in *Thomas & Betts Manufacturing* v *Harding*[45].

In many instances, the unfairness consists of a failure to set up and adhere to a proper selection procedure. Such a procedure may be simply one of practice, such as 'last in, first out', or some more complex scheme that has been arrived at, preferably in agreement with the employees or their trade union representatives. However, it must be emphasised that even a procedure that has been agreed with the trade union would be objectionable if it were to be sexually or racially discriminatory[46].

Guidance on what is good industrial practice in redundancy situations has been given by the Employment Appeals Tribunal in *Williams* v *Compair Maxam Ltd*[47]. In any event, selection for redundancy on the grounds of trade union membership or activity is automatically unfair dismissal by virtue of Section 59. Such an unfair selection would entitle the applicant to damages for unfair dismissal, entitling him in many instances to an award in excess of that to which he might have been entitled under a redundancy.

Claims in respect of both unfair dismissal and redundancy may arise from the one dismissal; but in all such cases, the compensation payable for unfair dismissal will be reduced by the award made in respect of redundancy (Section 73).

Redundancy procedures

Where employers recognise a trade union, they are required to consult with it over any redundancy proposals: in situations where more than one hundred employees are at risk of redundancy, this consultation must begin at least ninety days in advance; where at least ten employees are at risk, they must consult at least thirty days in advance (Section 99, Employment Protection Act). Failure to consult a trade union in the above circumstances can result in a 'protective award' being made by a Tribunal against the employer in favour of the employee or employees at risk (Section 101, Employment Protection Act). The duty to consult does not, in the last resort, give the union a power of veto over the proposals, and nor does it, of itself, invalidate any particular redundancy[48], but it may be a factor in determining whether or not the employer has fairly selected those made redundant (see above).

Further, employers proposing to make the redundancies referred to above must notify the Secretary of State on the same time scale; failure to do so constitutes a criminal offence under Section 100, Employment Protection Act.

6. CONTRACT OF EMPLOYMENT LITIGATION

(a) In the courts

Litigation involving issues of breach of contract of employment must be brought in the County Court or High Court as appropriate according to the financial limits of the claim. At present, the County Court may handle only claims of less than £5,000: all others go to the High Court.

The principal issues which are likely to come before the courts involve breach of the contract, particularly where the contract is of fixed duration or involves a substantial period of notice[49]. Such fixed term contracts are frequently negotiated by managers or directors[50]. Other frequently litigated issues include sick pay and restrictive covenants relating to the conduct of the employee during the contract or after the relationship of the employer and employee has ceased[50].

A major area of litigation in the High Court concerns questions of employer's liability for injuries arising from breaches of the duty to provide a safe working environment.

Section 131 of the E.P.C.A. gives power to the 'appropriate Minister' (in England and Wales, the Lord Chancellor) by order to transfer to the jurisdiction of the industrial tribunals, litigation involving claims for damages for breaches of the contract of employment. However, the section goes on to make it clear that the proposed extension of the industrial tribunals' jurisdiction shall not be exclusive, but will run concurrently with the courts: and further, that the Lord Chancellor's power may only be exercised in relation to litigation relating to the termination of the contract of employment, or litigation that at the same time involves issues otherwise within the jurisdiction of the industrial tribunals (for example, claims for redundancy payments).

So far, no such order has been made: thus litigation over employment contract disputes may still be somewhat unrealistically divided between the jurisdiction of the courts and that of the industrial tribunals[51].

The basic remedies available from the courts in contract of employment litigation are declarations of the rights of the parties, or an award of damages; it should, however, be borne in mind that the remedy of specific performance of the contract of employment is seldom available[54], both by long-standing practice[53], and more recently by statute[54]. A limited exception is the occasional grant of an injunction to prohibit breach of an express negative stipulation not to work for some rival employer[55].

(b) Before industrial tribunals

The jurisdiction of industrial tribunals is entirely created by statute. They were set up initially under the Industrial Training Act to hear appeals relating to industrial training levies; further responsibilities have been put upon them by successive statutes until they have at present upwards of thirty separate heads of jurisdiction, of which unfair dismissal claims and applications for redundancy payments form perhaps the bulk of their case-load.

An industrial tribunal consists of a legally qualified chairman (a barrister or solicitor of seven years' standing who may be a full-time or part-time appointment) together with two 'wingmen', each of whom is appointed after consultation with organisations of employers and employees respectively. The lay members are part-time appointments. Majority decisions are acceptable, although in practice most decisions are unanimous. The chairman does not possess a casting vote. Tribunal procedure is informal, consonant with the general object of facilitating the bringing of claims in person; for the same reason, access to tribunals is inexpensive, with absence of legal representation being commonplace and awards of costs being made only against parties who have conducted proceedings 'frivolously, vexatiously or otherwise unreasonably'[56].

Appeal lies from the decision of an industrial tribunal to the Employment Appeal Tribunal on a question of law under, *inter alia*, the Employment Protection Act and the Employment Protection (Consolidation) Act. An appeal in the Employment Appeal tribunal is heard by a bench consisting of one High Court judge, together with an equal number of members representing employers and employees, making up a tribunal of three, or exceptionally five, members. With the consent of the parties, the Tribunal may consist of one judge and one appointed member only.

Guidance to the types of situations where an appeal can lie was given in the case of *Palmer* v *Vauxhall Motors*[57] as follows:

(a) cases where the industrial tribunal's reading of the relevant law was mistaken;

(b) cases where there was no evidence on which the industrial tribunal could have reached the conclusion it did;

(c) cases where the industrial tribunal misunderstood the facts;

(d) cases where the industrial tribunal misapplied the facts.

In arriving at its decisions, the Employment Appeals Tribunal is bound by decisions of the Court of Appeal and the House of Lords.

A further appeal lies on a point of law to the Court of Appeal, and a further appeal to the House of Lords; in both instances, leave to appeal is required.

Proceedings in an industrial tribunal are initiated by an applicant completing a Form IT 1 and sending it to the secretary at the Central Office of Industrial Tribunals (COIT). The use of the official form is not mandatory providing that the relevant information, setting out the parties, the complaint, and the general ground upon which relief is sought, is made explicit. The exact nature of the relief sought need not be specified, as the industrial tribunal itself is free to grant whatever relief it deems appropriate, even if not specifically identified by the applicant. Time limits for making an application to an industrial tribunal vary according to the particular statutory provisions – for example, six months from the 'relevant date' in the case of redundancy payment claims, and three months from the 'effective date of termination' in the case of unfair dismissal claims. Other claims under the Employment Protection (Consolidation) Act must be brought within three months of the 'cause' of the complaint arising.

A copy of the original application will be sent by the COIT to the respondent: the latter has a right to 'enter an appearance' within fourteen days of its receipt. His response may be made upon Form IT 3, but it must in any event be in writing, stating, if it is intended to oppose the application, the grounds upon which this will be done. Copies of this response will, in their turn, be served upon the applicant. At this stage, a Conciliation Officer will endeavour to promote a settlement in, *inter alia*, unfair dismissal complaints. In these complaints, the Conciliation Officer is bound to advocate reinstatement or re-engagement as the most appropriate remedy, or, should this not be practicable, to promote an agreement over compensation.

Any information communicated to a Conciliation Officer by either party at this stage of the procedure is not admissible, without the consent of the party communicating it, in any subsequent industrial tribunal proceedings. Either party, or the industrial tribunal itself, may require the other party to produce further particulars of the grounds upon which he relies, and of any facts relevant thereto: orders for the discovery of documents may be made by the industrial tribunal, but only where this is considered 'necessary' after balancing the need to assure confidentiality against the need to deal fairly with the case[58].

Proceedings may be short-circuited by the holding of a pre-hearing assessment, held at the discretion of the chairman. At a pre-hearing assessment, all the relevant documents are scrutinised, and oral argument may be heard, but no witnesses may be heard. The industrial tribunal may express a view on the lack of strength of the application, or on any of the contentions put forward by either party, together with a warning that, if the application is not withdrawn, or the objectionable contentions are persisted in at the formal hearing, the offending party may be held liable to pay the costs.

The formal hearing

This will be held in public, except where there are overriding issues of confidentiality. The parties may present their case in person or through a lawyer or lay representative. No legal aid is available, but legal advice and assistance short of representation may be obtained through the 'Green Form' Legal Advice Scheme.

Evidence may be given on oath or affirmation, but the industrial tribunal is not bound by the rules of law relating to the admissibility of evidence in the courts. The legal onus of proof before an industrial tribunal may vary according to the nature of the claim. For instance, the burden of proof of 'cause' in unfair dismissal cases is placed by statute upon the employer; likewise, in redundancy payment claims, there is a presumption, rebuttable by the employer, that the dismissal was for redundancy.

The decision

The decision, with reasons, is generally given orally at the end of the hearing. Some time later, the written reasons, signed by the chairman, will be sent to the parties. An agreed settlement between the parties may be reached at any time before the industrial tribunal gives its decision. Costs will not normally be awarded, except where a party has acted 'frivolously or vexatiously, or otherwise improperly' (see above). The only really effective decision of an industrial tribunal is an award of money in cases involving employment issues. Whatever the formal description of the award (for example, in the case of a dismissal held to be 'unfair', an 'order' for reinstatement or re-engagement or an award of compensation), at the end of the day, in reality, any of these remedies can only be expressed in monetary terms. This is because there is no mechanism for the specific enforcement of the awards of an industrial tribunal; that tribunal has no power to punish a failure to comply with its order as some form of contempt; thus orders are in effect recommendations, a breach of which results in an additional award of compensation; and even the compensatory award itself can only be recovered through a County Court[59].

QUESTIONS

1. (a) Describe the circumstances under which an employee may make a claim for unfair dismissal.
   (b) In March this year Z Limited summarily dismissed their site forman Horace, who had been irregular in his hours of work and generally unsatisfactory in the performance of his duties, although his contract of employment provided for three months' notice. In April, they discoverd that Horace had in fact taken a number of tools from the site.
   Horace is now threatening to sue Z Limited for wrongful dismissal.
   Advise Z Limited.
   (Specimen paper)

2. The Employment Protection (Consolidation) Act 1978 states that an employee shall not be dismissed unfairly.
   Explain the circumstances which allow an employer to dismiss an employee fairly.
   Name the body which is empowered to decide if a dismissal was a fair dismissal and describe its composition and operation.
   (1985 paper)

3. A building company is suffering a substantial reduction in its work load and recognises that it will have to reduce its work force.
   Advise the company of the factors it must take into consideration if it decides to dismiss some of its:

   (a) senior managerial or professional staff, many of whom
       have individual contracts of employment;
   (b) craftsmen and labourers.
       (1986 paper)

NOTES TO CHAPTER 11

1. The Unfair Contracts Terms Act 1977, Section 2(1) renders void any
term of a contract which excludes or restricts libility for death or personal
injury resulting from negligence. These provisions extend to contracts of
employment.

2. *Langston* v *A.U.E.W.* (1974) I.C.R.180, C.A.
An employee involved in an industrial dispute was suspended on full pay
by his employer. His allegation that the employer was in breach of
contract could only be sustained on the basis that he had a contractual
right to be provided with work, since his wages were being paid. Lord
Denning M.R. favoured the existence of a duty to provide work, but
Cairns and Stevenson L.J.J. had considerable doubts.

3. *Robinson* v *Crompton Parkinson Ltd* (1978) I.R.L.R.61
An employer is under a duty not to destroy the mutual trust and
confidence that should subsist between himself and an employee, in this
instance by making irresponsible charges of theft against a blameless
employee on the basis of unsubstantiated evidence.

4. *Orman* v *Saville Sportswear Ltd* (1960) 1 W.L.R.1055
In this case, Pilcher J. suggested that there was a 'presumption' that the
employer's duty to pay wages continued during sickness unless an implied
term to the contrary could be identified; but the existence of this
'presumption' has been doubted in later cases.

5. *Pepper* v *Webb* (1969) 1 W.L.R.514
The summary dismissal of a gardener by his employer was upheld for
disobedience of an order relating to his work, together with 'insolence' to
his employer.

6. *Lister* v *Romford Ice and Cold Storage Ltd* (1957) A.C.555
A lorry driver injured a fellow-employee by negligent driving of his
vehicle. The House of Lords ruled that there was an implied term in the
driver's contract of employment tht he would drive his employer's lorry
with reasonable care and skill.

7. *Hivac Ltd* v *Park Royal Scientific Instruments Ltd* (1946) Ch.169
Workers employed by company A worked for company B in their spare
time. Both companies manufactured scientific instruments. A company
sought an injunction against B company to restrain them from employing
any of the A company employees. Injunction granted on the grounds that
the employees concerned were under contractual duty not to misuse the
confidential information that they had acquired through their employment with A company.

8. *National Coal Board* v *Galley* (1958) 1 W.L.R.16
An official in a coal mine was employed on the basis of 'the National
Agreements for the time being in force' (that is, the agreements between
the N.C.B. and the defendant's union). The agreements required officials
to work reasonable overtime if requested; so when he refused to work on
a particular Saturday, he was held to be in breach of his contract of
employment.

9. *Singh* v *British Steel Corporation* (1974) I.R.L.R.131
After an employee had resigned from his union, the latter negotiated with
the employer a change in the shift system under which the employee
worked. It was held that the employee's contract of employment was not
amended by the revised collective agreement, so that he was not obliged
to work the new shift system.

10. *McClelland* v *Northern Ireland General Health Services Board* (1957)
1 W.L.R.594
A woman's contract stated that her employment was permanent, and then
went on to provide for termination on a number of specified grounds. The
House of Lords held that the contract could only be terminated on those
grounds, as the customary right to terminate at any time by giving notice
had been excluded.

11. In *National Coal Board* v *Galley* (above) the employers claimed £535
for loss of profit through the employee's breach of contract. They were
awarded £3.18.2d. – the cost of hiring a substitute for the day.

12. *Cox* v *Phillips Industries* (1975) I.R.L.R.344
Damages awarded for wrongful termination of the contract of employment included an element for the depression, anxiety and illness caused to
the employee by the employer's breach of contract. However, the Court
of Appeal in *Bliss* v *S.E. Thames R.H.A.* (1985) I.R.L.R. 308, refused to
follow *Cox*.

13. *London Transport Executive* v *Clarke* (1981) I.C.R.355, C.A.
An employee was granted extended leave of absence on the understanding that, if he did not return to work by the stipulated date, he would be
deemed to have dismissed himself.

The employee returned some time after the agreed date and claimed
that he had been 'dismissed' by his employer, who had in the meantime
returned his employment documents to his last known address.

The Court of Appeal categorically rejected the principle of 'self
dismissal'. Although the employee's conduct amounted to a repudiation
of his contractual obligations, the ordinary rule of contract law applied,
namely, that the contract is terminated only by acceptance by one party of
the repudiatory conduct of the other party.

14. *Marshall* v *Harland and Wolff Ltd* (1972) 1 All.E.R.715
In deciding whether or not illness has frustrated a particular contract of
employment, the following factors should be considered:
    (i)   the terms of the contract;
    (ii) the likely duration of the contract if there were no sickness;

    (iii)   the nature of the employment;
    (iv)   the period of past employment.

These considerations should help to resolve the central question: was the employee's illness of such a nature, and of such a likely duration, as to render impossible the future performance of his obligations under the contract?

15. *Laws* v *London Chronicle Newspapers Ltd* (1959) 1 W.L.R.698
The plaintiff employee received conflicting orders from her departmental manager and the managing director of the firm. Her resulting disobedience to orders was held to be excusable as it did not show an intention not to be bound by her contract of employment.

16. *Adsett* v *K. & L. Steelfounders and Engineers Ltd* (1953) 1 All.E.R.97
An employee who worked in a foundry contracted silicosis through exposure to dust. His employers had previously installed an up-to-date dust extraction device, but there was evidence that the plaintiff's injury was due to exposure prior to its installation. It was held that the employer's duty was to install devices which were commercially available – he could not be liable for failing to install devices that had not been invented at the relevant time.

17. *Wright & Cassidy* v *Dunlop Ltd & I.C.I. Ltd* (1972) 13 K.I.R.255, C.A.
A chemical substance was manufactured by one company and used by another in its processes. After many years, cases of cancer were diagnosed among the latter company's employees. It was held that both companies were liable to the employees, as on the basis of scientific and medical knowledge available at the time when the plaintiffs must have first been injured by the chemical, both companies should have known of the risk, and should have respectively taken steps to warn, or to protect, the employees at risk.

18. *Paris* v *Stepney Borough Council* (1951) A.C.367
The plaintiff was a one-eyed fitter employed in the defendant's garage. While using a hammer and chisel, he dislodged a metal fragment which injured his one eye. Goggles were not worn by fitters in the garage as the risk of eye injury was considered remote. The House of Lords held that the defendants owed a higher duty of care to protect the eye of the plaintiff owing to his increased vulnerability to eye injury, and that they were in breach of this duty as they had not provided him with eye protection.

19. *McArdle* v *Andmac Roofing Co.* (1967) 1 All.E.R.367
A roofing company and a waterproofing company were laying a roof as subcontractors to the main contractor for the site. As the former company's employees laid the roofing, the latter came up behind to apply waterproofing. The roofers ceased work, leaving an opening in the roof into which the plaintiff, a waterproofing employee, fell and was injured. It was held that the main contractor was under a duty to co-ordinate the work of the subcontractors and was liable to the plaintiff for its breach of this duty towards him.

20. (1938) A.C.57

21. *Davie* v *New Merton Board Mills Ltd* (1959) A.C.604
A faulty tool was supplied to the plaintiff's employer by a reputable manufacturer. The tool had not been properly hardened by the manufacturer, and the resulting brittleness was not detectable by the employer's normal inspection procedures. When the plaintiff was injured by this faulty tool, it was held that the employers were under a duty of care to supply safe tools for the use of their employees, but they had discharged this duty by obtaining tools from a reputable manufacturer, and satisfying themselves by inspection that they were free from visible defects. (This decision was in effect reversed by the Employers Liability (Defective Equipment) Act 1969).

22. *Hudson* v *Ridge Manufacturing Co. Ltd* (1957) 2 Q.B.348
A fellow employee of the plaintiff habitually engaged in horseplay, such as tripping up his workmates, and ignored the supervisor's instructions to desist. When he injured the plaintiff by his conduct, it was held that in such a case, a clear duty lay on the employers to remove the danger, by dismissal if necessary.

23. *Marshall* v *Gotham Co. Ltd* (1954) A.C.360
An accident in a mine was due to a fall of unsupported rock. It was not the usual practice to provide systematic supports for the roof, but it would have been practicable to do so, though at great expense. Lord Reid, in the House of Lords, remarked (at page 373) that '. . . as mens' lives may be at stake, it should not lightly be held that to take a practicable precaution is unreasonable . . .', but went on to decide that in all the circumstances complete timbering of the roof was not a reasonable requirement.

24. *Qualcast (Wolverhampton) Ltd* v *Haynes* (1959) A.C.743
The plaintiff, an experienced foundry worker, worked in a foundry where there was a risk of hot metal splashing on his feet. Protective leggings and spats were provided by the employers, but the plaintiff did not wear them. The plaintiff sued his employers when his legs were burned by hot metal, arguing that they had not taken steps to ensure his wearing of the protective devices. The House of Lords held that the employers had done what was reasonable by providing equipment adequate to meet an obvious hazard, and that they were not under a duty to do more to enforce their use by a fully experienced foundry worker.

25. *Crookall* v *Vickers Armstrong Ltd* (1955) 2 All.E.R.12
The plaintiff, a labourer in a steel foundry, was exposed in his work to fine, frequently invisible dust. Dust masks were made available for his use, but the management did not take positive steps to secure the use of these masks by the plaintiff. When the plaintiff suffered from silicosis through inhaling the dust, it was held that the special circumstances, including the extreme hazard of the dust, and the insidiousness of the risk, imposed a duty on the employers to take more positive steps than they had done to secure the wearing of a dust mask by the plaintiff.

26. *Brookes* v *J.P. Coates (UK) Ltd* (1984) 1 All.E.R.762
The plaintiff had worked for many years in cotton spinning and later as a

gardener. In 1979, he was found to be suffering from bassinosis, a disease caused by cotton dust. There was evidence of dusty work conditions at his former workplace, but little evidence on which it could be established that his former employers knew, or ought to have known, at the relevant time that the dust was likely to be injurious. (The plaintiff succeeded on the basis of a breach of Section 63, Factories Act 1961, that is, that the dust was present '. . . to such extent as to be likely to be injurious').

27. *Williams* v *Port of Liverpool Stevedoring Co. Ltd* (1956) 2 All.E.R.69
A gang of six men disobeyed their foreman's orders to unload sacks from a ship's hold by a certain method; the method they chose to adopt was easier, but dangerous. One of the men was injured by the fall of a sack, and his damages were reduced by 50 per cent for his contributory negligence.

28. *Bowater* v *Rowley Regis Corporation* (1944) K.B.476
The plaintiff, a municipal dustman, was injured by an unruly carthorse, as to whose vicious habits he had complained to management on previous occasions. It was held that the evidence of his knowledge of the risk from the horse, shown by his protests, was not evidence of agreement to run this particular risk, so that his employers were liable for failing to take reasonable care for his safety.

29. *Merrington* v *Ironbridge Metal Works Ltd* (1952) 2 All. E.R.1101
A fireman was called to fight a fire at a factory containing quantities of aluminium dust. This dust represented an exceptional risk of explosion, but the fireman was not warned of this. It was held that the defence of *volenti* failed as, although the fireman might have had knowledge of the general risks of fire-fighting, he had no knowledge of the exceptional risk which had in fact caused his injury.

30. *Western Excavating Ltd* v *Sharp* (1978) Q.B.761
An employee, who had been refused an advance on his wages, resigned and, asserting that he was entitled to terminate the contract 'by reason of his employer's conduct', claimed that he had been unfairly dismissed. The Court of Appeal ruled that, in determining all such claims of 'constructive dismissal', the court's approach had to be on the basis of ordinary contract law. Thus the employer's conduct did not amount to the fundamental breach of contract that had to be established before the employee could show that he had been 'constructively dismissed'.

31. *R.S. Components Ltd* v *Irwin* (1973) I.C.R.535
The employer requested his employee to sign a new contract of employment containing a restrictive covenant protecting the employer's interests. The employee refused and was dismissed. It was held that the reasons for the dismissal could be justified as 'some other substantial reason'. The interpretation of this phrase was not to be limited to the class of preceding reasons set out in Section 57, but could include the reasonable requirements of the business.

32. *British Home Stores* v *Burchell* (1978) I.R.L.R.379
In considering an employer's decision to dismiss an employee on the basis

of an allegation of misconduct, a Tribunal must be satisfied that the decision to dismiss was based on a *bona fide* belief, held on reasonable grounds, which had only been arrived at after a reasonable investigation of the circumstances, including an opportunity for the employee concerned to state his case (allegation of theft).

33. *Alidair Ltd* v *Taylor* (1977) I.C.R.662
An airline pilot was guilty of an act of negligence that might have caused a crash. He was dismissed without warning for what was arguably a first offence. His dismissal was upheld because, in the circumstances, a warning would not have been enough to safeguard the airline's passengers.

34. *Nothman* v *Barnet London Borough Council* (1978) W.L.R.220
'Normal retiring age' for the purposes of E.P.C.A. Section 64 means the age at which the employee concerned must or should retire from his work under the terms of his contract of employment, unless his period of service is extended by mutual agreement between himself and his employer. This retiring age is not necessarily the same as the age at which the employee becomes eligible for a State retirement pension.

35. *Stock* v *Frank Jones (Tipton) Ltd* (1978) I.C.R.347, H.L.
A number of workers went out on strike. Their employer issued a warning that all who did not return to work by a certain day would be dismissed. Some returned and the rest were dismissed. The House of Lords held that a Tribunal had jurisdiction to hear a claim for unfair dismissal from the strikers who had been dismissed.

36. *Coleman* v *Magnet Joinery Ltd* (1975) I.C.R.46, C.A.
It is not 'practicable' to reinstate or re-engage an employee dismissed in circumstances involving industrial relations issues if his return to the workplace would give rise to a serious risk of industrial strife.

37. *Simmons* v *Hoover Ltd* (1977) Q.B.284
After the employee had been on strike for some time, he received a letter giving seven days' notice of dismissal, far less than he was entitled to under statute. The employee's claim for a redundancy payment was unsuccessful: the E.A.T. held (*inter alia*) that the strike in which the employee had participated amounted in law to gross misconduct justifying the dismissal (see above p. 209 for notice under the E.P.C.A.).

38. *O'Brien* v *Associated Fire Alarms Ltd* (1969) 1 All.E.R.93
Where the contract of employment gives the employer the right to move employees from one firm to another, all the firms contemplated can be regarded as the employee's 'workplace', so that the closing down of one of them is not a cessation of business in the place where the employee was employed. Thus any dismissal of an employee for refusing to re-locate (in this case a move from Liverpool to Cumberland) in these circumstances would not be for redundancy.

39. *Tyler* v *Cleveland Bridge and Engineering Co. Ltd* (1966) I.T.R.89
The applicant had been employed at a power station. He was dismissed and offered new work on better terms at Sheffield, 150 miles away. His

wife was not in good health and he had diet problems which might be exacerbated by living in lodgings. The tribunal held that it was not an offer of suitable alternative employment in relation to that employee.

40. *Fuller* v *Stephanie Bowman Ltd* (1977) 1 R.L.R.87
The applicant worked in an office in Mayfair: her employers wished to transfer her to Soho. As the new office was located above a sex shop, she objected to the move. The tribunal held that her objection to working near a sex shop was based on a personal whim, and that she had unreasonably refused alternative employment.

41. *Lesney Products Ltd* v *Nolan* (1977) I.C.R.235
Where a group of machine setters were required to work a 'double day shift' system, rather than a conventional day shift plus overtime, this was not a redundancy situation, because there was no reduction in the requirement for the services of employees to set up machines. Hence the dismissals of those employees who refused to work the new system were not for redundancy.

42. *Hindle* v *Percival Baats Ltd* (1969) 1 All.E.R.836
The applicant was a carpenter working in a boatyard. His employers changed over from wood to fibreglass construction, but retained Hindle as a boat repairer. It was later decided that Hindle was 'too good and too slow' and as his continued employment was uneconomic, he was discharged. The Court of Appeal accepted the employer's view that the employee was dismissed because his work was uneconomic in a changing situation, and not because there was a reduction in the requirement for employees of his particular kind.

43. *Woodhouse* v *Peter Brotherhood Ltd* (1972) 1 All.E.R.1047
The original owner of a factory used the premises and machinery to produce diesel engines. He sold both the premises and the machinery to a new owner, who used them for producing a different type of engineering product. There was no sale of the goodwill of the business. The Court of Appeal held that there was no 'transfer of the business': it was not relevant that particular employees may have worked at the same benches under the same supervisors.

44. *British United Shoe Machinery Co. Ltd* v *Clarke* (1977) 1 R.L.R.297
It is not an infrangible rule that employees should always be consulted about impending redundancy. If there is a genuine redundancy situation, and little can be done to mitigate it, the tribunal should be slow to find the resulting dismissals unfair; or if it does so find, it should not award compensation unless it is satisfied that the loss resulted from the particular unfairness.

45. *Thomas & Betts Manufacturing Ltd* v *Harding* (1980) 1 R.L.R.255
In deciding whether an employer has acted fairly in declaring a redundancy, the tribunal should ask whether he has considered the alternatives to redundancy, such as transfers elsewhere within his organisation. Thus, if an employer merely states that he decided not to offer alternative work to a redundant employee, without giving any

justification for his decision, the tribunal may well classify the resulting dismissal as unfair.

46. *Clarke* v *Eley Kynoch Ltd* (1982) 1 R.L.R.482
A redundancy agreement provided that part-timers should be selected for redundancy before full-timers. A smaller proportion of women than men worked full-time. The claimant, by virtue of her domestic situation, was forced to work part-time and not full-time. When she was selected for redundancy under the agreement, the E.A.T. ruled that the agreement amounted to unlawful sexual discrimination, which was unfair selection for redundancy.

47. *Williams* v *Compair Maxam Ltd* (1982) 1 R.L.R.83
In redundancy situations, unionised employers should act in accordance with the following principles:
    (a) give the union and the affected employees as much warning as possible;
    (b) consult the union as to the best means to achieve the necessary staff reductions fairly, and with as little hardship to the employees concerned as possible;
    (c) seek to establish 'objective' criteria for selection of those to be made redundant;
    (d) seek to make the selection fairly in accordance with these criteria;
    (e) seek to arrange alternative employment wherever possible.

48. *Foreman Construction Ltd* v *Kelly* (1977) 1 R.L.R.468, E.A.T.
The failure to consult a union on redundancies carried its own penalty under the E.P.C.A. Section 101, and it was not the policy of the E.A.T. to seek to enforce it by holding any particular redundancy arrived at without consultation to be unfair.

49. *Grundy* v *Sun Printing and Publishing Association* (1916) 33 T.L.R.77, C.A.
An editor was held to be entitled to twelve months' notice of termination of contract.

50. *Strange* v *Mann* (1965) 1 W.L.R.629
The defendant's employee was an assistant in a betting shop. He mostly took bets over the telephone and had little personal contact with customers. His contract contained a stipulation that he would not subsequently engage in a similar business within a twelve mile radius. Held that the restrictive stipulation was void, being an attempt to restrain future competition rather than an attempt to obtain protection for the business interests and connections of the employer.

51. *Treganowan* v *Robert Knee Ltd* (1975) I.T.R.121
An employee, who caused considerable embarrassment to her colleagues at work by her immodest conversation, was held by a tribunal to have been fairly dismissed. Her dismissal had been without notice: this did not invalidate the fairness of her dismissal, and although it might have been grounds for an action for damages at common law, it was outside the jurisdiction of the tribunal to deal with this aspect of the case.

52. *Hill* v *Parsons Ltd* (1972) Ch.305

An employee of thirty-five years' service was given notice by his employer to terminate his employment because he refused to join a certain union. The employer's action was taken under pressure from that union. An injunction was granted which had the effect of requiring specific performance of the contract of employment, that is, of treating it as subsisting despite wrongful termination. The Court of Appeal justified this special, and very limited exception, to the general rule on the grounds, *inter alia*, that the employer and the employee still had the necessary complete confidence in each other. This justified the judicial intervention to keep the contract in being.

53. *Chappell* v *Times Newspapers Ltd* (1975) I.C.R.145

An employee, who had been instructed by his union to take industrial action, was threatened with dismissal by his employer. He applied, unsuccessfully, for an injunction to restrain the threatened dismissal. Even though the threatened dismissal would have been 'wrongful', to grant the injunction would have been tantamount to ordering specific performance of the contract of employment, which was against the policy of the courts.

54. Trade Union and Labour Relations Act 1974, Section 16.

55. *Warner Bros Pictures Inc.* v *Nelson* (1937) 1 K.B.209

Bette Davies agreed to work as a film actress for Warner Bros for a stipulated period, and during that period, to work for no other employer in the film industry. In breach of this stipulation, she went to work for another film company. The grant of an injunction preventing breach of the stipulation was justified by the court on the ground that the injunction did not force Miss Davies to work for Warner Bros or starve, as there were plenty of other outlets for her talents that were not covered by the injunction.

56. Industrial Tribunal (Rules of Procedure) Regulations 1980 (Statutory Instrument No. 884); Schedule 1, Para.11(i).

57. (1977) I.C.R.24

58. *Scientific Research Council* v *Nasse* (1978) 3 W.L.R.754

An industrial tribunal may grant to a claimant 'discovery' and inspection of documents in the possession of the respondent which are relevant to his claim. In claims alleging discrimination in making appointments, the most vital documents may be confidential reports on the claimant and other applicants. The House of Lords confirmed that in such cases industrial tribunals have a wide discretion to order disclosure of such documents, subject to suitable safeguards, such as covering up the names of the applicants reported on.

See also Industrial Tribunal (Rules of Procedure) Regulations (above).

59. See Employment Protection Consolidation Act 1978, Schedule 9, para.7.

Appendix: Bankruptcy

The law relating to bankruptcy has been drastically altered by the Insolvency Act 1985 (now consolidated in the Insolvency Act 1986 along with the Receivership and Liquidation provisions of the Companies Act 1985), most of which, it is anticipated at the time of writing, will come into force towards the end of 1986. Some delegated legislation under the Act and the new Bankruptcy Rules are not expected to be effective until that time also.

Interim orders

The Act introduces a new method by which the debtor may make an arrangement with his creditors which is binding without so much court involvement. On presentation of a bankruptcy petition, a debtor may apply to the court for an interim order appointing a nominee to supervise an arrangement with his creditors, and the petition and any other proceedings may not then be proceeded with without the court's consent. The order ceases to have effect fourteen days after it is made, or, in certain circumstances, when the court specifies it shall.

In order to apply to the court for an interim order, the debtor must show that he intends to make a proposal for an arrangement with his creditors, that he himself could have petitioned for his own bankruptcy on the date the application was made, that he has not made any previous application for an interim order within the last twelve months, and that his nominee is willing to act as supervisor of any scheme.

If an interim order is made, the debtor must then furnish the nominee with a statement of his affairs and his proposals for a composition. The nominee then reports to the court, indicating whether or not he considers that a meeting of the creditors should be called. If he does consider this necessary, he must then call a meeting of all creditors of whom he is aware within twelve weeks. The meeting may approve the debtor's proposals, with or without modifications, but the debtor must consent to any modifications.

Modifications which would take the proposal outside the scope of the Act, or which would result in a secured or preferred creditor losing their security or preference, cannot be approved. The nominee appointed by the interim order, or some other person appointed by the meeting of the creditors, will be the supervisor of the scheme; he is under the overall supervision of the court, and the debtor or creditors can apply to the court to vary any orders of his.

Bankruptcy petitions

A bankruptcy petition may be presented to the court by the debtor on the ground that he is unable to pay his debts, by a creditor (or creditors jointly) who has first served a statutory demand on the debtor requiring him to pay, secure or compound his debt, or by the supervisor of a voluntary scheme or any person bound by such a scheme, or, where criminal proceedings may be involved, by the Director of Public Prosecutions.

A creditor must show that the debtor has failed to pay his debt for at least three weeks after service of the statutory demand, or that he has no reasonable prospect of paying it. The debt must be for a liquidated sum of at least £750. The court may dismiss the petition if the debtor shows that he has a reasonable prospect of paying the debt, or if the creditor has unreasonably refused to accept the debtor's offer to secure or compound the debt. The statutory demand replaces the old 'acts of bankruptcy'.

A debtor who petitions must put in a statement of his affairs to support his petition.

The supervisor of a voluntary scheme may petition on the grounds that the debtor is not co-operating with him in supplying all information and fulfilling his requirements.

Any disposition of property or payment made after a bankruptcy petition has been presented is void unless sanctioned by the court, and any such property or money becomes part of the debtor's estate. There are exceptions to this; probably the most important exception is in favour of a person who gives value and acts in good faith without notice of the bankruptcy petition, and any third person who takes from such a person.

After presentation of the petition, the court may make a bankruptcy order if it feels that this is appropriate and the voluntary scheme procedure is not to be implemented, but if the debts and assets involved are small (not exceeding an amount to be prescribed by delegated legislation) then the court may order a summary administration instead. Where a bankruptcy order is made, the court may appoint an interim receiver if it deems this necessary to deal with the sale of perishable goods, or goods likely to diminish in value, or a special manager if the debtor's property is highly specialised.

The trustee in bankruptcy

The court may appoint the supervisor of a voluntary scheme if it is his petition, or an insolvency practitioner appointed on the debtor's petition, to be the trustee in bankruptcy. If no trustee is appointed when the bankruptcy order is made however, then the official receiver will act as an interim receiver until one is appointed by a meeting of creditors called by the official receiver. The official receiver may call a meeting of creditors within twelve weeks of the order, and must do so if requested by one quarter of the creditors in value. If there is no meeting, then the official receiver will act as the trustee in bankruptcy. Where there is a criminal bankruptcy, the official receiver must act as the trustee in bankruptcy.

Both the official receiver and the trustee in bankruptcy have powers to seize goods, papers, books and other documents from the bankrupt or other persons, such as the bankrupt's spouse. Either the official receiver or one half of the creditors in value can apply to the court for a public examination.

It is the duty of the trustee in bankruptcy to realise the debtor's estate and distribute it in accordance with the Act, and the Act contains detailed provisions and powers as to the execution of his duties. His title to the bankrupt's property relates back to the date of the bankruptcy order, and he may serve written notice on the bankrupt claiming property subsequently acquired. He may disclaim onerous property, such as unprofitable contracts or unsaleable property, and must elect to do so within 28 days if notice is served upon him by any person interested in the property. Failure to elect within 28 days is deemed to be acceptance of the contract or property. The bankrupt's tools or equipment for use in his employment, and domestic and household equipment and clothes belonging to him and his family are excluded, as are any interests expressly made defeasible on bankruptcy, such as a building contract which expressly provides that the building materials are to vest in the client if the builder becomes bankrupt (Re *Keen and Keen* (1902) 1 K.B.555).

The trustee is accountable to the committee of creditors (appointed by the creditors' meeting) and the court, and must call a final meeting to report when the distribution is completed.

Distribution of the bankrupt's estate

The detailed procedure for this is to be prescribed by delegated legislation. The trustee must allow for expenses and creditors who prove late. Property which cannot be sold profitably may be distributed in specie if the committee of creditors consent to this. The trustee must give notice of his intention to declare a dividend, but a creditor who proves late in the bankruptcy cannot upset previously paid dividends.

Preferential claims are set out in the Fourth Schedule to the Act and include twelve months' PAYE tax, twelve months' deductions of payments of contributions in respect of subcontractors in the construction industry (Finance (No.2) Act 1975, Section 69), and employees' wages (including piece work), for four months prior to the date of the bankruptcy order or interim receiver's appointment.

Ordinary debts, which rank for payment after preferential debts, include trade debts, and they abate equally if there are insufficient funds to pay them in full.

Discharge from bankruptcy

The Insolvency Act 1976 introduced the concept of automatic discharge from bankruptcy by lapse of time, and this has been extended by the Insolvency Act 1985 which has removed the court's discretion to which this was subject. The court may still suspend the time from running if the bankrupt fails to comply with any of his obligations, however. Apart from this, discharge is automatic two years after the bankruptcy order in a summary administration, and three years after the order in other bankruptcies unless it is a criminal bankruptcy or a repeated bankruptcy.

INDEX